TO MY MOTHER

THREE NAPOLEONIC BATTLES

THREE
NAPOLEONIC
BATTLES

by

HAROLD T. PARKER

1983

DURHAM, NORTH CAROLINA

DUKE UNIVERSITY PRESS

Library of Congress Cataloging in Publication Data
Parker, Harold Talbot, 1907–
Three Napoleonic battles.
Reprint. Originally published: Durham, N.C. : Duke
University Press, 1944.
Bibliography: p.
Includes index.
1. Napoleonic Wars, 1800–1814—Campaigns. 2. Fried-
land, Battle of, 1807. 3. Aspern, Battle of, 1809.
4. Waterloo, Battle of, 1815. I. Title.
DC202.1.P3   1983   940.2′7   82–21082
ISBN 0-8223-0547-X (pbk.)

Contents

Maps

THE WORK OF Harold T. Parker needs no introduction. He is generally acknowledged to be one of the premier scholars of the French Revolutionary and Napoleonic period. Many of his works, including a study of the cult of antiquity in the French Revolution, a psychological examination of the young Napoleon Bonaparte, and a history of the development of the French bureaucracy and administrative system, are points of departure for additional serious scholarship.

Forty years ago, Professor Parker also made his mark as a military historian. His *Three Napoleonic Battles* dealt with the engagements at Friedland, Aspern-Essling, and Waterloo and provided a splendid analysis of Napoleon the commander at his best, in his decline, and at his very worst. Unfortunately, because of World War II and wartime shortages and rationing, the first edition of his book appeared in severely limited numbers and even more unfortunately has not until now been reissued.

Duke University Press is now printing a new edition of *Three Napoleonic Battles* with a new introduction and afterword by the author. Readers may well be struck by the fact that although Professor Parker's book is four decades old it is nonetheless fully in tune with the work of the most current and innovative military historians.

Military history has moved well beyond the drums and trumpets style of narrative. Scholars are now aware of the impact of social structures and technology on the battlefield. Historians have examined the impact of policy both foreign and domestic upon force composition and strategy and are aware of the influence of logistics and bureaucratic politics upon the conduct of military operations.

Innovative military historians including Cornelius Ryan, Bernard Fall, and John Keegan have sought to examine battles and campaigns from a dual point of view. They discuss the large issues—armament, organization, and strategy—and also describe the roles, feelings, and points of view of the fighting men. Keegan's *Face of Battle* was greeted as a welcome innovation in military historical writing for the particularly effective manner in which he merged large- and small-scale perspectives.

Professor Parker's book takes precisely this approach and also explores in detail the problem of employing effectively eyewitness accounts of an engagement. *Three Napoleonic Battles* not only describes important engagements of the French imperial era but also offers valuable insights into the nature of battle. This new edition of Professor Parker's work will thus be of interest to both Napoleonic and military historians who will find it in the forefront of current military scholarship.

STEVEN ROSS
Naval War College

THREE NAPOLEONIC BATTLES seems a legitimate subject of study, but why choose these three: Friedland, Aspern-Essling, and Waterloo? To answer that question, we need to go back a little, to the mid-eighteenth century.

Warfare then resembled a game of chess in the slowness of movement, the intricacies of maneuver, and the delay of final decision by battle. For the infrequency of decision, physical conditions in Europe, the technical equipment of the army, and traditional habits of military thought were responsible.

Roads were little better than muddy or dusty tracks, if wider than what we now term a track, so that instead of marching in threes or fours, troops *trudged* ten or twelve abreast. Rapid movement along such tracks was difficult.

Then too, in the backward condition of rural Europe few regions could support a large army closely concentrated unless it passed quickly onwards. But since bad roads slowed advance, only with difficulty could an army live off a region whose resources were soon exhausted. Supply depots, or magazines as they were called, had to be established along the country's frontiers. An army dependent on food brought up over poor roads by awkward carts could safely advance only three days' march from its magazines. Then it would normally have to wait until supplies were assembled at a new chain of magazines.

Another factor hampering the movement of armies was the circumstance that an army was held together on march and went forward on the same road almost in block formation. The absence of light artillery that could keep up with the infantry seemed to justify this procedure. A small detachment separated from its main force and without light artillery could be overwhelmed by a somewhat larger enemy group before reinforcements traveling over poor roads could arrive. The detachment, therefore, was not of much value on defense. Nor, before light artillery, was it of much value on offense. An infantry detachment armed mostly with muskets could not pin down by attack a stronger enemy force until its own main body could arrive over poor roads to administer a crushing blow. So it seemed best that the army march as a large, unwieldly unit.

The army also moved into battle as a unit. In an orthodox "model" eighteenth-century battle each army deployed from marching column into a line three ranks deep and several miles long. Then the line of one army, or segments of it, would advance against the opposing formation. As the line moved forward, each platoon in turn halted to fire a volley, after which it quickened its pace to recover its place in the advancing line. When close to the enemy the entire line charged with the bayonet. Peacetime parade drill was intended to speed deployment and advance. Nevertheless, since it still took hours to form a line, the enemy commander could perceive what was going on and, if he thought a battle would be to his disadvantage, withdraw and fight another day. So a battle usually occurred only in that rare situation when both commanders thought the outcome would be favorable. Casualties tended to be heavy. Yet battles were rarely decisive. Victorious commanders, fearful of desertion by mercenary troops from their own army, seldom pursued. A defeated army could usually march off and fight again. So battles of the mid-eighteenth century "tended to be infrequent, tactically rigid, strategically indecisive, and resultant in heavy casualties."[1]

These physical, technological, and psychological con-

---

[1] Steven Ross, *From Flintlock to Rifle: Infantry Tactics, 1740–1866* (Cranbury, N.J.: Associated University Presses, Inc., 1979), p. 30.

ditions making for immobility and tactical rigidity were changed in the French army before the French Revolution. Greatly to simplify a complicated story of military reform let us say that two men, Pierre Joseph Bourcet and Jacques-Antoine-Guibert, above all others, broke the way in the realm of strategic ideas. Bourcet, an able French chief of staff during the War of the Austrian Succession (1740–1748) and Seven Years' War (1756–1763), was the prophet of organized dispersion. A French army on march, he recommended, should be divided into several columns. They would move along parallel roads that would permit rapid concentration for attack or defense. Upon approaching the enemy each column was itself to be formed into three or more lesser columns, so that it took less than half an hour to deploy into line of battle. These simple reforms would speed the rate of movement cross-country and in deployment.

Guibert, whose *Essai général de tactique* appeared in 1772, can be called the prophet of mobility and tactical flexibility. In the interests of mobility he urged that the French army live off the enemy's country and not be tethered to a chain of magazines. He advised, like Bourcet, that the army on march be split into parallel columns accompanied by light field artillery that could work closely with the infantry. Moving rapidly and capable of being reunited swiftly for attack or defense, the columns would form a waving net in which the enemy might be entangled, or forced into a false maneuver and crushed. Or to use Liddell Hart's phrase: the columns would resemble the tentacles of an octopus: one column or tentacle would discover the enemy, fasten on him, and pin him down; the others would join in. Guibert suggested that a major maneuver might be to have this army of columns move on the enemy's rear. On the battlefield itself the introduction of the cadenced step had already speeded maneuver. Men marched together and in time, but the pace was still seventy steps per minute. Guibert recommended it be quickened to 120. In the continuing debate within the French army—whether in battle the army would stay with the three-rank linear formation (*ordre mince*) with its firepower or use massive multi-rank attack columns (*ordre profonde*) for alleged shock value—Guibert counseled tactical flexibility and ingenuity: use line, *or* column, *or* a mixture of line and column (*ordre mixte*), whichever seemed appropriate and effective at the moment, and if necessary change from one formation to another and back again as the battle roared on. Infantry of the line should be prepared to perform light infantry duties, as skirmishers, for example.

Two technical advances made possible the application of Guibert's ideas. Between the Seven Years' War and the Revolution, surfaced roads were constructed in western and central Europe. Their creation partially explained Napoleon's rapid marches. Then in 1765, Jean-Baptiste Vaquette de Gribeauval, inspector-general of the artillery of the French army, introduced a completely new system of guns, gun-carriages, limbers, ammunition chests, and servicing tools. His light, mobile 4-, 8-, and 12-pounder field guns, the best in Europe, were not replaced in France until 1825. This new field artillery could move as rapidly as infantry. It could defend an infantry detachment beset by a superior enemy force, and on offense pin down a larger enemy column. In military manuals Gribeauval and his disciples showed how under a skilled, knowledgeable overall commander the new artillery could work in with Guibert's theories of dispersion, mobility, and swift concentration. One disciple, the chevalier Jean du Teil, suggested that in battle the new artillery, by concentrating on the enemy's infantry, could help pound out a decision.

In the two decades before the French Revolution, the 1770s and 1780s, and in the first two years of peace of the Constituent Assembly the ideas of the reformers began to affect French army practice. In 1774 the crown finally adopted Gribeauval's new guns. It built up the artillery regiments until in 1789 the French artillery corps was the finest in Europe. It established two-brigade infantry divisions, and on peacetime maneuvers began to exercise them in interarm combined operations—infantry, artillery, and cavalry working together. For battlefield operations the cadenced pace was quickened to 120 steps per minute, and the new drill regulations of 1791, standard in the French army until 1831, encouraged the commander to use line, *or* column, *or* line and column formations according to the opportunities and necessities of combat.

In the desperate ordeal of nine years of land warfare, from 1792 to 1801, the French Republic, under a succession of governments, forged a new mass citizen army that inventively utilized and amplified in practice the new military doctrines. In August 1793 the Convention proclaimed a national *levée en masse*, the first national draft in modern European history. Under the Directory the draft was institutionalized in the Jourdan Conscription Law of 1798, which established machinery for calling up men from ages twenty to twenty-five. The Jourdan law has served as a model for European and American conscription laws ever since. The French army grew in size, on paper at least, to over one million men, though its actual numbers were somewhat less. Since supply depots could not be rapidly built for the six or seven component armies, they lived off the country, as Guibert had recommended. The armies were subdivided into multiarm infantry divisions that organically incorporated artillery and cavalry. The divisions came to be officered by sergeants, captains, majors, colonels, and generals who had proved their competence on campaign and in battle. Dealing at first with soldiers inexperienced in the exactitude of disciplined close-order drill, the officers often sent their men forward as skirmishers to wear down the enemy line and to screen the advance of assault columns. In the years of combat experience, officers and men learned how to march in dispersed divisions along parallel roads; to concentrate swiftly on eve of battle; to use infantry, cavalry, and artillery in overwhelming converging action; and on the battlefield to maneuver infantry as skirmishers and as line, column, or line and column with tactical versatility, proficiency, and address.

Bonaparte grew up within this development. As second lieutenant of artillery in the Royal Army from 1785, he learned the detailed minutiae of the military craft, he read the reform treatises of Guibert and the chevalier du Teil, he engaged in peacetime workshop exercises at Auxonne, probably the finest and most progessive artillery school in the world. As captain of artillery during the Revolution at the end of 1793 he "commanded a combined arms force at the siege of Toulon. In the final assault, he used assault columns covered by skirmishers while his artillery provided supporting fire"[2] As commanding general of the Army of Italy, 1796–1797, he utilized the new military doctrine and practice to win astounding victories.

Napoleon added nothing, at least nothing fundamental, in the realm of military ideas. His genius lay in the realm of administration and imaginative execution of the reform ideas and techniques on campaign and in battle. As first consul and emperor he refined the operation of the French military machine: tightened the administration of conscription; grouped three to four army divisions into multiarm army corps of 10,000 to 18,000 men and placed each corps under the command of a master tactician (Davout, Lannes, Massena, Mortier, Ney, Soult, Victor); formed an elite group, the Consular and then the Imperial Guard under Bessières, to serve as a model and a reserve; elaborated his headquarters staff and discovered in Berthier a chief of staff unexcelled in the clear and secure transmission of his orders; enlarged the artillery; strengthened the cavalry and entrusted it often to Murat; and during years of military peace on the European continent,

[2] Steven Ross, "Napoleonic Tactics," in *Proceedings* [*1981*] *of the Consortium on Revolutionary Europe 1750–1850* (Athens, Ga.: The Consortium, 1981).

1802–1805, subjected his Grand Army contingents to peace-time maneuvers and drill. With an organization thus finely tuned and himself at the height of his powers, he *orchestrated* with genius the movements of all elements of the French army on campaign and in battle to achieve the smashing victories of Austerlitz (1805), Jena-Auerstadt (1806), and Friedland (1807). Then ensued a decline.

We are now in a position to understand why the battles of Friedland, Aspern-Essling (1809), and Waterloo (1815) were selected. To compare Napoleon to the conductor of an orchestra is useful, if we keep in mind that unlike an orchestra conductor he had to improvise his own score as he went along and in response to enemy action. Napoleon expressed the spirit of the operation when he remarked of the commander at a battle, "He engages, and then he sees" (*On s'engage, et puis on voit*). Nevertheless, even with this reservation, the comparison with an orchestra has its value. It reminds us that in a Napoleonic battle everything depended on the initial decision of one man, Napoleon, and everyone in his army waited for it. Then once the decision was announced, its successful execution (again as in an orchestra) depended on the resourceful, intelligent initiative of everyone from Napoleon himself through the corps and cavalry commanders to the lone infantry skirmishers out front.

In the battle of Friedland everyone, including Napoleon, did his part, and everything clicked. To the military historian the campaign and battle of Friedland seem almost a textbook illustration of Napoleon's way of making war and of the new military doctrines and techniques of Guibert, Gribeauval, and the chevalier du Teil. In the fall and winter of 1806 / 1807 Napoleon was at war with Prussia, whose army he had smashed at the battle of Jena-Auerstadt (October 14, 1806), and with Russia. After the resumption of spring campaigning in early June 1807 and a standoff battle with the Russians at Heilsberg on June 11, Napoleon sent his six army corps cross-country, in organized dispersion, northward along the left bank of the Alle River in East Prussia in pursuit of the Russian army retreating on the right bank. Seeking to reach the Russian base of Königsberg before the Russians did, he was maneuvering on the rear of the enemy, as Guibert had once suggested. On the evening of June 13 an outpost of the Lannes army corps at Friedland on the left bank of the Alle made contact with the Russians on the right bank. The next morning the Russian commander, Bennigsen, moved his army across the Alle to the Friedland side. Lannes, as corps commander, now illustrated one principle of Napoleonic warfare: against a superior enemy force an army division could hold out for one hour, a corps for an entire day. With a skillful multiarm combination of skirmishers, mobile infantry columns, cavalry, and artillery, Lannes through the morning of June 14 held off the entire Russian army and pinned it down. Napoleon swiftly reinforced him by marching in the corps of Ney, Mortier, and Victor and the Imperial Guard. By the afternoon of June 14 he was ready to do battle with superior force.

For Napoleon each battle was a unique problem, to be solved en route by a flowing, unique combination of approaches and devices. By 1807 he had in mind an arsenal of approaches to choose from. He might initiate a perpendicular attack, a direct frontal assault at right angle to the enemy line. Or he might open with an enveloping flank attack of one variety or another. He might try to outflank the enemy, or he might in flanking try to move on the rear of the enemy's position. Then when the enveloping flank attack had succeeded, Napoleon would release the rest of his army for a crushing assault on the remainder of the enemy's line. At Friedland he chose to attack with the right flank that moved on the enemy's rear. (An outflanking attack was ruled out by the presence of the Alle.) He entrusted the management of the attack to Ney, who skillfully coordinated infantry, cavalry, and artillery in a combined assault by tactically proficient veteran soldiers. But Napoleon himself closely supervised the battle and at one point sent in under General Sénarmont a massed battery of thirty-odd field artillery guns, an illustration of his increasingly massive employment of artillery. In accord with the counsel of the chevalier du Teil the battery concentrated its fire on the Russian infantry. It opened at a range of over 1,000 yards. But then apparently on his own initiative Sénarmont had his cannoneers manhandle the mobile Gribeauval guns forward to ranges of 600, 300, 150, and finally 60 yards from the Russian troops. Once the French right flank had crushed the Russian left wing, Napoleon released his center and left for an overwhelming blow. The final act of a Napoleonic battle, the remorseless cavalry pursuit of the demoralized enemy, did not come off, perhaps because the battle started late in the day and closed in darkness.

Waterloo, on the other hand, is the example of a battle in which almost no one on the French side, above the level of the private soldiers and noncommissioned and subaltern officers, who fought well, did his part. It is almost a textbook illustration of Napoleon's way of making war, by showing in reverse how it should not be done.

Part of Napoleon's charm was the objectivity with which he could regard himself and events. Several weeks after Waterloo he remarked, "This battle was lost because to begin with me, no one did his duty." Napoleon's opening plan for the campaign had its old-time brilliance: namely, to assume a central position between the Anglo-Dutch and the Prussian armies, and to defeat first one and then the other as opportunities presented themselves. He defeated the Prussians at the battle of Ligny (June 16) and deputed Grouchy to pursue them with two corps while he turned to the British. But Napoleon thereafter carelessly managed his relations with Grouchy. The new chief of staff, Soult, unlike his predecessor Berthier, could not assure the clear and secure transmission of orders. Grouchy apparently did not understand how an isolated detachment in pursuit should operate and lost contact with both the Prussians and Napoleon. For the assault on the Anglo-Dutch line on June 18, Napoleon chose a perpendicular attack and entrusted its management (as at Friedland) to Ney. But Napoleon did not supervise Ney closely, as he had at Friedland. Ney did not skillfully coordinate infantry, cavalry, and artillery in a combined assault. He first sent up the infantry of D'Erlon's corps inadequately supported by cavalry, and later cavalry alone unsupported by artillery and infantry. D'Erlon advanced two of his divisions in massive columns twenty-four ranks deep, which smothered the tactical versatility and proficiency of the veteran soldiers. Only near the end, in the multiarm attack on the farm buildings of La Haye Sainte, did Ney finally bring all portions of his force into play. By then it was too late.

Friedland and Waterloo, radiant victory and total collapse, are thus two extremes of Napoleonic battles. The case for including them in this book is very clear: each illustrates the central theme of the volume: Napoleon's way of fighting a battle.

The case for including Aspern-Essling is less clear. It illustrates Napoleon and the French army working at the very special problem of getting a large force across a broad river in the presence of an enemy. Napoleon was just moving into a characteristic offensive battlefield maneuver when he was frustrated by the breaking of the slender pontoon bridge across the Danube.

However, Aspern-Essling belongs here because it illustrates and calls our attention to three other preoccupations of the volume. The constant in the battles of Friedland, Aspern-Essling, and Waterloo was the courage of the common soldier—French, Russian, Austrian, British, and German. Whatever their nationality or allegiance they fought stubbornly. Their experience in battle and in hospital forms one major theme of the volume. It so happens that for the battle of Aspern-Essling the clinical hospital reports are abundant, which is one good reason for including it.

Another theme of the book is the changing caliber of the French leadership. At Friedland Napoleon, his staff, and his general officers were still at the peak of their powers. At Aspern-Essling the top personnel under Napoleon was still intact: three able corps commanders (Massena, Lannes, and Davout), an excellent chief of staff (Berthier), and an irreproachable commander of the Imperial Guard (Bessières). But at Aspern-Essling Napoleon's personal military efficiency had already declined. This deterioration was noted at the time, by Napoleon himself and by his closest associates—Berthier, for example. Recently it has been attributed to a disease of the pituitary gland, whose symptoms include alternating periods of lassitude and vigorous activity. By Waterloo both Napoleon and the top French personnel were no longer what they had been. Aspern-Essling was thus an intermediate step on the way down and enables us to perceive some of the features of Napoleon's early degeneration.

Yet another theme of the three essays was the improvement of the opposition leadership. Bennigsen at Friedland was incompetent. Archduke Charles at Aspern-Essling showed tactical capability but lacked strategic drive. Wellington at Waterloo applied to Napoleon's way of making war a sophisticated answer developed in the Peninsular campaigns: a two-rank line to bring more muskets into play, field artillery guns placed in direct support, a covering skirmisher screen, skillful utilization of terrain for protection and tactical surprise, the total army backed by an excellent supply administration. Aspern-Essling is again valuable as a battle intermediate between Friedland and Waterloo.

Now read and try to see what the experience was.

THREE NAPOLEONIC BATTLES

FRIEDLAND

THE SMALL TOWN of Friedland lies in northeastern Europe, in East Prussia, on the left bank of the River Alle. It is built on a small peninsula of land, bounded on the south and east by the twisting Alle, on the north by the lake and marsh of the tributary Mill Stream. By land, it opens to the west.[1] In that direction, back from the town stretches an immense plain, which slopes gently upward from the river into the distance.[2] Around and beyond the plain, about two miles away, lies a forest. In a vast, irregular semicircle, with only a few breaks, it sweeps from the River Alle south of the town, around to the west, and then to the north until again its trees fringe the river.[3] In the plain thus enclosed on three sides by a forest and on the fourth by a river, there is only one notable irregularity: the Mill Stream, scarcely fordable, from the forest in the west to Friedland, cuts across at the bottom of a steep ravine.[4] It divides the plain into two sections, northern and southern.

Along that edge of the forest which borders the plain lie three villages: to the south of Friedland, on the river, the village of Sortlack; to the west, Posthenen, on the road

[1] M. le comte Mathieu Dumas, *Précis des événemens militaires ou essais historiques sur les campagnes de 1799 à 1814: Campagnes de 1806 et 1807* (Paris, 1826), V, 5-6; F. Loraine Petre, *Napoleon's Campaigns in Poland: 1806-7* (London, 1901), p. 305; Oscar von Lettow-Vorbeck, *Der Krieg von 1806 und 1807* (Berlin, 1896), IV, Map in pocket in back of the book.

[2] Petre, *op. cit.*, p. 305; Jean Marbot, *Mémoires* (Paris, 1891), I, 371.

[3] Robert Wilson, *Brief Remarks on the Character and Composition of the Russian Army and a Sketch of the Campaigns in Poland in the Years 1806 and 1807* (London, 1810), pp. 153-154; letters of Robert Wilson, June 16 and June 22, 1807 (Rev. Herbert Randolph, ed., Robert Thomas Wilson's *Life from Autobiographical Memoirs, Journals, Narratives, Correspondence*, etc., 2 vols., London, 1863, II, 268, 425).

[4] Petre, *op. cit.*, p. 305; Wilson, *op. cit.*, p. 153; letters of Wilson, June 16 and 22, 1807 (Randolph, *op. cit.*, II, 269, 424-425).

[3]

to Eylau; to the northwest, Henrichsdorff, on the road to Königsberg. At the opening of the nineteenth century these villages and Friedland were inhabited by Germans, then a frugal and industrious race. By good farming, which requires character as well as skill, their ancestors and they had raised the Friedland region to a high level of well-being, cleanliness, and comfort.[5] And in the spring of 1807, as they had done for many years before, they went into the Friedland plain, plowed and harrowed and sowed rye and wheat. The crop prospered. By the middle of June it stood so high that a kneeling man would be concealed behind it. Except then for gardens along the river, the entire plain was a vast field of grain stretching away to the forests which bound the horizon.[6]

Now, it so happened that on June 13, 1807, in the Friedland area just beyond the horizon to the south and southwest, armies were marching. Coming down the Alle from the south, the Russian Army was retreating along the river-road which passed Friedland on the opposite bank.[7] Coming cross-country from the southwest, the French, in pursuit, were scattered along a road which passed from the town of Eylau, Napoleon's headquarters, through the Friedland forest, through the village of Posthenen on the edge of that forest, and then across the two-mile plain into Friedland.[8] When the Russian advance cavalry arrived opposite Friedland at 3 P.M., June 13, they found the town occupied by a French regiment of hussars. The Russian cavalry crossed the river over a bridge, attacked, drove out the French, took

[5] Petre, *op. cit.*, pp. 52-53; Freiherr Reinhold von Vietinghoff, "Kriegstagebuch des Freiherrn Reinhold von Vietinghoff vom Jahre 1806/7," *Baltische Monatschrift,* XLVII (1899), 35.

[6] Petre, *op. cit.*, p. 305; Marbot, *op. cit.*, I, 371-372.

[7] Vietinghoff, *op. cit.*, p. 19.

[8] Napoleon to Soult, June 13, 1807, 11 A.M. and 10 P.M., Nos. 12750 and 12754, in Napoleon, *Correspondance de Napoléon Ier* (Paris, 1864), XV, 331, 333.

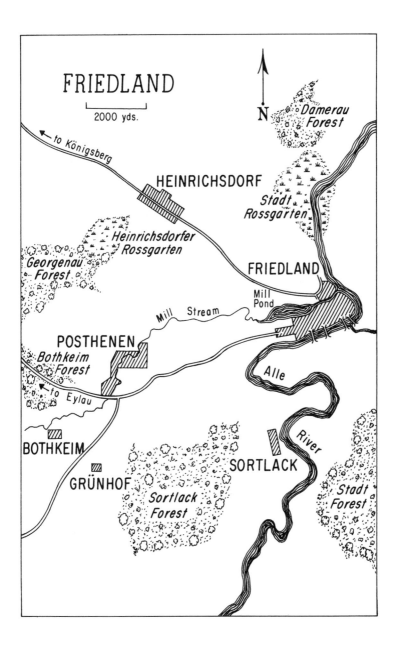

prisoners, and occupied the town.[9] From the prisoners, the Russian commander, General Bennigsen, who came up that night with the rest of the army, learned that only the French advance guard, a division or two, were on the Friedland plain.[10] He calculated, therefore, that he had time to cross the river with part of his army, whip the advance guard, and make off before Napoleon and the French Army could catch him.[11] In accordance with this calculation, the next

[9] 79e Bulletin de la Grande Armée, June 17, No. 12767, in *ibid.*, XV, 341; General Bennigsen to the Emperor Alexander, Wehlau, June 15 (Wilson, *op. cit.*, p. 250); *ibid.*, p. 152; letters of Wilson, June 16, 22, 1807 (Randolph, *op. cit.*, II, 267, 424).

[10] Wilson, *op. cit.*, p. 152; letters of Wilson, June 16, 22, 1807 (Randolph, *op. cit.*, II, 267, 424).

[11] Wilson, *op. cit.*, p. 152; letters of Wilson, June 16, 22, 1807 (Randolph, *op. cit.*, II, 267, 424). It is difficult to decide what was Bennigsen's purpose in transferring his army across the river. Three purposes have been alleged: (1) to pass through Friedland and then down the Henrichsdorff road to Königsberg, which was threatened by French forces; (2) to secure possession of Friedland, and hold off the French, so that the Russian troops might have a day of rest; (3) to crush the French advance guard. The first purpose has been attributed to Bennigsen by Napoleon, Grouchy, and French sources in general (79th Bulletin, No. 12767, in Napoleon, *Correspondance*, XV, 341; Grouchy only hints at it: Marquis Albert de Grouchy, *Mémoires du Maréchal de Grouchy*, Paris, 1873-74, III, 328). But they had no way of knowing what Bennigsen was thinking, and hence are only guessing; no Russian source gives this motive; and the failure of the Russians to make a really vigorous effort to clear the Königsberg road would suggest that Bennigsen did not intend to proceed to that city. Therefore, the first alleged motive may be rejected. The second purpose was given the next day by Bennigsen himself in a letter to the Emperor Alexander. The Russian commander wrote: "In order to keep possession of the town, that my troops might rest from their fatigue, I sent some infantry to the left bank of the Alle during the night. But in the morning at break of day, the enemy attacked my advanced posts, and at half after five the cannonade commenced. I, therefore, sent another division of my army across the river, to support the other troops, as I had reason to suppose that the enemy's van only had come up." (General Bennigsen to Emperor Alexander, Wehlau, June 15, in Wilson, *op. cit.*, p. 250). But in regard to this letter, two points may be made. First, Bennigsen is obviously trying to minimize his errors and their consequences. As a result, the letter is unreliable in many of its details and in the general picture of the battle. Hence, it may be unreliable in the statement of the purpose it gives for the crossing of the river. This is especially likely since to state what was probably the true purpose—to crush the advance guard because he thought he had time to do it before Napoleon could come up—would magnify the mistake and miscalculations of Bennigsen. Secondly, the purpose that Bennigsen gives (to rest his troops) may explain why he sent over one or two divisions. It does

morning at dawn, he ordered a division to cross the river and attack; that proving insufficient, he ordered another division across, and another, and another, and so on. As a result, through most of that June morning his entire army of forty-six thousand men,[12] like grains of sand in the neck of a huge hourglass, trickled across the long, frame town bridge[13] and the two pontoon army bridges,[14] worked their way through the narrow streets of Friedland,[15] and then fanned out into the plain beyond.[16]

On the French side, opposed to Bennigsen was first of all General Oudinot, a tall, dark, handsome man in uniform, who, though forty, was still slender, erect, and full of grace, a commander of men. His high forehead; his eyes half-closed under eyebrows that were slightly raised; his brown eyes, which constantly shifted and wandered; his serious mien—a smile was rare and fleeting though gracious —all gave him in repose the air of a dreamer.[17] But in action he was impetuous and formidable.[18] Napoleon had christened his division *la colonne infernale*.[19]

---

not explain why he transferred his entire army (cavalry and six infantry divisions) and except for one division did it by nine o'clock in the morning. For one does not rest an army by marching it toward the enemy. In fact, what Bennigsen really says is this: my purpose in marching my troops as fast as I could to meet the enemy was to rest them; this is ridiculous. He must, therefore, have had some other reason for his action, unless we assume that he moved forty-six thousand men without any reason whatsoever, merely from caprice. The third purpose is logical, and it is given by Wilson, who had some opportunity of knowing what was going on in Russian headquarters and whose account is otherwise reliable.

[12] This is the lowest possible figure, given by Wilson, a Russian partisan. Dumas on the French side states it was sixty-one thousand (Wilson, *op. cit.*, p. 155; Dumas, *op. cit.*, V, 10).   [13] Wilson, *op. cit.*, p. 153.

[14] Wilson says there were three pontoon bridges, Vietinghoff two (*ibid.*, p. 152; Vietinghoff, *op. cit.*, p. 21).   [15] Vietinghoff, *op. cit.*, p. 27.

[16] Wilson, *op. cit.*, p. 154; letters of Wilson, June 16, 22, 1807 (Randolph, *op. cit.*, II, 267, 424).

[17] Gaston Stiegler, *Récits de guerre et de foyer: Le maréchal Oudinot* (Paris, 1894), pp. 2, 88.

[18] *Ibid.*, pp. vii-viii, 4-5, 6-7, 9, 10-12, 15-16, 29, 36, 48-49, 549-550.

[19] *Ibid.*, p. 84.

Oudinot's immediate superior was Marshal Lannes, also present, a man of middling height, not much taller than Napoleon; a Gascon, that is to say, lively, excitable, cool only in danger; daring in action; loyal in peace, but in war artful, sly, insatiate of wiles.[20] Add to these a quality less typically Gascon: a desire to be better. As an obscure, youthful lieutenant he had demonstrated a desire to learn; as a marshal of France in times of peace he still at night studied his profession. He was a growing man.[21]

Also opposed to General Bennigsen was General Grouchy, in the absence of Murat commander-in-chief of the French cavalry, a sensitive, well-bred soldier of an old noble family, a failure in his own opinion.[22] His misfortune (in part) was this: though he had fought capably in all the wars of the Revolution and the Empire from 1792 to 1807, he had never fought under the eyes of Napoleon, never had his merit recognized. Thus, in 1793, when Bonaparte, a thin, energetic artillery captain of twenty-four, was serving effectively at the siege of Toulon, Grouchy, three years older, was general of a brigade in the Vendée, and was just being dismissed from the army for having once been a noble. In 1796, when Bonaparte was offered command of the Army of Italy, Grouchy, now general of a division, was offered the inspectorship of the cavalry of the Army of Italy. Bonaparte accepted; Grouchy refused to serve under an unknown of so slight a reputation. In the ensuing campaign Bonaparte, knowing the exhilaration of swift successful action and of swifter thought, defeated army after army, swept to victory and to glory; Grouchy, faithful and industrious chief of staff of the stagnant Army of the North, cursed himself for rejecting the inspectorship, bit his nails in envy.

[20] Marbot, *op. cit.,* I, 20; L. M. Poussereau, *Histoire du maréchal Lannes* (Nevers, 1910), pp. 19-20, 62, 168, 192, 346, 349, 350-351.

[21] Marbot, *op. cit.,* I, 20; Poussereau, *op. cit.,* pp. 5, 130, 346.

[22] Grouchy, *op. cit.,* I, iv-x, 1-2, 2-3, 183-184; II, 182, 224-225.

The campaign in Italy over, Bonaparte left with an army for adventures in Egypt; Grouchy, now too late, was transferred to Italy, where he cunningly intrigued the abdication of the King of Savoy, and later led a brilliant rear-guard action against the Austrians, in which he was wounded and taken prisoner. Bonaparte, back from Egypt, overthrew the French Republic, became First Consul, dictator of France; Grouchy remained general of a division. In 1800 Bonaparte crossed the St. Bernard, entered into Italy, defeated the Austrians at Marengo; Grouchy, on his return to France, fought brilliantly in this campaign, not, however, in Italy, but under Moreau at Hohenlinden. In 1805 Bonaparte, now Emperor Napoleon I, crowned in the presence of the Pope, again fought the Austrians, smashed them at Austerlitz; Grouchy, still general of a division, nearing forty, was away from the field observing another Austrian force.[23]

During these years, furthermore, Grouchy saw others, in his opinion less worthy than he, promoted over him. Grouchy, disgusted, was ready to quit.[24] But Napoleon, ever a master in kindling the ambition of men, graciously granted his request that his son Alphonse Grouchy be admitted to the imperial military school; and this grant led Grouchy to hope for further favors.[25] But in the succeeding campaign against Prussia, Grouchy's luck again held: at the Battle of Auerstädt he was in the reserve; at Prenzlau, where Grouchy performed brilliantly, Napoleon was not present; and in regard to the actions preceding Eylau, the official reports did not deign to mention the activity and bravery of his division.[26] Napoleon, however, still was gracious, markedly so after Prenzlau;[27] Grouchy still was

[23] On Grouchy's career see Grouchy, *op. cit.,* I, 66-67, 87-88, 220-223, 441-459; II, 82, 126-128, 143, 212-213.
[24] *Ibid.,* II, 224-225.   [25] *Ibid.,* II, 228-229.
[26] *Ibid.,* II, 239, 243, 322-323.   [27] *Ibid.,* II, 243, 252, 255-256.

hopeful;[28] and at Friedland an independent cavalry command was his opportunity.

These then were the men the Russian General Bennigsen had against him—Oudinot, Lannes, and Grouchy. And against him, also he had the little French infantryman, tough, sinewy, the best marcher in Europe, on offense a terrific fighter.[29]

The task of Lannes, who was in charge, was to withstand with ten thousand men the attacks of forty-six thousand until reinforcements and Napoleon should arrive.[30] How to do it was the problem. If he massed his men in an ordinary line of battle, several men deep, his line would not be long enough to cover the entire front of the line of the Russians, who would outflank him on both sides. But if he spread his ten thousand men out along the four-mile front, his line would be thin, and the Russians could break through the center, or indeed at every point. What Lannes did was this. On the Friedland plain just in front of the semi-circular forest, from Sortlack on the river to the right of Posthenen in his center and then part way to Henrichsdorff on his left, he stretched a long, thin line of sharpshooters, who lay in the long grass, or crouched in the grain, and kept up a steady musket fire on the Russians forming on the plain.[31] Then, screening his movements behind that curtain of fire and smoke and behind the slight irregularities of the ground, the height of the grain, the trees of the forest, he maneuvered a few mobile columns of infantry and cavalry, revealing them when he wished to give an im-

[28] *Ibid.*, II, 269, 320.

[29] Theodore Dodge, *Napoleon* (Boston, 1904-1907), II, 317, 320.

[30] Later, after nine o'clock, Bennigsen detached six thousand men, leaving only forty thousand (Wilson, *op. cit.*, p. 155). The figure for Lannes is given in Poussereau, *op. cit.*, p. 196.

[31] Wilson, *op. cit.*, pp. 152, 154, 155; Marbot, *op. cit.*, I, 363; Vietinghoff, *op. cit.*, p. 19; letters of Wilson, June 16, 22, 1807 (Randolph, *op. cit.*, II, 268-269, 426).

pression of strength, concealing them when he chose, and hurrying them to any point opposite which the Russians were massing.[32]

When the battle opened, about four in the morning, Grouchy and his cavalry were by Sortlack, at the edge of the forest, guarding the French right flank.[33] Oudinot and his grenadiers were in the forest between Sortlack and Posthenen. But as the Russians moved across the river into the plain, Lannes perceived their cavalry massing over by Henrichsdorff, preparing to turn his left flank.[34] From Sortlack to Henrichsdorff is nearly four miles.[35] Grouchy, therefore, on orders from Lannes,[36] with about two to three thousand men,[37] hurried along the forest, galloped across the plain,[38] barely arrived in time. Already the Russians occupied Henrichsdorff, and were preparing to detach troops in the rear of the French.[39] Grouchy, however, checked their advance, and about seven o'clock, with reinforcements, drove the Russians out of Henrichsdorff and beyond.[40]

Meanwhile, the Russian divisions continued to cross the Alle. By nine o'clock most were on the Friedland side.[41] Part of their infantry then marched up the river, trying to turn the French right at Sortlack.[42] Lannes brought up

[32] Dumas, op. cit., V, 13-14.

[33] Grouchy to Murat (Grouchy, op. cit., II, 326-327).

[34] Grouchy says he saw the massing (ibid.).

[35] By the approximate route Grouchy had to take, it measures 3.72 miles (Lettow-Vorbeck, op. cit., IV, map). Grouchy at first went only to a position somewhat this side of Henrichsdorff.

[36] Grouchy gives the impression he did it on his own responsibility (Grouchy, op. cit., II, 326-327).   [37] Ibid., II, 326-327.

[38] "Hurried" and "galloped" are assumptions.

[39] Grouchy, op. cit., II, 326-327.

[40] Ibid., pp. 327-328; Wilson, op. cit., p. 154; letters of Wilson, June 16, 22, 1807 (Randolph, op. cit., II, 269, 425).

[41] Wilson, op. cit., p. 155.

[42] Ibid., p. 155; letter of Wilson, June, 22, 1807 (Randolph, op. cit., II, 425).

troops;[43] Grouchy hastened over, or was already there;[44] Oudinot's division sacrificed itself; but the Russians continued to advance.

At the same time[45] the Russian cavalry, now reinforced, nearly surrounded the French at Henrichsdorff and threatened the town.[46] Again Grouchy hurried from Sortlack, reformed the fleeing French cavalry, charged, fell back, reformed, and charged again; fell back, reformed, and charged again; charged fifteen times until the lost ground was finally recovered.[47]

But it was obvious that despite the energy of the leaders, despite the stubborn defense of the troops, the French must give way unless aid came. Reinforcements, to be sure, had been arriving all morning; Lannes now had twenty-nine thousand; but they were not enough, and he dispatched courier after courier with appeals to Napoleon.[48] The first messenger was an aide-de-camp, Marbot, a boyish captain of twenty-five, round and smooth of face, a trustworthy youth.[49] Marbot first tried the road, but finding it thronged with troops hastening to Lannes, he took to the fields and cross-country galloped the fifteen miles to Eylau. Upon his arrival he joined Napoleon, now a mature man of thirty-seven, short, plump, and energetic. The Emperor was on horseback and, with Marbot riding beside him, set off for Friedland at a gallop. Even while galloping, however, he had Marbot explain what had occurred on the battlefield.

---

[43] Stiegler, *op. cit.*, p. 51.

[44] Grouchy, *op. cit.*, p. 328. "Hastened" is an assumption.

[45] Wilson describes the Russian infantry attack on the French right wing and the Russian cavalry attack on the French left wing as if they occurred at practically the same time. He places the infantry attack at about eleven o'clock. This agrees fairly well with Grouchy, who says the cavalry attack took place at eleven o'clock, while the infantry attack was still going on or just finishing (Wilson, *op. cit.*, pp. 155-156; Grouchy, *op. cit.*, II, 328).

[46] Wilson, *op. cit.*, p. 156; Grouchy, *op. cit.*, II, 328-329.

[47] *Ibid.* "Hurried" is an assumption.   [48] Marbot, *op. cit.*, I, 364.

[49] *Ibid.;* see also frontispiece—a picture of him as he looked in 1812.

The report finished, Napoleon said smilingly to Marbot: "Do you have a good memory?"

"Passable, Sire."

"Well then, what anniversary is today, June 14?"

"That of Marengo."

"Yes, yes," replied Napoleon, "that of Marengo and I shall beat the Russians as I beat the Austrians."[50] And saying this, he continued his gallop.

As Napoleon approached the troops on the road, they stood aside, and cheered him as he rode by. And the Emperor, skilled at lifting the spirits of those who are going into battle, did not cease to tell them: "Today is a happy day, the anniversary of Marengo."[51] And the troops would close in after him, continuing to advance rapidly.[52]

At the end of his fifteen-mile gallop on this hot June day,[53] Napoleon reached the Friedland forest about noon.[54] The wounded from Oudinot's division were passing: "Hurry," they said, "to the aid of our comrades. The Russians are stronger at this moment."[55] And Oudinot himself, his uniform riddled with shot, and his horse streaming blood, exclaimed: "Hurry, Sire, my grenadiers can do no more. But give me a reinforcement and I will throw all the Russians into the water."[56] Oudinot received a reinforcement, which checked the Russian attack.[57] Shortly afterwards Napoleon ordered the French soldiers to rest[58] while he considered what he should do.

[50] *Ibid.*, I, 364, 368.

[51] *Ibid.*, I, 364; Captain Coignet, *Les cahiers du capitaine Coignet (1799-1815)* (Paris, 1883), p. 148. Apparently Napoleon repeated this thought about Marengo many times that day. See 79th Bulletin, June 17, No. 12767, in Napoleon, *Correspondance,* XV, 341; Duc de Rovigo, *Mémoires du duc de Rovigo* (Paris and London, 1828), III, 88; Norvins, *op. cit.,* III, 205.

[52] Coignet, *op. cit.,* p. 148; Norvins, *op. cit.,* III, 204.

[53] Marbot, *op. cit.,* I, 365, 369, 371.

[54] Marbot said after 11 A.M. (*ibid.,* I, 365).

[55] Coignet, *op. cit.,* p. 148.

[56] Stiegler, *op. cit.,* p. 51.

[57] Wilson, *op. cit.,* p. 156.

[58] Marbot, *op. cit.,* I, 365, 369.

The arrival of Napoleon was not at once perceived by the Russians;[59] but an English officer, Colonel Hutchinson, stationed in a church tower at Friedland, gazing across the plain, past the forest, and down the road which Napoleon had used, observed the coming of long columns of French soldiers, numbered in the tens of thousands.[60] These continued to arrive during the late morning and afternoon, until the forest was "thronged by battalions which advanced upon the edge, and there reposed." From the town of Friedland, and in the late afternoon, the masses appeared "through the interstices of the trees and the partial interruption of the wood of enormous power and extensive depth" like dark clouds in a gathering storm. From the plain before Friedland "the horizon seemed to be bound by a deep girdle of glittering steel."[61]

While the French clung thus to the edge of the forest, the Russians stood exposed in the plain, facing the forest. In a fairly straight line parallel to the Alle River, the Russian position reached from the forest by Sortlack on the left, across the plain back of Friedland, across the Mill Stream and the plain beyond it, nearly to the forest on the right.[62] The Mill Stream cut the Russian forces in two, making difficult the reinforcement of the Russian left by the center and right. The river behind them, the Alle, was deep and flowed between precipitous banks thirty to forty feet high.[63] The only exit in case of disaster led through the narrow streets of Friedland and over the inflammable town and pontoon bridges.[64]

[59] Bennigsen and Wilson assumed he arrived at three in the afternoon (Bennigsen to Alexander, Wilson, *op. cit.*, p. 250; also letter of Wilson, June 22, 1807, in Randolph, *op. cit.*, II, 426).

[60] Lettow-Vorbeck, *op. cit.*, pp. 349, 353.

[61] Wilson, *op. cit.*, p. 157.   [62] Dumas, *op. cit.*, V, 10-11.

[63] Lettow-Vorbeck, *op. cit.*, IV, Map.

[64] Vietinghoff, *op. cit.*, p. 27.

Despite these circumstances and despite the French reinforcements, of which he knew, Bennigsen took no action. Indeed, in his position there was little he could do. He could not advance—the French were too strong. Nor could he retreat. It had taken him five hours to get his troops across the river onto the plain; it would take nearly that long to get them back. And in the meanwhile, the French with their immense power could fall upon his retreating columns and crush them. Bennigsen could only remain in the field and hope that the French would not attack; then with darkness he might slip away. But the decision no longer lay with him. Events were now beyond his control. His fate and that of his army depended on the decision of Bonaparte. And through the hot summer afternoon, while the sun moved from overhead to the forest in the west, the Russians stood in the plain, pending that decision.

Whatever the decision, an expert would make it: Napoleon was first of all a professional soldier. Among his qualities as a commander, he possessed a large store of technical experience and knowledge. He had attended military school from the age of nine to sixteen. Since his graduation he had become acquainted with every aspect of military life. He had known before the Revolution the boring routine of garrison existence. During and since the Revolution he had participated in thirty battles, commanded at most, been present a three formal sieges, commanded at two, planned and executed five major campaigns. He had studied with the understanding and appreciation of a connoisseur the campaigns of Alexander, Hannibal, and Caesar; of Condé, Turenne, and Frederick. Having risen from the lower grades of officership, he was master of every detail of his profession. He could handle a musket; work and point a cannon; give the correct command to a company, a battalion, a regiment, a brigade, a division, or an army corps; orient a map; apply a scale and read a map. He knew how many wagons were needed to transport fifty thousand rations of biscuit; how many yards of cloth were necessary to make twenty-five thousand military cloaks; how much flour was needed to feed one hundred and fifty thousand for ten days; how many days a pair of shoes would last a soldier on active campaign, in garrison, in good summer weather, or in winter. Over and above this store of technical knowledge he possessed, to quote one of his subordinates, General Foy, a cool and impassible courage, a well-calculated tenacity.[65] On campaign, he generally displayed a high level of intelligence, brilliance in conception, and a sustained drive in pressing execution of his projects. Not that he didn't make mistakes. Thus, seven years ago, the day before the Battle of Marengo to which he referred, he had detached from his army, when the enemy was near, five thousand men leaving him with only eighteen thousand to face a superior Austrian force; the next day when the Austrians attacked the main force under Napoleon, the French troops were at first forced to retreat, and were saved from disaster only by the arrival of the detachment sent off the day before, whose commander, hearing the cannonading, had started back without waiting for orders and whose arrival turned French defeat into victory. Or again, only three days ago, on June 11, he made a frontal attack on an entrenched position which Bennigsen and the Russians had prepared in advance and was thrown back with heavy loss—a waste of lives because Bennigsen could have been maneuvered out of his position without a gun being fired, as indeed Napoleon did do the very next day.

[65] General Foy's passage is quoted in J. C. Ropes, *The Campaign of Waterloo* (5th ed., New York, 1914), p. 23.

Today, however, Napoleon was careful, and he reconnoitered the Russian Army himself.[66] Its position seemed to him extraordinary. He could not understand why it should stay on this side of the river, inferior as it probably was to the forces he could bring against it. Indeed, at first he questioned whether it would remain, and he ordered an aide to ride along the forest to the right by Sortlack until the Friedland bridge was in view, then to observe the Russians, and see if they were recrossing the stream. The aide, Savary, accomplished his errand and reported that the Russians were not crossing back; that, in fact, more were coming over into the plain.[67]

But there were other things to consider. The Russian strength was unknown.[68] His own army was divided.[69] Thirty-two thousand were away under Murat, Davout, and Soult. Perhaps he should wait. Napoleon pondered, and wrote to Murat and Davout: "Try to be here by one o'clock in the morning. If I perceive at the beginning of the action, that the enemy is in too much force, I might content myself with cannonading and await your arrival."[70] Finally, however, he made up his mind for energetic attack, and, with characteristic snap and precision, he drew up the following order:

At the bivouac in the rear of Posthenen,
June 14, 1807.

Marshal Ney will take the right, from Sortlack to Posthenen, and he will bear toward the present position of General Oudinot.

[66] Rovigo, *op. cit.*, III, 87; 79th Bulletin, No. 12767, in Napoleon, *Correspondance*, XV, 341.

[67] Rovigo, *op. cit.*, III, 87-88. This report of Savary agrees with that of Vietinghoff, whose regiment crossed in the afternoon about four o'clock. Probably other regiments crossed before.

[68] See the following quotation from the letter to Murat.

[69] Figure given by Lettow-Vorbeck. Napoleon had about 87,500 on the field (Lettow-Vorbeck, *op. cit.*, IV, 350).

[70] Dumas, *op. cit.*, V, 16-17; Henri Jomini, *Vie politique et militaire de Napoléon* (Paris, 1827), II, 413-414.

Marshal Lannes will have the center, which will begin at the left of Marshal Ney from the village of Posthenen to Henrichsdorf. The grenadiers of Oudinot, which at present form the right of Marshal Lannes, will by slow degrees bear to the left, in order to attract the attention of the enemy to themselves. . . . The left will be formed by Marshal Mortier, holding Henrichsdorff and the road to Königsberg, and from there extending across the front of the Russian right wing. Marshal Mortier will never advance, the movement is to be made by our right which will pivot on our left.

The cavalry of General Espagne and the dragoons of General Grouchy, joined with the cavalry of the left wing, will maneuver to do the most harm to the enemy when the latter, pressed by the vigorous attack of our right, will find it necessary to retreat.

General Victor and the infantry and cavalry of the Imperial Guard will form the reserve and will be placed at Grünhof, Bothkeim, and behind Posthenen. . . .

I shall be with the reserve.

One should advance always by the right, and one should leave the initiative to Marshal Ney, who will await my orders to begin.

From the moment that the right advances on the enemy, all the cannon of the line must double their fire in a useful direction, to protect the attack of this wing.

Napoleon.[71]

Napoleon waited until the troops were in position,[72] allowed them a period of rest,[73] made sure by a minute inspection that every soldier possessed ammunition,[74] rode down his lines, returned at a gallop,[75] and then at five-thirty[76] gave

[71] No. 12756, in Napoleon, *Correspondance*, XV, 334-335.
[72] 79th Bulletin, No. 12767, in *ibid.*, XV, 341.
[73] Rovigo, *op. cit.*, III, 88.
[74] *Ibid.*   [75] Coignet, *op. cit.*, p. 148.
[76] Bennigsen thought the attack began at 6 P.M. (Bennigsen to Alexander, Wilson, *op. cit.*, p. 250). Napoleon said it began at 5:30 P.M. (79th Bulletin, No. 12767, in Napoleon, *Correspondance*, XV, 341). Wilson also said 5:30 P.M.,

the signal—twenty cannon firing salvos—for Ney to begin.[77]

In the battle which followed in accord with Napoleon's maneuver, Ney's corps of over ten thousand men may be compared to a huge hammerhead, swinging around, pivoting on the center. But if Ney's corps was the hammer, then the object to be hit was the left end of the Russian line. For Ney was not to back the Russians into the river by a frontal attack, but was to smite them in the side, press them sideways as it were toward Friedland, and then stuff them down that small pocket of land where every cannon shot would tell. He would thereupon seize or destroy the bridges, and cut off the retreat of the Russian center and right.

To accomplish all this, Ney needed to cover about one mile and a half, the distance from Sortlack forest to Friedland.[78] But much can happen in a mile and a half, and immediately did. When at a quick step his forces swung out of the forest, his right flank was in the air. It was at once attacked by cavalry, led by a swarm of Cossacks, who attempted to get in the rear.[79] This danger, however, had been foreseen and provided for; and the cavalry of Ney's reserve, forming at a gallop, repulsed the enemy charge.[80] But the right flank was now exposed to enemy cannon, firing from across the river, killing and wounding many.

---

but here he is obviously following the 79th Bulletin nearly word for word. Nevertheless, the fact that he repeats the hour given by Napoleon would suggest that he thought it was nearly correct (Wilson, *op. cit.*, p. 159). From Vietinghoff's narrative we can judge the battle began sometime between 4 P.M. and 6:30 P.M. (Vietinghoff, *op. cit.*, pp. 21, 22). Marbot says 1 P.M., which conflicts with all the other evidence (Marbot, *op. cit.*, I, 366).

[77] 79th Bulletin, No. 12767, in Napoleon, *Correspondance*, XV, 341.

[78] Lettow-Vorbeck, *op. cit.*, IV, Map.

[79] 79th Bulletin, No. 12767, in Napoleon, *Correspondance*, XV, 342; Wilson, *op. cit.*, p. 159.

[80] 79th Bulletin, No. 12767, in Napoleon, *Correspondance*, XV, 341, 342; Wilson, *op. cit.*, p. 159.

Napoleon learned of this and dispatched artillery, whose fire dismounted the Russian guns.[81] Ney's troops, now in the clear, quickened their pace and charged.[82] Beside them, helping them, guarding their left flank, marched the reserve, infantry and a massed battery of thirty cannon,[83] sent in by Napoleon. It was an attack of power.

What the French attack meant to a Russian who opposed it we happen to know because he kept a diary. His name was Vietinghoff, a Russian of German speech and descent, born in 1770 of noble family, a cavalry major. One can tell from his diary that he was proud of the regiment of which his squadron was part. And, indeed, it must have been a good one, for it was always chosen for dangerous service: in the advance guard on any forward movement, in the rear guard on retreat, and today with the left wing to help repel the French attack. When this evening, about six-thirty, the regiment reached its position behind the infantry, the enemy attack had already developed. Around the regiment, shells of every description—fireballs, canister shot, bombs, grenades, and cannonballs—fell and burst, fell so thick and fast that between one shell burst and the next Vietinghoff could not count one rapidly. The atmosphere was dense with gunpowder smoke, causing confusion. During the action the regiment received the order from a general who was in the rear to attack a French battery. Not knowing where the battery was, not being able to learn from the general's adjutant where it was, seeing before them nothing but flames and smoke, the members of the regiment charged blindly forward and rode down their own infantry scarce seventy paces ahead. Still unable to find a

<hr>

[81] Wilson, *op. cit.,* p. 159; Marbot, *op. cit.,* I, 366.

[82] Wilson, *op. cit.,* p. 159; letter of Wilson, June 22, 1807 (Randolph, *op. cit.,* II, 426).

[83] Rovigo, *op. cit.,* III, 90; 79th Bulletin, No. 12767, in Napoleon, *Correspondance,* XV, 342.

French battery or a passage through the infantry, the cavalry retired to its former position. The regiment operated as it were in a cloud, advanced, retreated, and stood in a cloud. In this murky atmosphere Vietinghoff could see little. He could only sit there on his horse and feel the heat of the enemy fire ("as if he stood before an immense bake oven"), feel the sweat run down the face and the eyes smart from powder fumes; and smell the sweat, the wounded, and the gunpowder; and hear through the cloud the roll and rattle of musketry ("like many thousand drums"), the incessant roar of cannon thunder, and the whistle of an approaching shell.

To keep his squadron steady, Major Vietinghoff stationed an officer behind each file of men with orders to saber any soldier who tried to withdraw. Perhaps for this reason, the squadron stood fast, and a man would move his horse slightly only when his neighbor happened to be torn from his by a cannonball. The Major confesses that he himself did not feel comfortable. He did not wish to show his feeling, and tried not to; but rode up and down the line exhorting his men to be brave, and spoke of the glory of a hero's death for fatherland and of the shame of the coward who runs away. So outwardly the Major maintained his calm; but inwardly, he prayed.[84]

Against such artillery fire—all the older Russian officers agreed that never had they experienced such a concentrated fire[85]—against the charges of Ney's infantry, and the pressure of overwhelming numbers, the Russians could not stand, and they retired into the town, fighting stubbornly.[86]

[84] Vietinghoff, *op. cit.,* pp. 22-24.   [85] *Ibid.*

[86] *Ibid.,* p. 24. The French, it is true, were checked for a time when as the French approached the town, the Russian Imperial Guard, which had been held in reserve near the marsh, charged a division of Ney's corps. The division fled; the Guard followed and entered the hole it had made in the French line. But one side of the hole collapsed on it, Napoleon's reserve which had stood firm on the Guard's right flank, and the Guard with the other Russians

There they continued to resist, sheltering themselves behind houses and shops, or fighting in the open roadways, until the streets were heaped with dead and wounded.[87] Gradually, however, the Russians were driven out of the town and across the river.[88] But before all were across, the French started to bombard the bridges, killing and wounding many.[89] The frame bridges caught fire and were consumed, leaving many Russian soldiers of the left wing stranded on the Friedland shore.[90] These sought escape from death by fording the stream, but the water was deep and many drowned.[91] Meanwhile a fire began in Friedland, spread, and destroyed the town.[92] As the fire progressed, some of the walls collapsed and blazing beams and furniture fell into the street. From the girders, the flames ate into the cloth of the uniform and the flesh of those who lay in the streets. In this way, the bodies of the dead were burned;[93] it is probable that the wounded who were not removed or could not drag themselves away were grilled alive.[94]

The French had now completed the first half of their maneuver. The right wing under Ney and the reserve had swung around, pressed the Russian left wing across the

was forced to withdraw into the town (Wilson, *op. cit.*, p. 160; Rovigo, *op. cit.*, p. 89; letters of Wilson, June 16, 22, 1807 (Randolph, *op. cit.*, II, 271, 426)).

[87] Marbot, *op. cit.*, I, 367; 79th Bulletin, No. 12767, in Napoleon, *Correspondance*, XV, 342.

[88] Wilson, *op. cit.*, p. 160; Marbot, *op. cit.*, I, 367; Vietinghoff, *op. cit.*, pp. 24-25; letters of Wilson, June 16, 22, 1807 (Randolph, *op. cit.*, II, 271, 426).

[89] Bennigsen to Alexander (Wilson, *op. cit.*, p. 251); Marbot, *op. cit.*, I, 366; Rovigo, *op. cit.*, III, 91.   [90] Wilson, *op. cit.*, p. 160.

[91] *Ibid.*, p. 160; Marbot, *op. cit.*, I, 367; Vietinghoff, *op. cit.*, p. 25; Rovigo, *op. cit.*, III, 91. Drowning is only implied by Wilson, who calls it "an almost impracticable ford."

[92] Marbot, *op. cit.*, I, 367; Coignet, *op. cit.*, p. 148; Dumas, *op. cit.*, V, 21.

[93] Marbot, *op. cit.*, I, 370-371.

[94] Inference from Marbot's account, but there is additional evidence in Wilson's letter, June 22, 1807 (Randolph, *op. cit.*, II, 426).

plain, through the town, and over the river, and had destroyed the only known means to retreat for the rest of the Russian Army. In the meanwhile, the French center and left had kept occupied the Russians opposed to them, but had purposely refrained from pushing them too hard for fear that they would fall back on Ney while he was still busy with the Russian left wing.[95] But now the French center and left advanced, pressing the Russians before them, while Ney in their rear did likewise, checking their attempts to cut a way through to Friedland.[96] The Russians, forming squares, faced forward, like cattle in a storm, and many were slaughtered where they stood.[97] Back toward the stream the living slowly retreated and continued the action until near eleven o'clock, when the French desisted.[98] The Russians who were left then made their way across the Alle, down the river from Friedland, by a ford which had just been discovered.

That evening Napoleon slept on the battlefield. The next morning he arose early and wrote to Josephine, his wife:

My dear, I write you only a line, for I am very tired; I have been bivouacking for many days on end. My children have worthily celebrated the anniversary of Marengo; the battle of

[95] Grouchy, *op. cit.,* II, 330.

[96] Marbot, *op. cit.,* I, 367, 372; Grouchy, *op. cit.,* II, 330; Wilson, *op. cit.,* p. 160; 79th Bulletin, No. 12767, in Napoleon, *Correspondance,* XV, 343-344.

[97] Rovigo, *op. cit.,* III, 92 (a description of the battlefield); Wilson, *op. cit.,* pp. 19, 160-161.

[98] Grouchy said it was 10 P.M.; Napoleon, 11 P.M.; Wilson, "near 11 o'clock at night." Wilson may have been following Napoleon's account, but the fact that he restates it strengthens Napoleon's assertion. Norvins states the battle lasted six hours, after beginning about five o'clock. Grouchy also implies that only after the Russians had crossed the stream, did the French stop. But Wilson, Vietinghoff, and Napoleon all agree in saying that the French desisted and then the Russians crossed (Grouchy, *op. cit.,* II, 330; Wilson, *op. cit.,* p. 160; 79th Bulletin, No. 12767, in Napoleon, *Correspondance,* XV, 343; Vietinghoff, *op. cit.,* p. 27; Marbot, *op. cit.,* I, 367-368; Norvins, *op. cit.,* III, 206).

Friedland will be equally famous and glorious for my people. The entire Russian Army is routed; 80 cannon, 30,000 men captured or killed; 25 Russian generals killed, wounded, or prisoners, the Russian Guard crushed; it is a worthy sister of Marengo, Austerlitz, Jena. The bulletin will tell you the rest. My loss is not considerable; I maneuvered the enemy with success.

Do not worry and be happy.

Adieu, my dear. I am just getting into the saddle.[99]

On horseback, he then rode along his line of troops, who were sleeping. Considerate of their rest, he forbade that anyone awake them to do him honor, as was the custom. He then rode out on the plain and inspected the battlefield. There, the former position of the Russian artillery was made apparent by the dead horses, the successive positions of the Russian infantry squares by the dead men.[100] In the town, the ruined houses of the natives, a frugal and industrious people, were still smoking;[101] in the field, their grain lay trampled and destroyed.

[99] Napoleon to the Empress, Friedland, June 15, 1807, No. 12758, in Napoleon, *Correspondance,* XV, 335-336.
[100] Rovigo, *op. cit.,* III, 92.   [101] Stiegler, *op. cit.,* p. 52.

From Friedland to Aspern-Essling

The crushing defeat at Friedland constrained the Tsar Alexander of Russia and his ally the King of Prussia to make peace. By the Peace of Tilsit, which concluded the war, and the accompanying protocols, Prussia ceded to Napoleon one third of her territory, agreed to pay a large indemnity and to accept in her major cities French garrisons which would be gradually withdrawn only as the large indemnity was paid. On the Tsar Alexander, Napoleon, who desired Russia as an ally, was more lenient. By the peace, Russia lost nothing (in fact, she gained a small section of Prussian Poland), and the Tsar promised to be Napoleon's ally and in effect to close Russian ports to the ships and goods of England with whom Napoleon was still at war.

Napoleon, who returned to Paris in July, 1807, now governed a large empire. He ruled directly through his administrators over an enlarged France which extended to the Rhine, the Alps, and the Pyrenees, and in addition included Savoy and Genoa. Using his relatives as subordinate (or sometimes insubordinate) kings, he ruled indirectly through his brother Louis over Holland; through his brother Jerome over Westphalia—a territory to the right of the Rhine in northwest Germany; through his brother Joseph over southern Italy (Kingdom of Naples); through his stepson Eugene as viceroy (Napoleon himself as King) over northern Italy. In addition, beyond this enlarged France and the circle of dependent kingdoms, he controlled the foreign policy of an outlying area of states. The Swiss Federation was a protectorate. The small German states then in existence outside of Prussia and Austria had formed the Confederation of the Rhine and accepted his protection. The Confederation was pledged to supply him in war with sixty-three thousand men. His troops also garrisoned the key northern ports of Bremen, Hamburg, Lübeck, and Danzig, and the major Prussian cities. Still farther to the east, a partial Poland, the Duchy of Warsaw, was virtually subject to his rule. Directly or indirectly, in brief, he governed France, Belgium, Holland, western Germany, northern and southern Italy—which comprised the wealthiest, the fairest, the most populous regions of Continental Europe in his time; he dominated the foreign policy of Switzerland and the small German states, and by his garrisons and his power he cowed a humiliated, bitter, and revengeful Prussia.

But Napoleon, a man of the South, dreamed of a Mediterranean empire. By the close of 1807, he had determined to master Spain and Portugal. He insinuated his troops into northern Spain, successfully intrigued the abdication of the royal family, and placed his brother Joseph on the Spanish throne. In the Spaniards, however, Napoleon encountered a people whose spirit of fierce independence would not brook a foreign ruler imposed upon them. They rose in rebellion against the French emperor; lacking a strong, standing army, they resorted to guerrilla warfare; and their resistance was stiffened by the presence of two successive English expeditionary forces—the first commanded by Sir John Moore, the second by Wellington. Napoleon's hold on his subject peoples depended on his benefits, his power, and his reputation for invincibility. Once engaged in Spain, he probably could not withdraw and confess defeat. But with an entire people in revolt, Napoleon was compelled to feed into Spain more and more infantry, cavalry, artillery—the flower of his army. He raised new levies by conscription; he was forced to come to terms with Prussia in regard to the indemnity so that he might withdraw from Prussia the French garrisons which he needed in Spain. Napoleon himself led a campaign in Spain; it was successful while he was present, but when he left, his lieutenants worked at cross-purposes, and the revolt continued.

The success of the Spaniards (merely to continue a revolt against Napoleon was a success) fired the hopes of others who were discontented with his rule. Austria, a major power and an old enemy, possessing a reorganized army and perceiving that Napoleon's best troops were occupied in Spain, declared war in the spring of 1809. The news of the declaration, which reached Napoleon in Paris on April 12, was not unexpected; and his army, consisting in part of new, inexperienced levies, was already in southern Germany around Augsburg and Ratisbon. Napoleon left Paris in the early morning of the thirteenth and after several hundred miles of carriage travel reached his army in the early morning of the seventeenth. When he arrived at the south German town of Donauwörth, his chief of staff, Berthier, a topnotch military secretary but a poor commander, had so misarranged the French Army corps that they were separated and spread over a line seventy-five miles long. The Austrian commander, the Archduke Charles, and the Austrian Army, which were near, had the opportunity to crush two of the corps. Fortunately, the Archduke, though capable, was slow. In a series of maneuvers Napoleon ordered his left wing to retire, his right to advance, and then in five successive days won five successive victories against the Austrians. The Austrian Army, however, though it suffered heavily, was not destroyed. Under the Archduke, it retired in a compact, orderly fashion north of the Danube River toward Bohemia. Napoleon, in turn, descended the Danube along the southern bank and reached Vienna, the enemy's capital, on May 10. He besieged it, and it capitulated three days later on May 13.

ASPERN-ESSLING

Though the Emperor was victor in a campaign and master of Vienna, he was still surrounded by difficulties. Before him, across the Danube, lay the main Austrian Army under the Archduke Charles, an army which would have to be destroyed before peace could be made. Even though Napoleon was in Vienna and the town had surrendered, its people were still exalted by a patriotic ardor and were disposed to riot and to resist.[1] To his right, not many miles distant, lay Hungary and the danger of an uprising of the Hungarian militia. Behind him was another Austrian Army under the Archduke Joseph coming up from Italy; though it was retreating before Napoleon's stepson Eugene, yet in a sense it was advancing on Vienna. It might make trouble, especially if the Archduke Charles should cross and attack Napoleon from the front while Joseph was engaging his forces in the rear.[2] Also behind Napoleon and to his left lay the uprising of the Austrian province of the Tyrol, only partly repressed, threatening his communications both with Italy and the Rhine.[3]

But except for the destruction of the Archduke's army, these were all problems and dangers which could be easily solved and provided for, at least for a time. General Andréossy could be appointed Governor of Vienna, and instructed to maintain a strict police;[4] Massena could be ordered to station patrols all along the Danube from Vienna to Press-

---

[1] General Rapp, *Mémoires du général Rapp* (Paris, n.d.), p. 144.

[2] Rovigo, *op. cit.*, II, Part II, p. 70.

[3] E. Driault, *Napoléon et l'Europe: Tilsit* (Paris, 1917), pp. 414-415.

[4] Napoleon to General Andréossy, Schönbrunn, May 15, 1809, No. 15214, in Napoleon, *Correspondance de Napoléon Ier* (Paris, 1866), XIX, 10-11.

burg, to watch for the Archduke Charles;[5] Bessières could be commanded to stretch out his cavalry reserve from the Danube at Pressburg on his left all along the Hungarian frontier around to the rear of the army, there to cover the army against surprise,[6] while Lefebvre could be directed to continue his successful campaign in the Tyrol.

But there were other difficulties and dangers, more intangible and more remote, that could not be solved so quickly or so easily by the movement of troops. In Italy the priests were stirring up the people. "The agents of the Emperor at Rome affirmed to him the connivance of the Pope with Austria, they maintained that at the first opportunity English troops would disembark at Civita-Vecchia and if by misfortune bad news would arrive from the army, all Italy would rise as in 1799 to drive out the French."[7] In Spain the natives were still unsubdued; and the tide of military conflict had once again turned against the French, as the English commander Wellington outmaneuvered the French marshals Soult and Ney on the road to Madrid.[8] Across the Channel, in England, another great expedition was preparing, destined for the Continent.[9]

Finally in Germany the people, on the whole, were no longer friendly to Napoleon or to his regime. French agents noted among the populace "a sceret effervescence, not a real agitation, but vague dispositions to act, an unhealthy desire for a sudden reversal of fortune, and a sympathy with those who would produce it."[10]

---

[5] Berthier to Masséna, Schönbrunn, May 16, 1809, No. 15216, in Napoleon, *op. cit.*, XIX, 12-13. As a further precaution, Davout had been ordered to keep his troops rested and also furnished with three or four days' supply of bread, so that they would be ready for the Archduke should he cross (Napoleon to Davout, May 15, 1809, No. 15212, in *ibid.*, XIX, 9).

[6] Napoleon to Berthier, Schönbrunn, May 14, 1809 (C. G. Saski, *Campagne de 1809 en Allemagne et en Autriche,* Paris and Nancy, 1899-1902, III, 272-274).

[7] Driault, *op. cit.*, p. 414.   [8] *Ibid.*, p. 410.
[9] *Ibid.*   [10] *Ibid.*, p. 412.

With a few German Army officers, hatred of the French had passed into action against Napoleon's brother Jerome, who as king ruled the French-held German territory of Westphalia. "At the beginning of April, a Prussian officer, Frederick-Charles de Katt, at the head of some partisans, tried to seize the Westphalian fortress of Magdeburg; he failed, but escaped into Bohemia."[11] Shortly afterwards a Colonel von Dörnberg, a Hessian in Jerome's royal guard, plotted to kidnap King Jerome and his French officers, sound the tocsin, and call the people to arms. On April 21, believing that his plot had been discovered, von Dörnberg fled to Homburg, roused the people of the region, gathered six hundred to eight hundred men. But he could not maintain himself against French troops sent by Jerome, and he, too, fled to Bohemia.[12] A few days later a Prussian Major Schill, "counting on the success of von Dörnberg's plot," led his regiment some distance out of Berlin, and then "announced to his men his intention to lead them into Westphalia and to drive the French out of Germany. They acclaimed him; with them he crossed the Elbe and entered Westphalia. But his band was very small; he knew that Dörnberg had failed and had been forced to flee"; and the people did not rally to his support. He retreated, therefore, toward the Baltic and entrenched himself in Stralsund, where he was now being besieged.[13] In the meantime, while these uprisings were occurring, yet a fourth was in preparation by the Duke of Brunswick-Oels, on his Silesian domains, a "legion of vengeance" of thirty-two thousand men.[14]

The real danger of the German situation, however, lay not in the vague unrest of the people, or in the pre-

[11] *Ibid.*
[12] *Ibid.* This passage concerning von Dörnberg is merely a compression of Driault's account, using Driault's words.
[13] *Ibid.*, p. 413.   [14] *Ibid.*

cipitate action of a few army hotheads, but in the more considered attitude of the Prussian government as it debated whether or not it should declare war on Napoleon, now that he was engaged in the heart of Austria. Napoleon, watchful, was aware of his peril, and though to others he scouted the idea that Prussia would declare war, yet he considered what he would do in case she should, and decided how he would march and what orders he would give.[15]

And then, as if the problems presented by these difficulties were not enough, there was always the administrative routine of the Empire to keep abreast of. The daily reports of the minister of police, Fouché, and the detailed reports and documents from the other ministers in Paris followed Napoleon wherever he went. When they arrived, he had then to perform his part in the endless routine of Empire from which he was seldom free—he had to read the reports, glance at the documents, and frame a reply—perhaps dictate a comment, ask a question, start an inquiry, administer a reprimand, communicate a decision, give a command. All this was accomplished on his part swiftly, unerringly, and without undue fatigue. But the ministers in Paris, less capable than he, sometimes blundered; and Napoleon, far away in Vienna, eight hundred miles or five days' travel distant from his capital, could only read about the mistake days after it had occurred and explode: "This measure has no sense. . . ."[16] These are 200,000 francs thrown into the water. . . ."[17] You have not employed enough prudence in

[15] Napoleon to General Clarke, Schönbrunn, May 17, 1809, No. 3175, in Napoleon, *Correspondance inédite de Napoléon Ier conservée aux archives de la guerre publiée par Ernest Picard et Louis Tuetey* (Paris, 1913), III, 59; Napoleon to General Clarke, Ebersdorf, May 19, 1809, No. 446, in Napoleon, *Lettres inédites publiées par Léon Lecestre* (Paris, 1897), I, 311; Napoleon to General Clarke, Ebersdorf, May 19, 1809, No. 15229, in Napoleon, *Correspondance*, XIX, 23-24.
[16] Napoleon, *Correspondance inédite* (Picard and Tuetey), No. 3178, in III, 61-62.   [17] *Ibid.*, No. 3180, in III, 62.

this affair . . . ,"[18] and then send off a reprimand and new instructions which would arrive in Paris five days later, nearly two weeks too late.[19]

In a situation so complex a loyal ally would have been a help, but Napoleon had only the Tsar Alexander of Russia. Alexander had allied with Napoleon in part to save his own country from invasion, in part perhaps to gain certain territorial advantages. But now in accord with his own and his country's interests, which were continually threatened by the presence of a strong, aggressive power dominating Western Europe, Alexander secretly hoped for Napoleon's defeat. Outwardly, it is true, he acted the true ally. At the beginning of hostilities, the Tsar in conversing with the French ambassador, Caulaincourt, "had been feverishly interested in the operations of the army of the Danube; he was impatient to know; he would that he were free to hasten there. When he received news of the five days' campaign in April, he burst into exclamations of admiration; he addressed to Caulaincourt for transmission to the Emperor the warmest compliments.

"But the troops which he had prepared at the Austrian frontier did not budge . . . and Napoleon remained alone on the Danube in front of the Archduke Charles."[20]

II

Napoleon's army was stretched out along the southern bank of the Danube, the left wing at Saint-Poelten under Marshal Davout; the center in and around Vienna under

[18] Napoleon to General Clarke, Ebersdorf, May 19, 1809, No. 15229, in Napoleon, *Correspondance,* XIX, 23-24.

[19] On the administrative routine during this period, see "Ordre du service pendant l'absence de l'empereur," Paris, April 13, 1809, No. 15065, in Napoleon, *Correspondance,* XVIII, 469-470; also *ibid.,* XVIII, 554, XIX, 22-24; Napoleon, *Correspondance inédite* (Picard and Tuetey), III, 59, 61-62; Napoleon, *Lettres inédites* (Lecestre), I, 311.

[20] Driault, *op. cit.,* pp. 415, 419; see also Rovigo, *op. cit.,* Part II, 69-70.

Marshal Lannes; the right down the river from Vienna all the way to Pressburg under Marshal Massena; the cavalry reserve under Marshal Bessières swinging south and east from Pressburg around to Neustadt in the rear: 109,272 men in all,[21] covering a front of 115 miles,[22] under the three most capable corps commanders the army possessed and an adequate cavalry chief. In front of the army, and a bar to its further march, was the Danube, an immense stream, here about one third of a mile wide, its waters now running high and strong from the spring thaws, and with all the bridges down for miles above and below Vienna.[23]

On the other side, just exactly where Napoleon did not know, lay the main Austrian Army under the Archduke Charles. It was Napoleon's hope that eventually, perhaps in a week or two, he would be able to smash the Austrian force with a single decisive blow, and then would come peace and an end to many difficulties. But all that was in the future, and in the meanwhile Napoleon's immediate task was to transfer his army across the Danube. To accomplish this, it was necessary to find a suitable place for

[21] This figure is an estimate. From the documents we learn, it is true, that on May 18 the Guard numbered 9,457 officers and men "présents sous les armes"; on May 15 the cavalry reserve numbered 13,491; on May 20 the Third Corps, 31,414; on May 15 the Fourth Corps, 25,617. But exact figures for the Demont division of recruits before the Battle of Aspern are lacking; after the battle, on May 25, it numbered 4,264 men, and, since its losses in the battle were slight, this figure has been used. Exact figures, moreover, for the Second Corps during the middle weeks of May are also lacking: we only know that of its divisions, the division Tharreau numbered 7,145, the division Claparède, 8,960 on April 15; the division Sainte-Hilaire numbered 9,541 on May 1. These figures have been used for the Second Corps, but 2,700 has been subtracted from them, 2,000 for the losses of the division Claparède at Ebersberg, 700 for the losses of the division Saint-Hilaire at Nussdorf. For the documents see the tables in Saski, *op. cit.*, II, 376-379; III, 396-406.

[22] Air-line distance from Saint-Poelten to Vienna to Pressburg to Neustadt.

[23] Coignet, *op. cit.*, p. 242; Vicomte de Pelleport, *Souvenirs militaires et intimes du général Vicomte de Pelleport de 1793 à 1853* (Paris and Bordeaux, 1857), I, 264; Jean Jacques Germain Pelet, *Mémoires sur la guerre de 1809 en Allemagne* (Paris, 1824-26), III, 258.

a pontoon bridge; to have materials gathered there—boats, pontoons, anchors, ropes, timber, planks, chains, forges, implements, tools, etc.—for its construction; to see to it that the army was ready for the next move—that the infantry was provided with shoes, cartridges, and food, and the artillery with munitions, and to collect reserves of the same; and then, when everything was ready, to concentrate his army of one hundred thousand men stretched out over one hundred miles, to build the bridge, to send the army and the supplies across, and to do all this swiftly, secretly, unobserved by Austrian eyes. It was an immense undertaking calling for skill, energy, and tremendous drive. Characteristically, Napoleon set to work at once.

On the evening of May 11, even before the surrender of Vienna had been assured, Napoleon instructed General Songis, who was in charge of the artillery, and General Bertrand, who was in command of the engineers, each to send an officer along the shore of the Danube below Vienna, searching for a place where a bridge could be built. Napoleon, after looking at a map whose scale was probably too small to show much detail,[24] suggested that Fischamend, thirteen miles below Vienna, would be a good location, since there the Danube flowed in a single bed, and did not divide into a broad, complex network of branches.[25] In accordance with these instructions the next day, May 12, was spent in reconnoitering, and on the morning of May 13, Generals Bertrand and Songis were ready with their reports.

[24] This is an inference. Pelet states: "Tel est le Danube, comme nous le montraient nos reconnaissances et l'excellente carte topographique des environs de Vienne par Louis Schmidt" (Pelet, *op. cit.*, III, 266). I assume this was the map Napoleon used. It may have been a good map for the day, but its scale was rather small, too small to show much detail. Napoleon, in fact, complained to the minister of war that the map division at Paris had not sent the detailed maps which were in the war office until it was too late. As a result, he had been forced to rely upon inadequate maps.

[25] Napoleon to Songis, Schönbrunn, May 11, 1809, 11:30 P.M. (Saski, *op. cit.*, III, 236).

That of Bertrand was brief: the bridge which had spanned the Danube at Vienna had been so completely destroyed by the Austrians in their retreat that it could not be restored, and the place was not suitable for the rapid construction of another. The report of Songis was longer: Fischamend, it said, was unsuitable as a bridge site, since the banks of the Danube were there too high and steep, the stream was too broad, and the boats near-by were insufficient. If the Emperor insisted on having a bridge below Vienna, Songis would recommend Kaiserebersdorf, five and three-tenths miles[26] below the capital, where the Danube was "a little narrower . . . and a few sand-banks which rose there would make it easy to use wooden horses (*chevalets*) and thus husband the supply of pontoons and boats."[27] But Songis advised that the bridge be constructed at Nussdorf, three miles[28] above Vienna. There, the Danube was narrow, a depot of stores and supplies was near, and a bridge had once before been erected, in 1806.[29] Napoleon was impressed, instructed Bertrand, who was present, to reconnoiter the Nussdorf crossing, and had a dispatch sent off to Massena, directing him to gather materials for a bridge at Kaiserebersdorf, as Songis had suggested.[30]

In accordance with his instructions Bertrand rode off from the imperial headquarters at Schönbrunn, and with the assistance of Lannes reconnoitered the Nussdorf crossing. To both men the location seemed extraordinarily

[26] Distance as measured from the fortification wall of Vienna to the center of Kaiserebersdorf by the most direct roads of the period.

[27] Songis to Berthier, Schönbrunn, May 13, 1809 (Saski, *op. cit.*, III, 261).

[28] Distance as measured from the fortification wall of Vienna to the center of Nussdorf by the most direct roads of the period.

[29] Songis to Berthier, Schönbrunn, May 13, 1809 (Saski. *op. cit.*, III, 260-261).

[30] Napoleon to Berthier, Schönbrunn, May 13, 1809, No. 15197, in Napoleon, *Correspondance*, XVIII, 555; Berthier to Masséna, Schönbrunn, May 13, 1809, 10 A.M. (Pelet, *op. cit.*, III, 433-434); Berthier to Masséna, Schönbrunn, May 13, 1809 (*ibid.*, 434).

favorable for the rapid construction of a pontoon bridge, and a messenger was dispatched to Napoleon to inform him of the fact and to ask him to order the collection of boats at the crossing. But without waiting for Napoleon's reply or for additional boats, Lannes, in his anxiety to possess the opposite shore before the Austrians took alarm, began incautiously in broad daylight to send across French troops in whatever boats happened to be at hand. Through the morning and part of the afternoon, he continued to have the soldiers rowed across until one thousand had been landed on the other side. This activity, however, had not been unperceived by Austrian scouts; an Austrian force gathered, and then attacked the isolated French detachment. The few French soldiers stood off the Austrian force as long as they could, thus enabling four hundred of their number to be transported back to the other side, but eventually the rest were surrounded and forced to surrender.[31]

In the meanwhile Napoleon had ridden down from Schönbrunn. He tried to send over cannon, but could not find boats sufficiently large. He and Lannes could see the conflict and struggle that was being fought out on the other side, and in their agitation they paced up and down the bank of the Danube, but could do nothing. When the fighting was over, Napoleon rode back to the palace. The order he sent off to Massena that night reflects his irritation and exasperation, and also his concern:

As I informed you, M. le duc, the intention of the Emperor is that you will personally, with General Molitor, repair to Ebersdorf to protect the construction of the bridge below Vienna. . . . This bridge becomes of the greatest importance, and with some activity the enemy can be surprised at this point. The bridge above Vienna, at Nussdorf, will offer greater diffi-

[31] Saski, *op. cit.*, III, 263, n. 1.

culty because the enemy has discovered our project. The mistake was made of throwing without precaution several companies of infantrymen on the other bank; and instead of establishing themselves in a house, they exposed themselves and were captured. It is necessary, M. le duc, that you collect boats, ropes, anchors, everything that is necessary, that you establish cannon on the right bank; that then you will have some men cross who will entrench themselves and will be protected by artillery. War has its rules which must be followed, the essential is to put forth the greatest activity, to bring together what is necessary for the bridge in such a manner as to throw it across quickly before the enemy can suspect and oppose it. The Emperor is counting on your bridge, for that of Nussdorf will present many difficulties.[32]

At Kaiserebersdorf, the Danube was divided by islands into four branches, necessitating the construction of four successive pontoon bridges. The first bridge would extend from the right bank across the water for 505 yards, over one fourth of a mile, to a small island, or rather sandbank, set in the midst of the stream. The second bridge would extend from the sandbank across 250 yards of swiftly flowing water, for here ran the current, to the first large island, which was called the Lobgrund and was about 630 yards wide. The third bridge would reach from the Lobgrund, over the smallest branch, only 30 yards broad, to the second large island, the Lobau, which was over a mile wide. Finally, the fourth bridge would go from the Lobau across the last branch of the Danube, only 83 yards wide, to the mainland. The total distance from the mainland on the right bank across the four branches and the three islands to the mainland on the left was about two miles.[33]

---

[32] Berthier to Masséna, Schönbrunn, May 13, 1809, 11 P.M. (Pelet, *op. cit.,* III, 434-435). Though the order was signed by Berthier, it was probably dictated by Napoleon. The tone as well as such a phrase as "La guerre a des règles qu'il faut suivre" is characteristic.

[33] Sources differ as to the width of the various branches of the Danube

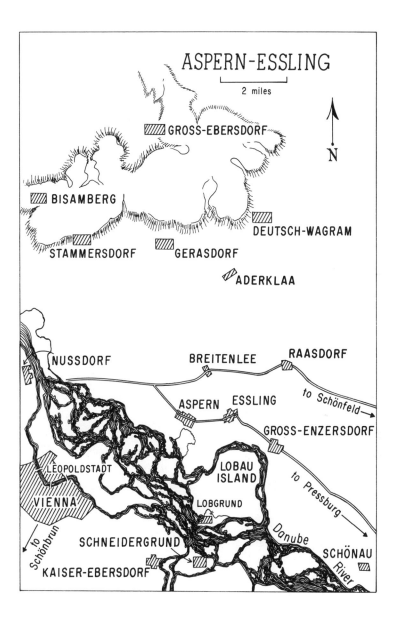

ASPERN-ESSLING

2 miles

N

GROSS-EBERSDORF

BISAMBERG

DEUTSCH-WAGRAM

STAMMERSDORF GERASDORF

ADERKLAA

NUSSDORF BREITENLEE RAASDORF

ASPERN ESSLING to Schönfeld→

GROSS-ENZERSDORF

LEOPOLDSTADT LOBAU ISLAND to Pressburg→

VIENNA LOBGRUND

to Schönbrun Danube SCHÖNAU

SCHNEIDERGRUND River

KAISER-EBERSDORF

At Kaiserebersdorf preparations were made for the construction of the bridge. Molitor's division of Massena's corps arrived and took up its quarters.[34] Just above the town a work-place was established, concealed from the Austrians by a small forest and situated on a little stream on which pontoons could be floated. Here, during the day soldier-workmen shaped up the materials for the bridge, while during the night engineers ventured forth on the broad Danube sounding the depths and the points of anchorage.[35]

at this point. The following table gives the estimates of the 10th Bulletin, the *Mémorial du dépôt de guerre,* Chapuis, Pelet, Marbot, and Drieu. The figures are in "toises" and a *toise* is 6.39 feet long or about two meters (10th Bulletin, No. 15246, in Napoleon, *Correspondance,* XIX, 34; France, Dépôt général de la guerre, *Mémorial du dépôt général de la guerre,* Paris, 1843, VIII, 356; Édouard Gachot, *Histoire militaire de Masséna,* Paris, 1913, p. 161, n. 2; Jean Marbot, *Mémoires,* Paris, 1891, II, 177; Pelet, *op. cit.,* III, 264-266). I have followed none of the sources, but have used the secondary account of Von Hoen and Kerchnawe, who have based their figures on Brinner, 1. Teil, II, 66 (M. von Hoen and H. Kerchnawe, *Krieg 1809,* Vienna, 1910, IV, 335). The figures given in Von Hoen and Kerchnawe check fairly well with measurements taken from the map in the back of Oskar Christe's *Erzherzog Carl von Österreich* (Vienna and Leipzig, 1912), Vol. III. According to that map the first branch was 460 meters wide, the sandbank 300 meters, the second branch 270 meters, the Lobgrund 660 meters, the third branch 30 meters, the Lobau 1,610 meters, the last branch 80 meters.

	10th Bulletin	*Mémorial du dépôt*	Chapuis	Pelet	Marbot	Drieu
1st branch	240	240		240	250	225
2d branch	120	120		170	180	185
3d branch				15	20	
4th branch	70	70	54	50-70	70	

[34] On May 14, Massena ordered Molitor to transfer his division to Kaiserebersdorf at once, "où vous recevrez des instructions ultérieures" (Massena to Molitor, Vienna, May 14, 1809, 5:30 A.M., in Saski, *op. cit.,* III, 274). It is possible that this order was countermanded, since Saski states, apparently on the basis of the "Rapport historique de la division Molitor," that from May 14 to 18 Molitor's division was quartered "en avant de Schwechat"; only on the eighteenth was the division placed "près du point de passage choisi sur le Danube" (Saski, *op. cit.,* III, 323, n. 2). Pelet also asserts that Molitor's division was encamped at Schwechat (Pelet, *op. cit.,* III, 266-267).

[35] Baron Lejeune, *Souvenirs d'un officier de l'empire* (Toulouse, 1851), I, 349, 353, 357-358. Despite what Lejeune says, I doubt if this activity went

Most of the materials, however, could not be found in the small suburban town of Kaiserebersdorf, but had to be sought in the city of Vienna, and here difficulties were encountered. Planks and beams and ropes in sufficient quantity could be located and shipped down to Ebersdorf; but a sufficient number of boats (General Bertrand estimated that he needed eighty, one to every 20 feet) and of anchors to hold them could not be found.[36] After two days' search only forty-eight boats had been collected;[37] after four days' search ninety had been assembled, but of these only seventy were as yet fit for use—the other twenty lacked ropes and oars and some needed to be calked; and of those seventy, some twelve to fifteen were too large to be used as pontoon boats to support a bridge, though they could transport troops.[38] In addition, anchors in sufficient quantity still were lacking.

Napoleon was kept informed of the situation by the reports of Bertrand and Massena and of the aides-de-camp who visited the work-place.[39] As the delay continued and when he learned that Archduke Charles was really on the other side of the Danube[40] and not in distant Moravia as he had hoped,[41] Napoleon considered the expedient of a flying bridge which could be constructed more rapidly. But this project was soon abandoned. It was really not needed, for as the reports came into headquarters on May 16 and 17, it was seen that the situation both on the Danube and elsewhere had cleared. Boats in sufficient number had

on at the work-place until May 18. The first convoy of boats loaded with materials apparently did not leave Vienna until the evening of May 17. A sounding of the river took place on the night of May 18.

[36] Bertrand to Napoleon, Vienna, May 15, 1809, at midnight (Saski, *op. cit.*, III, 287, n. 2).

[37] *Ibid.*

[38] Bertrand to Napoleon, Vienna, May 17, in the evening (*ibid.*).

[39] Lejeune, *op. cit.*, I, 353.

[40] Saski, *op. cit.*, III, 322-323.   [41] *Ibid.*, III, 257.

finally been assembled at Vienna, and the construction of the bridge could begin on the eighteenth.[42] In the meanwhile, Vienna was quiet. The other Austrian Army under Archduke Joseph was in full retreat. The pursuing Italo-French force would soon join and reinforce the main Napoleonic army. Marshal Lefebvre had captured Innsbruck, and the Tyrolean rebellion was nearly finished. Prince Poniatowski had driven the Austrians out of Poland, and was now ready to invade Austrian Galicia. Best of all, news was received from St. Petersburg that Russian troops were on the march against Austria, and had been ordered to invade the country.[43] From Paris, it is true, came a dispatch from the minister of war, General Clarke, reporting that he had been informed that the Prussian Blücher had invaded Westphalia with thirteen thousand men.[44] But Napoleon considered this information to be false,[45] and in a sanguine mood he dictated the conclusion of a letter to his stepson, the Prince Eugene: "The enemy is thus beaten on all sides. The immense materials that are needed for a bridge over the Danube have been assembled; I hope to

[42] *Ibid.*, III, 287. Napoleon also made other preparations for the coming operation. On May 15 he ordered General Songis of the artillery to collect all the munitions which could be found at Vienna, "de la poudre, cartouches à canon et autres." "On doit avoir de quoi donner une bataille," concluded Napoleon (Napoleon, *Correspondance inédite*, Picard and Tuetey, No. 3171, III, 58). On May 18 he ordered the distribution "dans la journée des souliers qui se trouvent en magasin": 12,000 pairs to the division of general Oudinot; 10,000 to the Guard; 6,000 to the Saint-Hilaire division; 3,000 to the Demont division: total 31,000 pairs of shoes. He concluded: "Faites-moi connaître ce qui reste en magasin après cette distribution" (Napoleon to Berthier, Schönbrunn, May 18, 1809, in Pelet, *op. cit.*, III, 437).

[43] That Napoleon was aware of these occurrences is shown by two dispatches: Napoleon to Eugene, Schönbrunn, May 17, 1809, No. 15224, in Napoleon, *Correspondance*, XIX, 19; Berthier to Poniatowski, May 18, 1809 (*Mémorial du dépôt de la guerre*, VIII, 363-364).

[44] Clarke to Napoleon, Paris, May 8, 1809, 7 A.M. (Saski, *op. cit.*, III, 310-312).

[45] Napoleon to Clarke, Schönbrunn, May 17, 1809, No. 3175, in Napoleon, *Correspondance inédite* (Picard and Tuetey), III, 59.

cross the 18th or the 19th and scatter the armies which are found *(réunies)* between the Danube and Moravia."[46]

When on May 18 Napoleon learned that the materials for the bridge were nearly ready, he left Schönbrunn for Kaiserebersdorf, arriving with a small staff in the late afternoon.[47] The materials for the bridge had been gathered

[46] Napoleon to Eugene, Schönbrunn, May 17, 1809, No. 15224, in Napoleon, *Correspondance*, XIX, 19-20.

[47] In regard to certain facts which are stated in the following paragraph, the sources disagree. Accounts in the memoirs—Pelet, Marbot (who is copying Pelet), and Savary—have Napoleon arrive at Ebersdorf on May 19 (Pelet, *op. cit.*, III, 272; Marbot, *op. cit.*, II, 70-71. Much of Marbot, on p. 179, at least, is taken word for word from Pelet). But contemporary accounts—the May 18 and May 19 reports of two Württemberg aides who were attached to Napoleon's headquarters, and the account of Castellane, which was probably based on the daily letter he wrote to his father—place Napoleon's departure from Schönbrunn and his arrival at Kaiserebersdorf on the eighteenth (Von Hoen and Kerchnawe, *op. cit.*, IV, 351; Esprit Victor, le comte de Castellane, *Journal du Maréchal de Castellane*, Paris, 1897, I, 54).

The memoirs state that the embarkation of the first companies of Molitor's division occurred on May 19 (Pelet, *op. cit.*, III, 272-273; Marbot, *op. cit.*, II, 179; Savary, *op. cit.*, II, 70-71). But the 9th Bulletin, written on May 19; the 10th Bulletin, written on May 23; the *Rapport historique de la division Molitor*, written shortly after the events; and the Austrian reports of May 18 state that the operation began in the afternoon of May 18 (9th Bulletin, Vienna, May 19, 1809, No. 15239, in Napoleon, *Correspondance*, XIX, 28-30; 10th Bulletin, Kaiserebersdorf, May 23, 1809, No. 15246, in *ibid.*, XIX, 34; Saski, *op. cit.*, III, 323, n. 2; Von Hoen and Kerchnawe, *op. cit.*, IV, 351-352). The 9th Bulletin was not dictated or written at Vienna. Both Napoleon and Berthier were in Kaiserebersdorf on May 19, and all other letters and dispatches of that day bear the place-line of Kaiserebersdorf. It is possible that the 9th Bulletin was issued from or published in Vienna.

The memoirs have the first companies of Molitor's division land on the second large island, the Lobau (Pelleport, *op. cit.*, I, 265; Pelet, *op. cit.*, III, 272-273; Marbot, *op. cit.*, II, 179; Savary, *op. cit.*, II, 70-71; Lejeune, *op. cit.*, I, 358). From the Austrian reports of that evening, the later commands given to Molitor, and the *Rapport historique de la division Molitor*, it is clear, however, that the first companies landed on the first large island, the Lobgrund (Von Hoen and Kerchnawe, *op. cit.*, IV, 351; Saski, *op. cit.*, III, 323 and n. 2).

The sources also differ on the time when these events occurred. From the report of the Württemberg aide, we learn that Napoleon left Schönbrunn at one o'clock in the afternoon (Von Hoen and Kerchnawe, *op. cit.*, IV, 351); by the 9th Bulletin we are informed that the operation—Molitor's embarkation and the start of the construction of the bridge—began at 4 P.M. (No. 15239, in Napoleon, *Correspondance*, XIX, 28-30); but Pelet states that Napoleon

together a few hundred yards above Kaiserebersdorf on the edge of the river and along the creek, and Napoleon examined them in the greatest detail. When he had made sure "that they had assembled everything that the circumstances would permit being procured,"[48] he gave the order that a few companies from Molitor's division, Massena's corps,

---

did not arrive at Kaiserebersdorf until "vers cinq heures du soir" and that the embarkation occurred after that (Pelet, *op. cit.*, III, 272); Saski, apparently basing his statement on the *Rapport historique de la division Molitor*, asserts that "quelques détachements de cette division prirent pied dans l'île dite Lobgrund . . . à 5 heures du soir" (Saski, *op. cit.*, III, 323, n. 2); Von Hoen and Kerchnawe, writing from the Austrian reports of that evening, state that Molitor approached the Austrian shore toward six o'clock (Von Hoen and Kerchnawe, *op. cit.*, IV, 351); while Savary, who took part in the expedition, has Molitor embark in the twilight, probably after eight o'clock on a northern spring evening, and cross in the dark (Savary, *op. cit.*, II, 70-72).

Exact accuracy in statements of time is not, of course, to be expected— after all, these men were not holding watches in their hands, noting the time when each event occurred in order that the hour and minute might be transmitted to historians. Their statements of time are likely to be estimates, and if only for this reason some disagreement is natural. Nevertheless, a comparison of accounts sometimes reveals the truth, and in this case a comparison reveals that the most contemporary accounts—the report of the Württemberg aide, the 9th Bulletin, the Austrian report, and even the *Rapport historique de la division Molitor,* which was written shortly after—really agree with each other, and that the facts given by them fit together to form a plausible, logical succession of events: Napoleon leaves Schönbrunn at one o'clock, arrives at Kaiserebersdorf at four or before, inspects the materials, orders the embarkation of troops, the embarkation takes some time, the troops push off, are rowed across, reach the Lobgrund sometime after five and probably toward six o'clock in the evening. In view of the essential agreement of the contemporary sources, Savary's picture of a night crossing may be rejected; and Pelet's statement that Napoleon did not arrive at Kaiserebersdorf until "toward five o'clock" becomes unlikely for two reasons: first, because it assumes that Napoleon took nearly four hours to cover on horseback the distance from Schönbrunn to Kaiserebersdorf, a matter of two or three leagues—though of course Napoleon may have stopped on the way; second, because the statement assumes that after Napoleon arrived, it took less than an hour for him to inspect the materials and have the troops embark and be rowed across the Danube—this rapidity of execution is of course possible, but it is more likely that the operation began earlier, at four o'clock, as the 9th Bulletin states, and lasted longer.

[48] Pelet, *op. cit.*, III, 272-273. This detail of Napoleon examining the materials rests on the single authority of Pelet, who, however, is usually accurate. The apparent confirmation of Marbot is worthless since he is merely quoting Pelet, without giving credit.

should embark, cross the Danube, and establish themselves on the island of the Lobgrund to cover the construction of the bridge. Napoleon himself supervised the embarkation and took charge of those details usually left to subordinates. He placed the soldiers in the boats, and arranged the men so that the greatest possible number were crowded into each boat; he had cartridges distributed to them before his eyes; he spoke a word to nearly every soldier; and after the six large boats containing infantry had pushed off, he sent after them a boat containing two cannon and "bottes" of grapeshot sufficient for the undertaking.[49]

It was nearly six o'clock in the evening when the boats approached the wooded shore of the first large island, the Lobgrund.[50]   The Austrian sentinels gave the alarm, but the boats landed and the French troops disembarked before the small Austrian detachment which was stationed on the island could come up. The French greatly outnumbered the Austrians, and after a brief skirmish the latter retreated across the island, across the third branch of the Danube into the Lobau, where the Austrian officer in charge sent back the warning to his superior that the French were landing troops on the Austrian side.[51]

In the meanwhile, the French did not at once pursue

[49] Saski, *op. cit.*, III, 323, n. 2.

[50] Rovigo, *op. cit.*, II, 70-71. This description rests on Savary—an eyewitness—but one who makes mistakes. Nevertheless, it may be noted that Laborde, in a secondary account published in 1822 and based on the oral reminiscences of eyewitnesses, also says: "C'étoit un spectacle intéressant de voir Napoléon, sur le rivage, s'occuper des moindres détails de l'embarcation de ses troupes, indiquer comment elles devoient faire entrer les canons dans les bateux, ce qu'on devoit observer pour ne pas être entrainé par le courant" (A. L. J. Laborde, *Voyage pittoresque en Autriche, avec un précis historique de la guerre entre la France et l'Autriche, 1809,* 3 vols., Paris, 1821-23, III, 60). Laborde, however, is not always accurate; his source in this case is unknown (it might have been Savary); his testimony, therefore, is of uncertain value. It tends to confirm, however, Savary's description of the personal activity of Napoleon.

[51] Von Hoen and Kerchnawe, *op. cit.*, IV, 351-352.

the Austrians into the Lobau, but consolidated their position. Having gained a foothold on the opposite shore, the war machine of Napoleon now smoothly moved into action to maintain and to extend that advantage. During the night the rest of Molitor's division was rowed across the Danube;[52] the other divisions of Massena's corps—those of Legrand, Carra, Saint Cyr, and Boudet—broke camp and by a night march concentrated on Kaiserebersdorf;[53] and a detachment of workmen landed on the small sandbank—in the midst of the stream, the Schneidergrund.[54] In the very early morning, Molitor began cautiously to advance his forces through woods and marshes of the Lobau,[55] while the pontonniers started to construct the bridge.[56]

Continuance of the forward movement was halted, however, when a high wind arose in the morning (May 19) and continued through most of the day, making the muddy waters of the Danube so rough that work on the bridge had to be discontinued and reinforcements could not be rowed across to Molitor's division, which was thus left isolated and exposed on the Austrian side.[57] Napoleon, who was quartered at Kaiserebersdorf in an Austrian "country house which was very pleasant, surrounded by a garden,"[58] took advantage of the delay to turn from the immediate problems which the transfer of an army across the Danube involved to those which the governing of a vast Empire presented, and he dictated a few letters: two officials had surrendered the island colonies of Cayenne and Martinique to the English too easily—Napoleon ordered an investigation;[59] in Spain the navy had been unable to

[52] Ibid., IV, 352.
[53] Ibid.
[54] Ibid.
[55] Ibid.
[56] Ibid.
[57] Ibid., IV, 353.
[58] Laborde, op. cit., III, 60.
[59] Napoleon to Decrès, Ebersdorf, May 19, 1809, No. 15230, in Napoleon, Correspondance, XIX, 24.

land some provisions at Barcelona—land them at Rosas;[60] in western France a gendarme had been assassinated—punish the town which allowed this to happen, and if necessary send troops;[61] at Mainz, Marshal Kellermann had diverted to Westphalia troops which were destined for the army—don't do it again, if he does "I shall be obliged to deprive him of his command of the Westphalian corps";[62] in Paris, the minister of war, still excited by the possibility of war with Prussia, imprudently gave the alarm to other officials and to public opinion—two successive reprimands by Napoleon, who, sanguine as ever, dictated: "General Blücher hasn't moved. Prussia doesn't think of making war on me; the Russians are marching against the Austrians." Besides, even if Prussia had attacked, why worry: "Prussia is a mere trifle."[63] Napoleon also dictated the ninth bulletin of the campaign, which reviewed the story of recent events from the retreat of the Archduke Charles, the capture of Vienna, the assembling of materials for the bridge, the transfer of Molitor's division, and the beginning of work on the bridge, which Napoleon "hoped would be finished tomorrow."[64]

In the late afternoon, as the wind began to die down, the army resumed its activity.[65] From Napoleon's headquarters, from three to five in the afternoon, orders were issued prescribing the movements for that night and the

[60] Ibid.

[61] Napoleon to Clarke, Ebersdorf, May 19, 1809, No. 446, in Napoleon, Lettres inédites (Lecestre), I, 311.

[62] Napoleon to Berthier, Ebersdorf, May 19, 1809, No. 15231, in Napoleon, Correspondance, XIX, 24.

[63] Napoleon to Clarke, Ebersdorf, May 19, 1809, No. 15229, in Napoleon, Correspondance, XIX, 23-24; Napoleon to Clarke, Ebersdorf, May 19, 1809, No. 446, in Napoleon, Lettres inédites (Lecestre), I, 311.

[64] 9th Bulletin, Vienna [sic], May 19, 1809, in Adrien Pascal, Les bulletins de la grande armée précédés et accompagnés des rapports sur les armées françaises de 1792 à 1815 (Paris, 1844), V, 55-59.

[65] Von Hoen and Kerchnawe, op. cit., IV, 375.

next day: an order to Massena to have his infantry ready to cross the bridge very early on May 20, probably at dawn, and to have cavalry ready at 5 A.M.;[66] an order to Bessières, in charge of the cavalry reserve, to have his four divisions of cavalry at Kaiserebersdorf the next morning, two divisions at five o'clock, one at six and one at eight;[67] an order to Lannes to have his corps at Kaiserebersdorf by 9 A.M., ready to cross;[68] an order to Davout to move his corps down the river from Saint-Poelten to Vienna by noon the next day;[69] an order to Daru, the quartermaster general, to send all his caissons to Kaiserebersdorf filled with "de pain et de biscuit."[70] In the meanwhile from Molitor on the other shore, word was received that his division was safe and that he had driven the Austrians out of the Lobau.[71] In

[66] Berthier to Massena, Ebersdorf, May 19, 1809, 3:30 P.M., No. 15234, in Napoleon, *Correspondance,* XIX, 26; *Mémorial du dépôt de la guerre,* VIII, 366.

[67] Berthier to Bessières, Ebersdorf, May 19, 1809, 3 P.M., No. 15233, in Napoleon, *Correspondance,* XIX, 25-26. In addition, Bessières was instructed to order General. Colbert to set out for Kaiserebersdorf with his cavalry brigade. General Colbert belonged to the corps of Lannes.

[68] Berthier to Lannes, Ebersdorf, May 19, 1809, 4 P.M., No. 15235, in *ibid.,* XIX, 26-27.

[69] Berthier to Davout, Ebersdorf, May 19, 1809, 8 P.M., No. 15238, in *ibid.,* XIX, 27-28. From these orders, the intention of Napoleon is clear: after the infantry of one corps (Massena's) had passed, he would send across all his cavalry (except Davout's) thirty thousand men in all, to clear the plain on the other side of the Danube; then would follow the infantry of Lannes and Davout. The emphasis would be on a strong cavalry reconnaissance and attack. This supposition is confirmed by an order which Berthier sent to Davout on the evening of May 19. The order is interesting also because it reflects the optimism which existed at French headquarters. The order reads: "Berthier au Davout, Ebersdorf, le 19 mai 1809, sept heures du soir. Vous ordonnerez qu'on ramasse toutes les barques, aussitôt que la rive gauche sera libre; ce qui doit être dans la journée de demain, puisque les ponts que l'Empereur fait jeter à Ebersdorf, à deux lieues au-dessous de Vienne, seront prêts avant midi, et que notre cavalerie inondera la plaine" (Pelet, *op. cit.,* III, 438). It is probable that this optimism regarding the events of the next day was shared by Napoleon.

[70] Berthier to Daru, Ebersdorf, May 19, 1809 (Saski, *op. cit.,* III, 326).

[71] Molitor to Massena, May 19, 1809, 3 P.M. (Saski, *op. cit.,* III, 323-324). When Massena received this dispatch, I do not know. It is logical to suppose that he received it sometime in the late afternoon or evening of May 19. See

the evening the pontonniers resumed work on the bridge[72] and worked all night.[73] The party of men building the second section of the bridge from the Schneidergrund to the Lobgrund finished their work by morning. But those working on the first section from the right bank to the Schneidergrund did not finish until noon.[74] Even when complete, however, despite the superhuman efforts of the engineers, the long slender bridge across the first two branches of the Danube remained a patchwork construction: in the absence of anchors for many of the boats, fisherman's boxes filled with grapeshot had been used; the boats and pontoons were of varying sorts and sizes;[75] and the entire bridge was menaced by the Danube, which, already in flood-stage, now on May 20 began visibly to rise higher.[76]

During the second delay, while the men were still working to complete the bridge, Napoleon sent off several letters—a reprimand to Fouché;[77] another to Cambacérès;[78] a series of minor instructions for Clarke[79]—the last letters Napoleon would dictate before entering into the experi-

---

also "Rapport historique de la division Molitor" (Saski, *op. cit.*, III, 323, n. 2). It may be noted that Gachot in his biography of Massena states that "Le 20 à six heures du matin, l'Empereur lisait ce rapport que lui faisait Masséna" concerning the activities of Molitor and then quotes Massena's report. But the report which Gachot prints as Massena's is in reality a report which General Rapp, an aide-de-camp of the Emperor, made to the latter (Saski, *op. cit.*, III, 324, n. 1). As a result, Gachot's statement throws no light on the question as to when Molitor's dispatch of 3 P.M., May 19, reached Massena and then Napoleon (Gachot, *op. cit.*, p. 160).

[72] Gachot, *op. cit.*, p. 160.   [73] Pelet, *op. cit.*, III, 272-273.

[74] Saski, *op. cit.*, III, 337; Von Hoen and Kerchnawe, *op. cit.*, IV, 375; Pelet, *op. cit.*, III, 272-273.

[75] Saski, *op. cit.*, III, 337; Von Hoen and Kerchnawe, *op. cit.*, IV, 375.

[76] Von Hoen and Kerchnawe, *op. cit.*, IV, 375; Pelet, *op. cit.*, III, 272-273.

[77] Napoleon to Fouché, Ebersdorf, May 20, 1809, No. 448, in Napoleon, *Lettres inédites* (Lecestre), I, 312.

[78] Napoleon to Cambacérès, Ebersdorf, May 20, 1809, No. 447, in *ibid.*, I, 311.

[79] Napoleon to Clarke, Ebersdorf, May 20, 1809, No. 3182, in Napoleon, *Correspondance inédite* (Picard and Tuetey), III, 63; Nos. 15240 and 15241, in Napoleon, *Correspondance*, XIX, 31-32.

ence of the next few days. Confident as ever, in his instructions to Clarke he recurred once again to the subject of Prussia: "Once more, Prussia will not budge; if she moves, I will be there to punish her. Extraordinary events can no longer take place. Besides, I am in a position to provide for everything."[80] But Napoleon's confidence in the ultimate success of his ventures did not preclude a measure of caution: he added that should "unforeseen events" occur, Clarke might provide for the defense of the frontier fortresses of Mayence, Wesel, and Strasbourg without waiting for instructions;[81] and, remembering the possibility of an English invasion, Napoleon urged Clarke to hasten the preparation of a force destined to resist that attack.[82]

Then, having done what he could to protect his empire, sanguine and yet cautious, and alone in the responsibility of command, Napoleon left Kaiserebersdorf in the early afternoon and set out for the Austrian side. Accompanied by his marshals, Berthier, Massena, Lannes, and Bessières, and followed by his usual escort of Guides and Mamelukes, a few hundred of his Guard in their brightly colored uniforms,[83] he crossed the long, slender bridge over the first two branches of the Danube; crossed the first large island, the Lobgrund, and the bridge over the third branch which Molitor had built;[84] crossed the second large island, the Lobau, and after a journey of two miles shortly before three o'clock arrived at the point on the fourth branch of the Danube where Molitor proposed to build the fourth bridge to the mainland.[85] Napoleon approved the location; the

[80] Napoleon to Clarke, Ebersdorf, May 20, 1809, No. 15240, in Napoleon, *Correspondance*, XIX, 31.   [81] *Ibid.*, p. 31.   [82] *Ibid.*, pp. 31-32.
[83] Von Hoen and Kerchnawe, *op. cit.*, IV, 376.
[84] Rapp to Napoleon, May 19, 1809 (Saski, *op. cit.*, III, 324, n. 1).
[85] Von Hoen and Kerchnawe, *op. cit.*, IV, 378-379; Pelet, *op. cit.*, III, 277; Pelleport, *op. cit.*, I, 266; Saski, *op. cit.*, III, 336, 337; 10th Bulletin, No. 15246, in Napoleon, *Correspondance*, XIX, 34; *Mémorial du dépôt de guerre*, VIII, 367.

construction of the bridge began at once; it was finished by six o'clock in the evening, and Napoleon after days of struggle and planning finally stood on the left bank of the Danube with a few of his troops.

In the meanwhile, during the afternoon the French Army which had assembled at Kaiserebersdorf began slowly to file across the long, slender bridge over the Danube, the infantry "à pas rompus," the cavalry leading their horses, in order that the fragile pontoon bridge might not be pounded to destruction.[86]

III

When on May 11 Napoleon began to prepare for the transfer of his army across the Danube, the Archduke Charles with the main Austrian Army was seventy miles away, northwest of Vienna,[87] and there was only a single Austrian corps to oppose Napoleon's passage. But the failure of the French attempt to cross at Nussdorf, and the unavoidable delay in securing materials for the bridge at Kaiserebersdorf had given the Archduke time to bring up the Austrian Army, and from May 16 on it was present on the northern side of the Danube.[88] It numbered about 120,000 men.[89]

[86] Von Hoen and Kerchnawe, op. cit., IV, 375-377; Pelleport, op. cit., I, 266; Saski, op. cit., III, 337; Pelet, op. cit., III, 273.

[87] On May 12, the Archduke was at Horn and Mold, which were about sixty miles northwest of Vienna. On May 11 he was farther away at Neu-Polla, ten miles from Horn (F. Loraine Petre, Napoleon and the Archduke Charles, London, 1909, p. 257).   [88] Criste, op. cit., III, 116.

[89] The secondary authorities disagree as to the exact size of the Archduke's army. Petre places it at 133,916; the Archduke's biographer, Angeli, at 121,700. The latter figure is probably nearer the truth, for while Angeli has a pro-Austrian bias, yet he worked from the Austrian archives, and in questions of fact tends to be exact; but Petre, though impartial, tends to be unreliable. It may be noted, furthermore, that another Austrian biographer of the Archduke, Criste, who has based his work on the best secondary accounts, states that the Archduke went into the Battle of Aspern-Essling with 98,250 men. But the Archduke left some troops behind as a reserve. If we take Angeli's figures for the corps which made up this reserve and add them to 98,250, we

The Archduke, sometimes vacillating and slow, but still the most capable of all the commanders who had yet opposed Napoleon, had placed his forces rather skillfully. He had camped the several corps in a line perpendicular to the Danube, along the base of the chain of hills which crossed the Danube just above Vienna,[90] a position from which the army could easily descend into the vast plain below whenever news was received that the French were crossing. The Archduke himself—a tall, lean man of thirty-nine, dark-complexioned, with high cheek-bones (the eyes of a commander, a long thick nose which hooked over a protruding underlip and a rather small chin)—took up his quarters at Gross-Ebersdorf, a small town about eight miles back from the Danube, and there he remained during the succeeding days, with his back to the valley hills, his glance as it were going across the plain to the Danube and beyond, trying to divine from a medley of rumors and reports what was happening on the French side of the stream and what Napoleon intended, ready to move his army in any threatened direction, yet not desiring to be misled into any false maneuver by misinformation.

The Archduke drew his information from three sources: from an Austrian observation post on the Bisamberg, a mountain which stood across and up the Danube from Vienna, a short distance back from the stream, and which commanded a view for miles down the valley; from Austrian scouts who were stationed all along the river from the Bisamberg down to Hungary; and from loyal Austrian inhabitants of the southern bank, who, unobserved by the French, stole across the Danube and brought word of the

---

get 114,450, which is fairly close to Angeli's figure of 121,700. It is probably safe to say that the Austrian force numbered about 120,000 men. See Moriz edler von Angeli, *Erzherzog Carl von Österreich als Feldherr und Heeresorganisator* (Vienna and Leipzig, 1897), IV, 292; Criste, *op. cit.*, III, 126-127; Petre, *op. cit.*, p. 264. [90] Petre, *op. cit.*, p. 264.

French activities. The Archduke's most reliable reports came at first from this latter source, the unsolicited communications of craftsmen, peasants, tradesmen, humble subjects who risked their lives thus to serve their monarchy. On the evening of May 17, one of these men, an inhabitant of Vienna, arrived with the news that a detachment of French had left Viennese waters with a consignment of boats and pontoons and dropped downstream. The Archduke thought this activity was merely preparation for a demonstration of some sort, presumably to distract his attention from the real point of crossing. But he gave the order that the chain of Austrian outposts along the Danube should be on the alert.[91] The same evening, May 17, another Austrian from a small town near Kaiserebersdorf slipped across the Danube and informed the Austrian Colonel Bakonyi stationed opposite that a large number of French troops were camped above Kaiserebersdorf, and that as soon as the boats arrived they would begin to cross. The Colonel, however, supposed that the French would land not on the Lobau but several miles lower down at the village of Schönau, and he requested permission of his superior to strengthen the post at the latter point.[92]

On May 18, early in the morning, an Austrian spy notified the Colonel that in the waters below Vienna the French had gathered ninety-six boats. The Colonel became convinced that the moment of crossing was approaching. Again he asked his superior for reinforcements and then rode off to Schönau, which seemed to him to be the place most threatened.[93] The Colonel's second request for aid reached his superior, Field Marshal Hiller of the Sixth Corps, in the early afternoon, and the Field Marshal decided to reconnoiter on his own account. On this afternoon

[91] Von Hoen and Kerchnawe, *op. cit.*, IV, 348.
[92] *Ibid.*, p. 348. [93] *Ibid.*

reconnaissance he noted the boats gathered by the French along the opposite shore, became convinced that the Colonel was right and that a crossing was imminent, ordered, therefore, that two cannon be sent to Gross-Enzersdorf, a village back of the Lobau, and then late in the evening rode back to the headquarters of the Sixth Corps to prepare his report to the Archduke.[94]

In the meanwhile, on the same day, May 18, the Archduke, as he thought over the information which had come to him, had also become convinced that the French intended to cross at some spot below Vienna, probably at the Lobau, with a large number of troops. But he believed, however (just why is not clear), that the main French force would cross above Vienna at Nussdorf and that the detachment which crossed downstream would be used only to outflank the Austrians as they repelled this main French attack. With this supposition in mind, the Archduke ordered Field Marshal Hiller to fortify the island which lay on the Austrian side of the Nussdorf crossing. This island could then be defended by a few thousand men, and the rest of the Austrian Army would be free to move against any French force wherever it appeared.[95]

Thus by May 18 the Austrian command had divined Napoleon's intention to cross below Vienna with at least a portion of his army; they had foreseen that this crossing would be made in the vicinity of the Lobau; they did not know, it is true, exactly where the landing would be made or at what time, and they had not yet divined to the full Napoleon's intention—namely, to cross with all his army— but it was probably with no great surprise that first the Colonel Bakonyi, then the Field Marshal Hiller, and finally the Archduke learned that at about 6 P.M. on May 18 a

[94] *Ibid.*, p. 349.   [95] *Ibid.*, pp. 353-354.

detachment of French troops had landed on the Lobgrund, and driven back the Austrian outposts stationed there.[96]

In the morning of May 19 the Archduke, still uncertain as to whether or not the Lobgrund landing was a blind, but realizing that the moment of decision was near, ordered his army corps to place themselves in readiness to march and to send their baggage trains to the rear.[97] In the afternoon, when the Austrian outposts brought in word of the further concentration of French troops around Kaiserebersdorf, of the clouds of dust raised by marching columns and the flash of weapons in the sun, and when a spy brought news of the transfer of Napoleon's headquarters to Kaiserebersdorf,[98] the Archduke took the further step of dividing his army into three parts: the Fifth and Sixth Corps of twenty-six thousand men, who were quartered near the Danube at Stammersdorf opposite Vienna, he constituted as a defensive group to remain where it was and to defend the Nussdorf crossing and the Bisamberg against attack; the First Corps of twenty-three thousand men which lay back of the Fifth and Sixth at Hagenbrunn, he constituted as a reserve; the Second, Fourth, and Reserve Corps of fifty-five thousand men who were situated back of the First Corps, from eight to twelve miles distant from the Danube around his headquarters at Gross Ebersdorf,[99] he formed into a mobile offensive group to be led by himself and to operate against the French as they issued into the plain from the Lobau.[100]

In the evening, as protection for a reconnaissance he proposed to make in the morning, the Archduke sent an ad-

[96] *Ibid.*, pp. 350, 354. It seems likely that the Archduke did not receive the news until the next morning, May 19.

[97] *Ibid.*, p. 365.　　　　　　　　[98] *Ibid.*

[99] In the villages of Königsbrunn, Enzersfeld, Gross Ebersdorf, Eibersbrunn, and Pillichsdorf.

[100] *Ibid.*, pp. 366-367; Criste, *op. cit.*, III, 116.

vance guard of infantry and cavalry halfway across the valley plain toward the Lobau to Deutsch-Wagram and Aderklaa.[101] Upon receiving news of the French advance in the Lobau, he ordered his offensive group to move down from the hills and take up a station in the plain, along the line of Seyring-Reuhof, one fourth of the distance to the Lobau.[102] Then when this double movement had been accomplished by dawn, the next morning, May 20, the Archduke rode off from Gross Ebersdorf and joined the advance guard at Aderklaa.[103]

Upon his arrival at Aderklaa, however, the Archduke at first did little. The French were inactive, and the Archduke waited for events to develop.[104] In the early afternoon, however, he received word by semaphore from the observation post on the Bisamberg that the French had completed their bridge across the Danube, and their troops were filing across.[105] Shortly afterwards Field Marshal Hiller rode up at full gallop to report that a French detachment had crossed to the mainland from the Lobau and that a passage of the river by the French was under way. Now was the time, the Field Marshal insisted, for the Austrian Army to advance and to attack the French before they had time to develop their full strength on the plain.[106] To this advice, however, the Archduke gave little heed.[107] A battle, he knew, must come between the two armies before peace could be made. For the Austrian Army to advance now and to check the French from issuing forth into the plain would only postpone the conflict; the French Army would only pile up in the Lobau, from which it could not be dis-

[101] Von Hoen and Kerchnawe, *op. cit.*, IV, 367.
[102] *Ibid.*, p. 368.
[103] *Ibid.*, pp. 368, 369.   [104] Criste, *op. cit.*, III, 119-120.
[105] Von Hoen and Kerchnawe, *op. cit.*, IV, 379-380; Petre, *op. cit.*, p, 271.
[106] Von Hoen and Kerchnawe, *op. cit.*, IV, 379.
[107] *Ibid.*, IV, 380.

lodged, and then would break out at some other point, perhaps surprising the Archduke, perhaps forcing him to fight on ground with which he was not familiar and unfavorable to Austrian tactics. No, the Archduke now knew where the French were, he was familiar with the ground on which he must fight, it was favorable to Austrian methods of fighting. He would allow the French, therefore, to cross unmolested, and perhaps to advance into the plain, and then he would fight it out to a decision.[108]

That evening of May 20, consequently, he prepared for the battle which would come on the following day: sent forward an advance guard of cavalry to observe the French and to hem in their scouts;[109] issued a proclamation to his troops;[110] ordered his mobile offensive group to move further forward across the plain and to occupy the line of Wagram-Gerasdorf, halfway between the valley hills and the Danube and about six and a half miles from the Lobau;[111] brought up his reserve of twenty-three thousand

---

[108] The intentions of the Archduke at this point are obscure, especially in regard to two points: Did he intend to let all the French Army or only a portion of it cross? Did he intend to attack the French once they had crossed, or wait and let them attack him? Angeli states that the Archduke's intention was to let only a portion of the French cross to the left bank, but "a sufficiently large number . . . as to make their destruction decisive of the fate of the whole army." But this statement, which is not supported by proof, seems incorrect, for the very next morning, only twelve hours later, when the Archduke arranged his troops and then ordered them to move forward, he made his arrangements and his advance on the assumption that he would find the French forces far out on the plain, and when he had finished his march and still did not find them, he was astonished and had to rearrange his plans and his troops before he could move forward again. Apparently he thought he had given the French time enough to get across the Danube and into the plain, and apparently it was his intention to let them do so.

As to the second point: Did he intend to attack or to wait and let the French attack him? there is no evidence. His proclamation to his troops, issued on the afternoon of May 20, states: "To-morrow, or the following day, there will be a great battle." It is clear, therefore, that he intended to fight it out. But how he expected to bring on the conflict is not certain.

[109] Von Hoen and Kerchnawe, *op. cit.*, IV, 380-381.

[110] Petre, *op. cit.*, pp. 271-272.   [111] Criste, *op. cit.*, III, 122.

men to the same line of maneuver;[112] commanded the Sixth Corps at Stammersdorf to make ready to march,[113] left only the small Fifth Corps to guard the Nussdorf crossing.[114]

Due to faulty work on the part of his staff, there was some delay in the transmission of the Archduke's orders, and the First, Second, and Fourth Corps did not receive theirs until late. As a result, they marched into position during the night, and (the fact is important) they had no campfires burning. By dawn the next day, however—it was Whitsunday—the entire Austrian Army was in position. In the gray light of early morning, the long Austrian line of nearly one hundred thousand men, arranged in columns, stretched across the plain from Wagram to Stammersdorf, poised, ready to move forward to the attack.

IV

The opening stages of the battle may be summarized briefly. In the late afternoon of May 20, about five-thirty, a derelict boat, floated by the flood, crashed the pontoon bridge and broke through, carrying several pontoons with it.[115] With only improvised materials, the French engineers were unable to complete repair of the bridge until three o'clock the next morning.[116] The movement of French troops across the Danube was thus halted. In the meanwhile, the few French squadrons of cavalry which had crossed under Lassalle skirmished with the enemy on the mainland, but were unable to penetrate the screen of the Austrian cavalry and discover what was happening on the plain.[117]

That night while awaiting further troops, Napoleon dispatched Massena to the first small village on the mainland, Aspern, which the French cavalry had occupied, to

[112] *Ibid.*   [113] *Ibid.*   [114] *Ibid.*
[115] Von Hoen and Kerchnawe, *op. cit.,* IV, 377.
[116] *Ibid.,* p. 416.   [117] *Ibid.,* pp. 384-388.

ascend the church tower.[118] Massena arrived at midnight
when everything lay in deep sleep. He ascended the tower
with an aide. Looking up the Danube, he perceived campfires near Bisamberg which, judging from their number, he
correctly inferred were those of an auxiliary corps. But the
bulk of the Austrian Army was on the march, their campfires had not been lit or were extinguished, and their presence on the plain and in the darkness was not betrayed.
Massena about one o'clock returned to Napoleon and reported that the Austrian Army was not in presence.[119]

At the time of the crossing of the Molitor division on
May 18, Napoleon had been extremely cautious, and when
on May 19 it had been cut off on the left bank by a high
wind, extremely concerned. But once Molitor's division was
not attacked by the Austrians, there was in Napoleon a certain relaxation of concern. Now, in accord with his sanguine
temper, from little direct evidence, simply from the fact
that the Austrians had not disturbed the initial crossing
and from Massena's observation made in the dark, Napoleon
assumed that the Archduke and the Austrian Army were
nowhere near, and he neglected some, not all, of those precautions (such as fortifications) which it might have been
wise to take in establishing a bridgehead on an enemy shore.

By three o'clock in the morning of the twenty-first, the
bridge over the Danube had been repaired, and the French
troops again began to work across the series of bridges.[120]
During the morning other minor breaks occurred, and the
movement of troops was momentarily held up; but those
breaks were soon patched, and the flow of men across the
fragile pontoon bridges continued, if slowly and interrupt-
edly.[121] Napoleon was in the saddle early.[122] If one stood

[118] *Ibid.*, p. 393.
[119] *Ibid.*, pp. 393-394.
[120] *Ibid.*, p. 416.
[121] *Ibid.*, pp. 418-419.
[122] *Ibid.*, p. 399.

at the last bridge which crossed from the Lobau to the mainland, then the first three small peasant villages on the valley plain formed a semicircle about two miles distant: the village of Aspern to the left center, the village of Essling to the right center, and the village of Gross-Enzersdorf to the right. The small villages with their stone churches, their stone peasant-houses, their garden walls offered good positions.[123] In addition, a ravine ran from Aspern to Essling. Napoleon with his staff rode forward to reconnoiter, but the Austrian cavalry held him to the line of Aspern and Essling.[124] He ordered Massena to occupy those villages and Gross-Enzersdorf with the troops at his disposal, while he himself hastened to the Danube bridge to press on the movement of troops.[125]

The Archduke Charles, in the meanwhile, with his army in the plain, awaited news. By nine o'clock in the morning he received a report of the French occupation of Aspern, Essling, and Gross-Enzersdorf. He concluded that all of the French Army was in the process of crossing, and he decided to attack. He ordered a general advance.[126] The Austrians numbered in infantry 83,600, in cavalry 14,250, and possessed 292 guns. But as the Austrians, unaware of the night breakage of the bridge, expected to meet the French farther out on the plain than Aspern-Essling, they approached rather hesitantly.

The French perceived the Austrian advance, probably from the Aspern church tower about one o'clock in the afternoon.[127] It was reported to Napoleon that huge masses were on the plain. At first he could not credit the report, but dispatched an aide, Flahault, to Aspern. The aide returned, confirmed the report, and estimated the advancing columns at eighty thousand men.[128] Napoleon now

[123] *Ibid.*, pp. 428-429, 433-435.   [124] *Ibid.*, p. 399.
[125] *Ibid.*, p. 400.   [126] *Ibid.*, pp. 401-402.
[127] *Ibid.*, p. 419.   [128] *Ibid.*

faced a decision: should he stand out on the plain or should he retire to the Lobau. Napoleon vacillated. He had on his side of the Danube only 26,300, of which only 20,000 were infantry.[129] He decided on retreat and ordered Molitor's division near Aspern to withdraw toward the Lobau.[130] But the marshals around Napoleon were for acceptance of combat on the Aspern-Essling line. It offered a good defensive position; it was already early afternoon; it need be held only until night; French reinforcements were steadily crossing. These objections, the news that a recent rent in the bridge had been repaired, the sound of cannon-thunder over by Aspern indicating that the engagement had already started, changed Napoleon's mind, and he decided to accept battle.[131] Massena was placed in charge of Aspern, Lannes of Essling, and cavalry occupied the field between.[132] The Austrians began to attack Aspern about three-thirty,[133] Essling somewhat later, their approach clumsy in formation. After concentrated, desperate fighting the Austrians by nightfall won part of Aspern, but Massena retained a portion, while the French were able to hold Essling and the line between the two villages.[134]

During the late afternoon and evening the French with inferior forces had thus maintained their ground. The French and Austrian positions at the close of the day can be compared to an opened fan. The handle of the fan was the bridge from the Lobau to the mainland; the French troops halfway out on the fan stretched from the left of Aspern through Aspern along the ravine to Essling through Essling and then around to the right of Essling; the Austrian troops in a semicircle were along the outer edge. For the French the distance from the left of Aspern to the right

[129] *Ibid.*, p. 420.
[130] *Ibid.*
[131] *Ibid.*, pp. 420-421.
[132] *Ibid.*, p. 422.
[133] *Ibid.*, p. 440. Some skirmishes preceded the major attack.
[134] *Ibid.*, pp. 440-501.

of Essling was perhaps a mile and a half; for the Austrians it was nearly five miles. Condemned to operate along exterior lines, the Austrians could reinforce a given point only slowly and with difficulty. In the distribution of their forces, furthermore, the Austrian line was unbalanced. Three large columns were attacking Aspern from the left; one large column was attacking Essling from the front; another large column was approaching Essling from the right from Gross-Enzersdorf. The Austrian center between Aspern and Essling was weak. The disadvantage of the Austrian position and the weakness of its center had been perceived by Napoleon, and after the afternoon battle of May 21 he decided with reinforcements to take the offensive in the morning and win as usual a victory. To be sure, the reinforcements of munitions and of men and in case of disaster the route of retreat depended on a single pontoon bridge of proven unreliability which might break again and permanently. But in accord with the sanguine nature of his character, Napoleon either did not consider that possibility, or took the risk.

With the offensive in mind, Napoleon at nine o'clock in the evening dispatched an order to Davout to concentrate at once the Third Corps at Kaiserebersdorf preparatory to crossing.[135] During the night the infantry of the Second Corps (Lannes)—the divisions of Saint-Hilaire, Tharreau, and Claparède, and in the early morning the division of Demont crossed the Danube into the plain.[136] By early morning Napoleon had the Fourth Corps (Massena), the Second Corps (Lannes), the cavalry reserve of Bessières, and the Guard on the left bank of the Danube—numbering in all about seventy-seven thousand men.[137] During the night Napoleon took little rest. He supervised the passage of

[135] *Ibid.*, p. 509.
[136] *Ibid.*, pp. 510-511.
[137] *Ibid.*, pp. 780-781.

troops over the Stadtler arm from the Lobau to the mainland. By three o'clock, when it began to become light, he
was in the saddle.[138] In Napoleon's plan Lannes with the
infantry of the Second Corps and the cavalry of Bessières
was to break through the Austrian center between Aspern
and Essling, and toward Breitenlee, then turn to the left
and with the troops of Massena overwhelm the Austrian
right flank; in the meanwhile Davout with the Third Corps
would cross into the firing line, turn to the right, and overwhelm the Austrian left flank.[139]

The plan required that the French secure and clear their
own flanks. Early in the morning, beginning about four
o'clock, Massena began the retaking of that part of Aspern
which the Austrians possessed. By seven o'clock all of
Aspern had been reconquered. At about the same time
Lannes brushed the Austrians to the right of Essling back
to Gross-Enzersdorf.[140] In the meantime, the infantry of
the Second Corps (except the division Demont), numbering
about thirty thousand, were in position behind the ravine
which ran from Aspern to Essling. A thick fog covered
the lowland and the troops, but still the Austrian artillery
fired into the masses of men, and by seven o'clock the fog
began to clear.[141] At the same time (7 A.M.) Napoleon
received word that the Third Corps (Davout) had arrived
at Kaiserebersdorf, that the bridge after a minor break had
again been repaired, and that reinforcements were crossing.[142] The reserve park of munitions, however, was still on
the right bank; it would also take several hours for Davout's
corps to file across the two-mile length of bridges and islands
and then the mile from the Lobau bridge into the battle
line. It might have been well, perhaps, if Napoleon had
waited until the reinforcements of munitions and of men

[138] *Ibid.*, p. 518.
[139] *Ibid.*, p. 517.
[140] *Ibid.*, pp. 519-532.
[141] *Ibid.*, pp. 532-533.
[142] *Ibid.*, p. 533.

were in hand. But by seven o'clock he could not hesitate. His attacking force was being bombarded by the Austrians and was in an increasingly uncomfortable position. The Austrians might advance before him. His own flanks were secure. He ordered, therefore, Lannes to advance through the Austrian center, relying on Davout to back him up and carry the blow to a triumphant conclusion.[143]

Lannes's corps fitted in the space between Aspern and Essling, division Tharreau on the left, division Clarapède in the center, division Saint-Hilaire on the right. Lannes was to break through the Austrian center and turn it back to the left. For that purpose the three divisions advanced across the plain echeloned from the right, the right-hand division, Saint-Hilaire's division forward first, then Claparède's, and finally Tharreau. They were at first successful. Under the impact of the attack the Austrian line was bent back; some Austrian regiments fell into confusion. But the Archduke was among them, he brought up what reinforcements he could, spurred on the troops by his example, and the Austrian line held. Lannes ordered in the heavy cavalry near Saint-Hilaire's position. The cavalry drove the Austrians back, caused them to fall into disorder, some of them to flee, and nearly saw light. But the Archduke, seeing the case desperate, a break-through near, threw himself into the mêlée, seized the colors of a fleeing regiment, brought it back to order.

Thus the situation stood at eight o'clock in the morning—with the Austrians in confusion, but held together by the will and activity of the Archduke, the French attack beginning to slacken, but still continuing, with Victory, as it were, poised between either side, when Napoleon, who was some distance behind the lines surrounded by his staff, received word that the slender bridge across the Danube had

[143] *Ibid.*, p. 534.

again been broken, that Davout's corps would, therefore, be delayed in its crossing. Napoleon took the news quietly, mastering whatever emotion of discouragement or of despair he may have felt. He quietly ordered one aide to tell Lannes to suspend his attack, but to hold what he had gained until it was learned if the bridge could be repaired. He sent another aide back to the Danube to investigate the disaster. These orders were delivered with so much calm that Napoleon's staff which was around him was still unaware of what had happened or what was going on, and when in the distance they saw Lannes halt the deployment of his troops, they wondered why this had been done. After an hour of waiting, Lannes meanwhile holding his own, the Austrians reforming their lines, Napoleon learned that the bridge had been severely damaged. While the pontonniers were repairing the first break of that morning, which had not been very serious, a huge mill, built on boats, abandoned to the rapid current by some Austrian officers upstream and set afire by them, bore down upon the bridge and crashed with its enormous mass against it. The mill caused a break so severe that many of the pontoons and boats, and with them the pontonniers, their officers, and General Pernetti of the engineers were helplessly carried several miles downstream.[144] It would be hours, Napoleon was informed, before the bridge could be reconstructed; hours, therefore, before the reserves of ammunition and Davout's corps could cross. Napoleon still retained the hope that the bridge might be repaired that day, but with no troops to support the attack of Lannes, he ordered him to retreat and to take up his former position between Aspern and Essling.[145]

[144] Dumas, *op. cit.*, II, 191; Pelet, *op. cit.*, III, 343-344; Rovigo, *op. cit.*, II, 78; Gachot, *op. cit.*, p. 173, n. 1.

[145] In discussing the rupture of the bridge and the events surrounding it, the tendency of some of the sources is to make two errors: first, to simplify

This order Lannes executed bravely, skillfully, even serenely, as he did everything in the moment of danger. His friend and subordinate, General Saint-Hilaire, had just been wounded; Lannes took his place at the head of the

---

the story by omitting events, thus making the action appear more rapid and dramatic than it really was; and second, to give the impression that Napoleon and his marshals and aides by ten o'clock in the morning were aware of the full extent of the disaster and understood its entire significance. Pelet and Pelleport, though otherwise accurate, make this second mistake; Lejeune makes the first one mentioned; Rovigo, Ségur (based on the oral testimony of eye-witnesses and a source in this sense), and the 10th Bulletin make both mistakes (Pelet, *op. cit.*, III, 318-321; Pelleport, *op. cit.*, I, 272-273; Lejeune, *op. cit.*, I, 380-382; Rovigo, *op. cit.*, II, 77-78; Comte Philippe Paul Ségur, *Histoire et mémoires,* Paris, 1873, III, 351; 10th Bulletin, May 23, No. 15246, in Napoleon, *Correspondance,* XIX, 36). The tendency of these sources, in other words, is to say: Lannes was at the moment of victory, Napoleon and his aides were looking forward to a triumph, when the bridge is irreparably destroyed, the news is brought to Napoleon, he at once understands that the bridge cannot be repaired that day, that it is useless to expect reinforcements, and he quickly dispatches an aide to Lannes with the order to retreat.

But it is apparent that this account errs in several particulars:

(1) It may be doubted if Lannes was at the moment of victory. The Austrians were still holding. Lannes needed help.

(2) These sources give the impression that the bridge was broken only once that morning. As a matter of fact two breaks occurred: the first, a minor one which could have been repaired, about seven o'clock; the second, more disastrous, about nine o'clock (Pelet, *op. cit.,* III, 318-319). I have assumed that the first report which Napoleon received concerned the first break, and that the second report dealt with the second break. This is an assumption, but the timing of the breaks of the bridges and the arrival of the reports fit together.

(3) Even after news of the second break reached him, Napoleon did not at first realize that the bridge could not be repaired. At twelve-thirty o'clock he was still writing to Davout: Repair the bridges . . . as soon as the bridge is ready or at nightfall, come over to the Lobau. (See p. 68.) Apparently, he still had hope that he might be reinforced later on during the day. Only at two o'clock did he finally learn from an aide that the bridges were irreparably destroyed, and that reinforcements could not be gotten across. (See p. 68.) Only then did he realize the full extent of the accident on the river; only then did he understand that he and his army were definitely cut off from all aid and that they must fight alone. The process by which Napoleon became fully aware of his really desperate situation was thus a slow one.

(4) The first order to Lannes was not to retreat but to halt and hold what he had gained. Lannes halted, and waited for an hour (Marbot, *op. cit.,* III, 194-196; Pelet, *op. cit.,* III, 318. Marbot was with Lannes). The order to retreat came later.

troops, and, communicating to them all his calm and
serenity, "he reminded them while smiling that at Marengo
he had in the same way led them in retreat under a similar
Austrian fire and that the day had ended in a brilliant victory. 'Come, come, friends! the enemy is not worth more
and we are not worth less than at Marengo!' Marching
tranquilly on foot in the midst of his men who shared his
confidence, the Marshal forced back several charges of
cavalry which attempted to attack him."[146] Thus retreating, then turning to repel an attack, then retreating, he
finally toward ten o'clock in the morning reached the position which had been assigned to him between Aspern and
Essling. On his left was the corps of Massena still holding
Aspern, on his right the division of Boudet in Essling, behind him, as a reserve, the Imperial Guard under
Bessières.[147]

The rest of that day was for the French one long endurance, and it passed, I imagine, like a long dream, or rather
a nightmare. Upon the retreat of Lannes, the Austrians
readvanced, brought up their artillery, and for hours bombarded his line and the Imperial Guard which was stationed
some distance behind. To this cannonade, the French were
unable to reply. Most of their guns were already dismounted, many of the cannoneers were killed, and the supply of munitions was so depleted that what little was left
could not be used, but had to be conserved for an emer-
gency.[148] The Sergeant Coignet of the Guard who went
through that day, standing on the plain, exposed to Austrian fire, writes:

[146] Lejeune, op. cit., I, 384-385.
[147] Ibid.
[148] On the Austrian cannonade see ibid., I, 393; 10th Bulletin, May 23,
No. 15246, in Napoleon, Correspondance, XIX, 36; Castellane, op. cit., I, 55-56;
Pelet, op. cit., III, 320-321; Armand Alexandre de Bonneval, Mémoires anec-
dotiques du général marquis de Bonneval (1786-1873) (Paris, 1900), p. 28.

The fifty Austrian cannon thundered on us without our being able to take one step forward, or fire a single musket shot. . . . Let one imagine the agony which each one endured in such a position, it cannot be described; we had four cannon in front of us, two before the chasseurs to answer to fifty. Cannonballs fell in our ranks and carried off files of three men at once, shells made the *bonnets à poil* jump 20 feet high.

[The men, however, held steady.] As soon as a file was carried away, I said: "Bear to the right, close ranks!" And these brave grenadiers would bear to the right without lifting an eyebrow. The Austrian cannon were so close that the Frenchmen could see the Austrians work their guns. Yet the French grenadiers would even joke, and would say "in seeing the fire put to the match-hole 'This is for me.—All right, I'll stay behind you, it's a good place, set your mind at ease.'"

The two cannons of the regiment no longer had any gunners to serve them. General Dorsenne replaced them with twelve grenadiers and gave them the cross, but all these brave men perished near their guns. No more horses, no more artillerymen, no more wheels, the gun-carriages in pieces, the guns on the ground like logs! impossible to use them. A shell arrives which bursts near our good general and covers him with earth, he gets up again like a good warrior: "Your general is not hurt," he says, "count on him, he will know how to die at his post. . . ."

A ball carries away a file near me, I am struck in the arm, my musket falls; I think my arm is gone, I no longer feel it. I look: I see attached to the small of my arm a piece of flesh. I think that my arm is shattered. Not at all. It was a piece of one of my brave comrades which had struck me with such force that it stuck to my arm.

The lieutenant arrives near me, takes my arm, shakes it and the piece of flesh falls off; I see the cloth of my coat. He shakes me and says, "It is only numb." You cannot imagine my joy to move my fingers.

Marshal Bessières of the Guard remained near us. He, too, was dismounted. A portion of the corps of Lannes, frightened, had thrown themselves on us and covered our line of battle.

As we were formed in line, our grenadiers took them by the collar and put them behind them saying: "You will no longer be afraid."

Fortunately, they had all their arms and cartridges. . . . Calm having been somewhat re-established . . . among them . . . Marshal Bessières came to take them, and reassuring them he said: "I am going to lead you as sharpshooters and I, like you, will be on foot."

All these soldiers left with this good general, he had them form in a single line within musket shot of the fifty cannon which had been firing on us since eleven o'clock in the morning. This line of sharpshooters protected the fire which the file had begun on the Austrian artillery. The brave marshal, hands behind his back, not stopping from one end to the other, silenced for a moment their fury against us. That gave us a little respite, but time is very long when one awaits death without being able to defend oneself. The hours are centuries.[149]

In the meanwhile, against the right of the French position, the village of Essling, the Austrians upon the retreat of Lannes concentrated their greatest number of troops. These stormed the town repeatedly, managed to win a small foothold, but on the whole were held in check. By three o'clock, however, the French defenders of the town, the division of Boudet, weakened by losses and by fatigue, were barely holding on.[150]

The Austrians also renewed their attacks on Aspern, stubbornly pressed the French back, occupied a part of the town, both sides furiously fighting. Again and again through that long morning and afternoon other portions of the village were taken and then retaken by one side or the other, ever with greater ease and facility by the more numerous, fresher Austrian troops, ever with greater

---

[149] Coignet, *op. cit.*, pp. 246-250. The first two sentences of the sixth paragraph of the quotation are paraphrased, not quoted.

[150] Pelet, *op. cit.*, III, 325; Marbot, *op. cit.*, II, 198-199.

weariness and difficulty by the diminishing number of French, ever courageous. And thus the struggle continued.[151]

During this long ordeal, where an army of seventy thousand men was standing off the attacks of one hundred thousand, Napoleon took up a position from which he could direct the defense of the French center and right, leaving to Massena the defense of Aspern. He stationed himself back of Essling, but in front of that portion of the Guard in which Coignet served. Napoleon, like the Guard, was thus exposed to the Austrian cannonade, to cannon balls and shells which came in from various directions, but with his usual courage he remained there with a small staff during the late morning and early afternoon and sent out those orders that seemed to be needed.[152] After two or three hours of endurance, Napoleon dispatched an order, it was nearly an appeal, to Davout. Briefly he described the situation in which the army found itself: "The interruption of the bridge has prevented us from receiving supplies; at ten o'clock we no longer had any munitions. The enemy perceived this and remarched upon us. Two hundred guns, to which since ten o'clock we have been unable to reply, have done us a good deal of harm." He then outlined the measures to be taken, not forgetting to provide for the broader situation of difficulty which existed behind him because he was operating in an enemy's country. "In this state of affairs," the dispatch continues, "to repair the bridges, to send us munitions and food, to keep an eye on Vienna, is extremely important. Write to the Prince of Ponte-Corvo

---

[151] "Report of General Beker, chief of staff of the 4th corps, May 23, 1809," Saski, *op. cit.*, III, 377-378; Molitor to Massena, May 23, 1809, *ibid.*, III, 380; Dumas, *op. cit.*, II, 192; Pelleport, *op. cit.*, I, 272-273; Pelet, *op. cit.*, III, 322-324.

[152] M. le comte Mathieu Dumas, *Memoirs of His Own Time* (Philadelphia, 1839), II, 192-193. Hereinafter cited as Dumas, *Memoirs*.

that he may not become engaged in Bohemia, and to General Lauriston that he may be ready to draw near us. See Daru that he will send us field-hospital supplies and food of all kinds." Napoleon concluded with an invitation to conference: "As soon as the bridge is ready, or in the night, come to confer with the Emperor."[153]

The long cannonade was interrupted for a time when about two o'clock in the afternoon the Austrians launched a general attack against the French center and right. For this attack the Austrians made careful preparation, massing infantry, cavalry, and artillery opposite the corps of Lannes, which occupied the weak portion of the French line.[154] The appearance of these Austrian masses, just at the most indefensible point, gave the French officers serious concern. Napoleon, realizing the danger, hastened over from his position near Essling to a station back of the corps of Lannes and began preparations to meet the Austrian attack.[155] At the same time, while the attack was impending, Napoleon received word from an aide who had just come from the Danube, that neither troops nor munitions could be gotten across.[156] The bridge was damaged beyond repair—here and there five or six, or sometimes a dozen, pontoons held together, but there were long empty spaces between; the current was of incredible swiftness; "the waves rolled in a fearful manner and were filled with a large number of floating objects. . . . Large boats and rafts of wood, arriving with the speed of a trotting horse, fell crosswise on the untouched portions of the bridge."[157] Small skiffs, coming from Davout's side, could with difficulty make the crossing; boats of any size loaded with men or

Berthier to Davout, May 22, 1809, 12:30 P.M., No. 15243, in Napoleon, *Correspondance,* XIX, 32-33.
Lejeune, *op. cit.,* I, 388; Pelet, *op. cit.,* III, 325-326.
Ibid. [156] Lejeune, *op. cit.,* I, 388.
Quoted and paraphrased from *ibid.,* I, 389.

munitions were carried out of reach, far downstream, into territory held by the Austrians.[158]   It was clear by now that the French were facing disaster.   Napoleon and the French were now in the same position that Bennigsen and the Russians had been at Friedland: their backs to a stream, themselves ringed about by a superior enemy force, which was taking the offensive. Napoleon, however, unlike Bennigsen, was not inactive; he continued his preparations for the Austrian attack: gathered what artillery was available, and sent it to the center; ordered Bessières to collect what cavalry was left, and prepare to charge; directed toward the Austrian flanks some available troops, already worn out with fatigue; kept the Guard in reserve; and dispatched an aide to look after the preservation of the small bridge which led from the mainland to the Lobau, the bridge over which the army must retreat in case of defeat.[159]

After some delay the Austrian masses of infantry began to move, advancing toward the left of Lannes' line. They were allowed to approach until they were within close gunshot range, and then received with grapeshot and musket fire "so brisk," that they stopped to reply, then refused to advance farther, despite the exhortations of their generals. At this moment Bessières charged and overthrew "a few sections of the Austrian line." The Austrian commander withdrew his first line of infantry and advanced his reserve of Hungarian grenadiers. They, too, were allowed by the French to approach nearly to their guns; then a hail of grapeshot was poured upon them. The grenadiers stopped,

[158] *Ibid.*, I, 392; see also Dumas, *Memoirs,* II, 192.

[159] Pelet, *op. cit.,* III, 325-326; Dumas, *Memoirs,* II, 193. According to Lejeune, Napoleon received the news that the bridge was irreparably destroyed and that reinforcements could not be gotten across when he was preparing to meet the Austrian attack. I do not know what preparations occurred before the reception of the news and what after. Putting a description of them after, especially the dispatching of the aide back to look after the small bridge to the Lobau, is purely arbitrary.

gave ground, readvanced, were again received with a terrible fire, and were forced to retire. In the meanwhile, the Austrian cavalry tried to penetrate the French line between the corps of Lannes and Essling. "Several squadrons of French light cavalry tried to oppose these charges; they were vigorously thrown back. Behind them were the brave 3d and 93d regiments of infantry (division Boudet) deployed into line. Fririon, who commanded these regiments, had his half-companies divide in two. Our horsemen passed on through; but those of the enemy soon found themselves facing a wall of bayonets. The general ordered the fire only at point-blank range. Then placing himself at the head of his battalions, he pursued for some distance the Austrian cavalry which the musketry had put in the greatest disorder."[160]

The Archduke, baffled by the courage and steadiness of the French troops in the center, shifted his attack to the French right at Essling. He again ordered in his infantry reserve, the Hungarian grenadiers, who stormed, then swarmed over the town; the division Boudet, entrenched in part behind corpses, was pressed back, and finally forced to evacuate the town. Essling was a key position. Napoleon sent in a part of his reserve—the fusiliers of the Guard—under one of his most trusted aides—the General Mouton. It was three o'clock in the afternoon. The French fusiliers "rushed on the Hungarian grenadiers. . . . These wished to resist, and opposed their mass to *la furie française*. In vain. They were routed from the several points which they tried to defend" and driven out of most of Essling. Boudet was thus disengaged, but Mouton's fusiliers soon found themselves hard-pressed when the Austrians returned to the attack. Napoleon sent in another portion of his reserve,

[160] This paragraph is quoted and condensed from Pelet, *op. cit.*, III, 327; see also Lejeune, *op. cit.*, I, 393-394; Pelleport, *op. cit.*, I, 273-274; Marbot, *op. cit.*, II, 198-199.

under General Rapp, with orders to rescue Mouton, then to abandon Essling as untenable and retreat to a position between Essling and the Lobau. Rapp, however, disobeyed orders. Instead of retreating, he attacked. Under his direction, his own troops and Mouton's moved forward from Essling, fell on the advancing Austrian column, and dispersed it "with the bayonet." This bold counterstroke ended the Austrian attack on the French center and right. The cautious Archduke, astonished by the French resistance and their counterattack, thinking that Napoleon had received reinforcements and was about to resume the offensive, suspended his own attacks and began the withdrawal of his own troops to a more practicable defensive position. Even when the French failed to follow, the Archduke, though he stopped the withdrawal of his troops, did not renew his offensive. His troops, too, were weary, diminished in number, and much shaken by the handling they had received from the French.[161]

Thus, rather suddenly for the French, about four o'clock in the afternoon, the crisis of the Austrian attack was past. The battle, however, was not yet over. Along the French center and right, the Austrians reopened their merciless cannonade, killing and wounding many who had survived thus far.[162] Over in Aspern, the Austrians continued their attacks against Massena, who, with the remnant of his corps, still managed to maintain himself in the town.[163]

Napoleon, perceiving that except in Aspern the battle had settled down into a steady cannonade and that his

[161] On the final repulse of the Austrians at Essling see: 10th Bulletin, May 23, No. 15246, in Napoleon, *Correspondance*, XIX, 36-37; Rapp, *op. cit.*, pp. 143-144; Dumas, *Memoirs*, II, 192; Lejeune, *op. cit.*, I, 394-395; *Mémorial du dépôt*, VIII, 372; Castellane, *op. cit.*, I, 55-56; Pelet, *op. cit.*, III, 328-329; Lieutenant Général Comte François Roguet, *Mémoires militaires du lieutenant général comte Roguet* (Paris, 1865), IV, 49; Napoleon, *Mémoires pour servir à l'histoire de France sous Napoléon écrits à Sainte-Hélène* (London, 1823), VI, 81.   [162] Lejeune, *op. cit.*, I, 395-396, 398, 402.

[163] *Ibid.*, I, 397; Dumas, *Memoirs*, II, 192; Pelleport, *op. cit.*, I, 274.

presence was no longer needed, moved from place to place behind the lines, gradually withdrew to the small bridge which led from the mainland to the Lobau.[164] Because of the sudden rise in all the branches of the Danube, this small, fragile bridge had broken repeatedly during the day, and as the waters rose, it had been necessary to lengthen and to repair it several times, and to struggle constantly to keep it in place.[165]   Around the head of the bridge on the mainland a huge multitude of soldiers had gathered, perhaps ten or fifteen thousand in all, waiting to cross. Among them were a great number of wounded who had dragged themselves thither or had been helped there by their comrades—all of them in pain, many in agony. For these, too, it had been a long day. Mixed in with the wounded were soldiers who had run away, dismounted cavalrymen, even horses, some of them wounded, some not, who had lost their riders and strayed toward this agglomeration of people. The entire crowd was pressing forward, each one trying to be among the first to cross the bridge during those periods when it was in repair.[166]

On the outer edge of the crowd, in a small forest which screened the crowd from the battle line, Larrey, the great surgeon of the Imperial Guard, and several other doctors of the army had set up a small field hospital. There they dressed the wounds of those who had been most seriously hurt, performing amputations and incisions when these seemed necessary. Those who had received less dangerous wounds were sent over to the Lobau to be treated by the doctors who had been stationed there.[167]

On his way back to the Lobau, Napoleon, now on foot,

[164] Ségur, *op. cit.*, III, 354; Lejeune, *op. cit.*, I, 400.

[165] Dumas, *Memoirs*, II, 193; Lejeune, *op. cit.*, I, 397-398, 399-400.

[166] Dumas, *Memoirs*, II, 193; Ségur, *op. cit.*, III, 354; Lejeune, *op. cit.*, I, 399-400.

[167] D. J. Larrey, *Mémoires de chirurgie militaire et campagnes de D. J. Larrey* (Paris, 1812), III, 277.

accompanied by his aides, passed through the small forest in which Larrey was operating, then reached the outer edge of the crowd of soldiers, most of them wounded, who were gathered around the bridge. On perceiving Napoleon, all of these men, so says the source, shouted "Vive l'Empereur," and pressed aside to open for him a path through the multitude. Napoleon, still accompanied by his aides, made his way through the crowd, with what emotion we do not know, and crossed to the Lobau in a small skiff.[168]

There he set to work at once to prepare for the withdrawal of his troops from their exposed position on the plain. He directed that the entrenchments around the bridgehead should be completed, the bridge strengthened, and the wounded brought across. He reconnoitered the island, to see if it could be defended against an Austrian assault, and ordered that batteries should be placed all along the shore which faced the mainland.[169]

Having taken what precautions he could, he then summoned his marshals to conference. This was rather an unusual step for Napoleon to take. On the battlefield it was not his habit to confer with subordinates—usually he gave orders and they obeyed. And indeed in this case, he probably called the conference not because he wanted advice—he doubtless knew already what he intended to do—but because he felt that in order to retain his hold on his marshals in a moment of near defeat, he needed to talk things over with them, listen to their suggestions, gain acceptance for his plans, discuss and persuade.[170] The conference was one of Napoleon's many maneuvers in the management of men.

[168] Lejeune, *op. cit.*, I, 400; Roustam, "Mémoirs inédite de Roustam Mameluck de Napoléon Ier," *Revue Retrospective Recueil de pièces intéressantes et de citations curieuses*, VIII (Jan.-June, 1888), 162.
[169] Pelet, *op. cit.*, III, 330; Rovigo, *op. cit.*, II, 79.
[170] Ségur, *op. cit.*, III, 355. The suggestion is Ségur's.

Of the marshals, Berthier, the chief of staff, and Davout, who had come over from the other side,[171] were already present; after some delay Massena was able to leave his troops to a subordinate, and finally appeared; since Lannes was slow in showing up, Napoleon went ahead without him.[172] It was already late, about seven o'clock in the evening. Napoleon, tired from the day's exertion, was seated against a large tree not far from a small bridge which led from the mainland to the Lobau.[173] Around him stood the three marshals, the men he had to convince, and a few other members of the military circle.

Napoleon began by asking the marshals what they thought should be done in the present situation—with a part of the army isolated on the left bank of the Danube, without munitions, exhausted by fatigue, weakened by losses, barely maintaining itself in the presence of a superior Austrian force which would probably renew its attack the next day. All the marshals spoke in favor of retreat to the right bank of the Danube. Napoleon, though of a different opinion, listened to what they had to say, and then he spoke calmly, trying to win his hearers to his views.

"You wish," he said to Berthier, Davout, and Massena, "to re-cross the Danube! And how? Are not the bridges destroyed? Without that, would we not be united, victors, and already far from here? We can, it is true, have the men and horses cross on boats; but what will become of the artillery? Shall we abandon our wounded? Shall we add to the loss of the last two days that of all these brave men and of those lost in the woods? Shall we say thus to the enemy, to Europe, that victors today are vanquished? And if the Archduke, more puffed up by our retreat than by his earlier, pretended success, crosses the Danube behind us at Tulln, at Krems, at Lintz . . . if he brings

---

[171] Saski, *op. cit.*, III, 355, n. 1.   [172] Pelet, *op. cit.*, III, 330.
[173] This sentence is in part a quotation from Ségur, *op. cit.*, III, 355. For support from the sources, see Roustam, *op. cit.*, VIII, 162.

together his different corps . . . where shall we retire? Will it be to the positions which I have intrenched on the Traun, on the Inn, on the Lech? . . . No! we must run as far as the Rhine; for those allies which victory and fortune have given us, an apparent defeat will take from us and even turn against us. . . . We must remain here [in the Lobau]. We must threaten an enemy accustomed to fear us and keep him before us. Before he has made up his mind, before he has begun to act, the bridges will be repaired in a manner to defy all accident, the corps will be able to unite and fight on either bank. The army of Italy soon followed by that of Lefebvre will bring us the aid of its strength and its victories; it will open through Styria a line of communications which is still closed to us, and which will if necessary even replace that of Bavaria. Then we shall be complete masters of our operations."[174]

The persuasion was effective. Enlightened by his reasoning, the marshals expressed agreement with his views. Massena, the impulsive Italian, even exclaimed in admiration: "That's true! that's right! Ah, there is the great spirit, the genius worthy to command us! Yes, the Danube alone has conquered us, and not the Archduke! Let us remain on the island where soon having become masters of the one and checking the other, we shall return to finish with this prince."[175]

Napoleon arose, turned to Massena, and speaking in that caressing voice of friendship which he knew so well how to assume, he said: "Massena, it is up to you to defend the island of the Lobau, to finish what you have so gloriously begun! You alone can overawe the Archduke, and hold

[174] Pelet, op. cit., III, 330-332.
[175] Ségur, op. cit., III, 356. Ségur's book is a secondary account based in large part on the oral testimony of eyewitnesses. Ségur is usually accurate, but generally revises speeches so that it seems that they were spoken in good literary style. Massena probably said something like the words Ségur attributed to him; but it may be doubted if he spoke in phrases so nearly balanced or in words so elegantly chosen.

him immoble before this island! I have just travelled over it; the ground will be favourable to you. . . ." Napoleon having ceased to speak to them as a group, "the circle which had formed around him gradually broke up, the various personages of the military court took their places at a considerable distance. The Emperor remained alone with Massena, walking near the little bridge, resolving upon what these difficult circumstances demanded. . . . It was decided that the troops should fall back at two o'clock in the morning. . . . The command of everything that was on the left bank and in the islands of the Danube was given to Massena."[176]

While Napoleon was talking thus with Massena, an officer approached with the news that Lannes, the excitable Gascon, cool only in the moment of danger, had been wounded. Shortly after, Lannes himself was seen, lying unconscious on a stretcher which was being carried past by a group of grenadiers. His wound had been the result of that long Austrian cannonade, which still continued. In the late afternoon he had been walking up and down behind the French line not far from Essling. With him was his friend, General Pouzet, who, fifteen years before as a sergeant, had taught the young second lieutenant Lannes the elements of maneuver. Partly as a result of this instruction, Lannes had become an excellent tactician, and in gratitude to his teacher, Lannes, as he himself advanced, had also secured the advancement of Pouzet. Now, as they were walking together behind the French line, a "spent bullet" struck the forehead of Pouzet, and Lannes saw his friend fall dead at his feet. Lannes, "deeply moved" and "wishing to get away from the corpse, took a hundred steps in the direction of Stadt-Enzersdorf, and sat down in a thoughtful

[176] Pelet, op. cit., III, 332-333. Pelet was present at the conference; see ibid., p. 333. On the council, see also Ségur, op. cit., III, 355-356.

mood on the side of a ditch from where he watched the troops. After a quarter of an hour, four soldiers, laboriously carrying in a cloak a dead officer, whose face could not be seen, stopped to rest opposite the marshal. The cloak half-opened, Lannes recognized Pouzet! "Ah!" he cried, this frightful spectacle will follow me then everywhere." He got up and went and sat down on the edge of another ditch, has hand over his eyes and his legs crossed. "He was there . . . when a small cannon ball shot by the cannon of Enzersdorf arrived ricocheting and struck the marshal where his two legs were crossed," breaking the kneecap of the left leg and tearing the flesh of the right thigh. Lannes tried to rise, but could not. An aide and a few infantrymen from a near-by regiment improvised a stretcher of tree branches and carried him back to the small field hospital where Larrey was operating.[177]

When he arrived at the hospital, his condition was already serious, his face livid, lips pale, eyes dull and watery, the voice feeble, the pulse scarcely perceptible, the muscles of the right thigh torn, the wound of the left knee "alarming for the smashing of the bones, the laceration of the ligaments, the rupture of the tendons and of the popliteal artery,"[178] the man himself in a state of stupor and extreme prostration. The doctors had little hope of saving his life. But they dressed the wound on the right thigh, which was not serious, and amputated the left leg above the knee, Larrey performing the amputation rapidly in about two minutes, Lannes "giving very few signs of pain." Lannes was then placed in a stretcher, and was carried now unconscious across the small bridge which led into the Lobau, where Napoleon perceived him. Napoleon hastened over. In tears he knelt beside the stretcher and embraced his un-

[177] The account of the wounding of Lannes is quoted and paraphrased from Marbot, *op. cit.*, II, 200-202. [178] Larrey, *op. cit.*, III, 278.

conscious friend, saying, "Lannes, my friend, do you recognize me? It is I . . . it is the Emperor. It is Bonaparte, your friend. . . . Lannes, you will be saved." Lannes returned to consciousness, answered with a few affectionate words, and then was carried farther on into the Lobau, there, like many others, to suffer in agony.[179]

Napoleon continued his conference with Massena for a few minutes, and then they separated. Massena returned to Aspern to await the time set for retreat; Napoleon remained in the Lobau until nightfall, occupied with the transfer of the wounded and the preparation of the means of defense.[180] Since seven o'clock the battle on the mainland had been gradually slowing down. "Toward nine o'clock all was over. To that horrible din which shook the earth . . . succeeded a vast silence," broken only by occasional, sporadic firing and "the vigilant voice of the sentinels."[181] Fortunately for the French the night was extremely dark; it was at the time of a new moon, and thick clouds covered the stars. A strong, almost tempestuous wind blew in the darkness, rustling the trees, muffling any sounds the French might make in retreat.[182] Napoleon, feeling perhaps that under the circumstances Massena could be relied on to conduct the retreat satisfactorily and wishing to expedite the reconstruction of the bridge and the transport of provisions, decided to recross the Danube that night. About ten o'clock an aide was sent back to get ready a boat for the passage.[183]

---

[179] The accounts differ as to exactly what Napoleon and Lannes said. I have selected one of the shorter versions. See Pelet, op. cit., III, 333-335; 10th Bulletin, May 23, No. 15246, in Napoleon, Correspondance, XIX, 37; Lejeune, op. cit., I, 400-401; Castellane, op. cit., I, 55-56; Coignet, op. cit., p. 248; Ségur, op. cit., III, 357; Dumas, Memoirs, II, 194; Roustam, op. cit., VIII, 162-163; Marbot, op. cit., II, 202-203. The sources agree on the general picture: the embrace and the tears of the Emperor, the general import of his words, the affectionate reply of Lannes.   [180] Ségur, op. cit., III, 358.

[181] Pelet, op. cit., III, 329-330, 337-338; see also Pelleport, op. cit., I, 274.   [182] Lejeune, op. cit., I, 403.   [183] Ibid., I, 403.

With Berthier and one or two aides Napoleon soon followed, wearily feeling his way in the dark back through the mile-wide Lobau to the Danube.[184] When he arrived at the edge of the water and at the point where the boat, manned by fourteen rowers, was moored, Napoleon ordered Berthier to dictate a set of last-minute instructions for Massena. An aide lit and held a torch; in the flickering light of its flame blown by the wind, another aide wrote, while Berthier dictated:

The Emperor arrives at the bridge (between the Lobau and the Lobgrund). The bridge of wooden horses (chevalets) is broken. . . . It is necessary that you send sappers to construct two bridges of wooden horses instead of one. . . . The bridge over the large branch of the Danube is half destroyed. . . . It is therefore necessary that you strongly hold the head of the first bridge, which you will cross tomorrow morning, that is that you will place artillery and withdraw the pontoons and send them at once to the bridge of the large branch. . . . You understand how all of this requires activity and dispatch.

The Emperor is crossing to the other side to expedite all necessary measures, and to forward you food. The important thing is for you to stand firmly and with a great many cannon on the first island, and to send your pontoons to the broken bridge.[185]

[184] *Ibid.*, I, 403-404.

[185] Berthier to Massena, Ebersdorf, May 23, 1809, after midnight, No. 15244, in Napoleon, *Correspondance*, XIX, 33. The editors of Napoleon's *Correspondance*, following Pelet who first printed this order in his *Mémoires*, have given this dispatch the place-line of Ebersdorf. This, it seems to me, is a mistake. The first line of the dispatch says clearly: "L'Empereur arrive au premier pont sur le petit bras." Since Berthier then speaks of "le pont de chevalets," the Emperor has arrived at the small bridge which connected the Lobau with the Lobgrund. Later on the dispatch says: "L'Empereur passe de l'autre côté pour activer tous les moyens." The dispatch says the Emperor *crosses*, that is *will cross*, to the other side; evidently he is still on the Lobau. It does not say that "the Emperor has crossed," which would be natural if the dispatch was sent out of Ebersdorf.

Lejeune, by his own account, carried a dispatch from Berthier to Massena. I have assumed that the dispatch he carried was the one printed in Napoleon's *Correspondance*.

The dictation finished, Berthier's signature affixed to the dispatch, the aide who wrote it instructed to carry it to Massena, Napoleon stepped into the boat, followed by Berthier and two aides. It was nearly midnight. "The ropes were unlashed, and the boat, shot like an arrow (in the dark), disappeared instantly. The raging wind extinguished the torch four steps from the bank; nothing more indicated the direction it had taken."[186] The boat, carried downstream by the current, finally managed to make the other bank, some distance below Ebersdorf. The Emperor, exhausted by fatigue, leaning on the arm of an aide-de-camp, made his way to the house he had occupied before the battle.[187]

A meal was prepared in haste, and Napoleon sat down to eat. He was now alone with his valet, the Mameluke Rustam, and with Berthier. As he sat there at the table, tears filled Napoleon's eyes, and as he ate his soup, they streamed down his cheeks and fell into his spoon. Of what was he thinking? Was he thinking, perhaps, of Lannes? Or were, as sometimes happens at the end of a day of nervous excitement, a whole series of pictures of recent events going through his mind—the evening crossing of Molitor's division, the building of the bridge, himself crossing accompanied by his marshals and his staff . . . the arrival of the news that the bridge had been broken, the endurance of the Guard under the long cannonade, the appearance of the Austrian columns as they massed for their last attack, the crowd of wounded near the small bridge leading to the Lobau, the conference with the marshals, the appearance of the wounded Lannes, the crossing of the Danube in the dark—pictures mingled, perhaps, with thoughts of what might have been if only. . . . Or was Napoleon's fatigue so extreme that his mind was in a daze, thinking and

<hr>

[186] Lejeune, *op. cit.,* I, 404-405.   [187] Rovigo, *op. cit.,* II, 83.

feeling were at a stop, and tears merely a physical response to the general situation?

In the meantime, on the opposite shore the French Army under Massena's direction commenced its withdrawal. When Napoleon left the small bridge which led from the mainland to the Lobau, the wounded had already been brought across to the island.[188] Shortly after his departure, about midnight,[189] the retreat of the army itself began. Quietly the troops on the French right and center withdrew from their positions and crossed the bridge into the Lobau; then followed the troops of Massena's corps on the French left.[190] By morning,[191] when the Austrian sharpshooters began to approach the river and to open fire on the group of Frenchmen around the bridge, most of the French Army was in safety, the last column of the infantry of the Guard

[188] Pelet, *op. cit.*, III, 341.

[189] *Ibid.*, III, 342; Lejeune, *op. cit.*, I, 407, 408-409. Pelleport says toward eleven o'clock (Pelleport, *op. cit.*, I, 275). But he includes the transportation of the wounded in the retreat. The army itself did not begin to move until midnight or after.

[190] There is some disagreement among the sources as to the order in which the various divisions withdrew from their positions and crossed the bridge. But as a general statement, the above sentence will probably hold, though certain regiments of the Guard which were on the French right and center, crossed almost last of all (Pelleport, *op. cit.*, I, 275; Pelet, *op. cit.*, pp. 341-343; Lejeune, *op. cit.*, I, 408-409; Saski, *op. cit.*, III, 378).

[191] There is little agreement among the sources as to exactly when the French retreat into the Lobau was finished, and the fire of the Austrian sharpshooters began. The source most worthy of belief is the report which Beker, Massena's chief of staff, drew up on May 23. He states that by seven o'clock in the morning of the twenty-third, all the army had passed over to the Lobau (Saski, *op. cit.*, III, 378). Lejeune states that the army entered the Lobau "fort avant le jour"; but he adds: "laissant . . . quelques compagnies pour garder la tête du pont." These were evidently not withdrawn until later (Lejeune, *op. cit.*, I, 408-409). Pelet says that Massena, one of the last to cross, entered the Lobau at three o'clock. A few Austrian cavalrymen approached at five o'clock (Pelet, *op. cit.*, III, 343). Pelleport writes that the bridge was withdrawn at 3:30 A.M. and that the last French troops passed over to the Lobau in boats at four o'clock, after exchanging shots with enemy sharpshooters (Pelleport, *op. cit.*, I, 275). Dumas, who was at the bridge all night, states that French troops were still defiling across the bridge at seven o'clock, when the Austrian sharpshooters opened fire (Dumas, *Memoirs*, II, 195).

was just defiling across the bridge, and only Massena with a small rear guard of three companies of Legrand's grenadiers remained on the mainland near the bridge.[192] Undisturbed by the Austrian musket fire, Massena waited until all the French arms and cuirasses lying around the bridgehead had been collected and carried into the Lobau. He then ordered all troops except a single company of riflemen to pass across the bridge before him, he himself followed, and the bridge was taken up after him.[193] The single company of riflemen on the mainland then came across in two boats which had been placed at their disposal.[194] Since the Austrians did not choose to attack the French in the Lobau or even to cannonade their position, the Battle of Aspern-Essling was thus definitely at an end.

The next two days were spent by the French in pushing forward the repair of the bridges and the provisioning of the troops left on the Lobau,[195] and then Napoleon returned to that routine of empire from which he was seldom free. Indefatigable as ever, he began once again to read the reports of his officials, to dictate replies, and to consider the difficult situation in which he and his empire found themselves, a situation rendered more difficult by the battle which had just occurred.[196]

V

Conceivably, now, we could close the account of the battle here, adding perhaps a few words on the number killed and wounded (4,000 French killed, 15,000 wounded; 4,012 Austrians killed, 16,020 wounded),[197] a few reflec-

[192] Dumas, *Memoirs,* II, 195.
[193] *Ibid.;* Pelleport, *op. cit.,* I, 275; Pelet, *op. cit.,* III, 343; Castellane, *op. cit.,* I, 56.
[194] Pelleport, *op. cit.,* I, 275; Castellane, *op. cit.,* I, 56.
[195] Rovigo, *op. cit.,* II, 83-84; Roguet, *op. cit.,* IV, 51-52.
[196] Napoleon, *Correspondance,* XIX, 42 ff.; Napoleon, *Correspondance inédite* (Picard and Tuetey), III, 63.
[197] These figures are estimates, but are probably fairly accurate. They are

tions on the generalship of Napoleon and the Archduke Charles (Napoleon was too sanguine before the battle in not preparing a defense on the mainland, overconfident in launching an offensive the second day, but then superb in holding on to the end of the day and in bringing the army off in safety from its exposed position; the Archduke's strategy was good up to the battle, but during the conflict itself he failed except toward the end to launch an attack on the weak center of the French line, and he never did push any attack home—however, the Austrian Army was always unwieldy), add a moral comment or so on the dangers of pride and overconfidence, and then feel that we had given an adequate picture (at least from the French point of view) of a terrible struggle. In fact, however, the picture is still incomplete; it contains no adequate conception of the immense suffering a battle entails. Perhaps there is no better way to convey an idea of what that suffering was like than to paraphrase the *Mémoires* of the surgeon Larrey as he tells of what he saw and what he did in the days which followed the Battle of Aspern-Essling.

During the night of May 22, while Napoleon was crossing the Danube to Ebersdorf and the army was retreating into the Lobau, Larrey and his aides continued operating until every wounded person who was on the island had been taken care of. Only then did the doctors rest.[198] Despite the care of the doctors, however, the condition of the wounded was distressing. Until the bridges were repaired, it was impossible to transport them to the hospitals which had been made ready on the right bank of the Danube. They lay, therefore, stretched out on the dry, rather barren, ground of the Lobau, thousands of them assembled in groups on the bank of the river, the others scattered by twos or threes or

taken from Von Hoen and Kerchnawe, *op. cit.,* IV, 700, 786. See also Saski, *op. cit.,* III, 380, n. 1.   [198] Larrey, *op. cit.,* III, 280.

singly through the interior of the island.[199]   As they lay
there, they were exposed to the heat of the summer day and
to the humid and glacial air of night.   The winds, which
blew frequently, at every moment covered them with clouds
of dust; the branches of trees and the marsh reeds which
had been placed over some protected them only imperfectly
from the rays of the sun.[200]   Along with the other soldiers
on the island, they suffered from lack of food and drink.
The water of the river was muddy and filthy[201]—some soldiers refused at first to touch it[202]—and food could not be
gotten across from Ebersdorf in sufficient quantities. Larrey,
therefore, had a bouillon prepared for the wounded, using
horse meat seasoned (since there was no salt) with gunpowder.   The bouillon, Larrey assures us, was very good;
those who had been able to keep their ration of biscuit made
excellent soup.[203]

This scarcity of provisions, however, lasted for only
forty-eight hours.   On the third day after the battle, provisions were available in abundance.   On the fourth day, the
bridges having been repaired, the wounded were all transported to the hospitals which the Inspector-General, M.
Heurteloup, had prepared at Ebersdorf and at Vienna.[204]

On that day Larrey took occasion to revisit Marshal
Lannes, who, as a warrior of eminence, had been rowed
across the Danube to Ebersdorf on the first day after the
battle.[205]   Larrey found Lannes "extremely weak, in pro-
found depression, and with a deathlike paleness. His ideas
were incoherent and his voice broken; he complained of a
heaviness in the head; he was restless, felt oppression, and

---

[199] Dumas, *Memoirs*, II, 195.

[200] Larrey, *op. cit.*, III, 281.   [201] Pelet, *op. cit.*, III, 339-340.

[202] Marbot, *op. cit.*, II, 203-204.   [203] Larrey, *op. cit.*, III, 281.

[204] *Ibid.*, III, 282; Bonneval, *op. cit.*, pp. 28-30; Coignet, *op. cit.*, p. 251.
Roguet says it was on the third day (Roguet, *op. cit.*, IV, 51-52).

[205] Marbot, *op. cit.*, I, 204-205.

sighed frequently; he could not bear the weight of his bed-coverings, although they were very light. . . . Larrey's presence seemed to make an agreeable impression."[206]

The doctors in attendance had been giving him "iced, acidulated drinks." The weather, however, having just changed from extreme heat to cold, Larrey proposed to cover the Marshal "with flannel, to give him good broth frequently, and to omit the iced drinks." This was done and the strength of Lannes "revived a little and his sleep was more calm. The next day, the wounds were redressed for the first time; the old dressings were soaked with a purulent serosity; the wound of the stump had a favorable appearance, and that of the right thigh gave no hint of trouble, part of its edges had already healed. The first lint" was then covered "with a simple digestive and the later compresses were soaked with warm, sugared wine. The first twenty-four hours passed rather well,"[207] and Larrey began to hope that Lannes would recover. "But during the night of the sixth to the seventh day of the accident, a dangerous attack of fever came on."[208] After a consultation of the four doctors in attendance, a strong dose of quinine was administered, to which was added sulphuric ether. Twelve hours later, however, "a second attack, less alarming however than the first, declared itself. . . ; a third appeared during the next day, with delirium, and was followed by an almost complete prostration of the vital forces."[209]

Napoleon, who during Lannes' illness had visited his friend every day and sometimes twice a day and who had been confident that he would recover,[210] was now informed of the danger the Marshal was in, and came over to see him

[206] Larrey, *op. cit.*, III, 282.   [207] *Ibid.*, p. 283.
[208] *Ibid.*, pp. 283-284.   [209] *Ibid.*, p. 284.
[210] Marbot, *op. cit.*, II, 210-211; Pelet, *op. cit.*, III, 335-336; Napoleon to Fouché, Ebersdorf, May 25, 1809, No. 15253, in Napoleon, *Correspondance*, XIX, 43.

once again. M. le docteur Franck of Vienna, one of the most celebrated physicians in Europe, "was called into consultation"; as is usual with a visiting doctor, "he approved the treatment which had been used," and then remained with the other doctors "near the patient whose strength was progressively declining. The Marshal finally entered complete delirium, which was of short duration, and he died a few hours later in a rather calm condition. It was at the close of the ninth day of the accident and of the battle."[211] Everything that medical care of the time knew how to do had been done, but it was not enough, and as Napoleon said in the bulletin which announced the death of Lannes, "Thus came to an end one of the most distinguished soldiers France has had."[212]

The body of Lannes was transported to the palace of the Schönbrunn, where it was embalmed by Larrey. This disagreeable task completed, Larrey then took up his quarters at the hospital of the Guard in the Reneveck barracks at Vienna, and returned to his duties as surgeon of the Guard and director-general "du service de santé," giving special attention to the care of the wounded.[213]

Among the wounded in his hospital, there were a large number who had undergone amputation of a leg or an arm; in fact, an amputation was the type of operation most frequently performed. Occasionally both legs had to be cut off, and then Larrey was always careful to make the stumps of equal length, so that in later civilian life the men could walk about more easily on their wooden legs.[214] Whether or not a man survived an amputation depended on many

---

[211] Larrey, *op. cit.,* III, 284; see also Napoleon to Cambacérès, Ebersdorf, May 31, 1809, No. 15281, in Napoleon, *Correspondance,* XIX, 61; Marbot, *op. cit.,* II, 210-211.

[212] 14th Bulletin, June 1, 1809, No. 15287, in Napoleon, *Correspondance,* XIX, 66.

[213] Larrey, *op. cit.,* III, 285.   [214] *Ibid.,* pp. 378-379.

factors, on so many in fact that two individuals might have nearly identical wounds, be brought to the ambulance within the same elapsed time after the injury, undergo the same type of amputation, receive the same care, and yet their cases would develop entirely differently. Larrey noticed this in regard to two grenadiers, both of whom had received somewhat similar wounds at Essling. "The first,"[215] Larrey says, "had his leg carried away at a point above the knee joint. A fracture of the lower part of the femur" forced Larrey to amputate. The operation was successful. "The wound passed through the normal course of suppuration without the slightest accident. The soldier did not have even a quarter-of-an hour of fever, and he was well on the road to recovery at the end of the second month, when" Larrey "left him."

The second, struck in the knee by a ball of the same caliber but at the end of its course, had the articular extremities broken, the femur quite extensively fractured, and the soft parts abraded. He already felt painful spasms in the wounded limb; the pulse was small, the paleness of death was diffused over his face, and he was in a condition of mental aberration. In this last wounded person, as in a large number of others, the resistance of the parts struck by a ball whose rectilinear force had diminished had spread the blow: there was consequently concussion and shock which had affected the internal organs.

The first grenadier, having had his limb entirely carried away by a ball which being in full career acted like a cutting instrument, had not experienced the least complication, and his recovery had been prompt. All the effects of the blow were concentrated in the injured part.

But in the second, on the contrary, the ball being at the end of its parabola, had not been able to cut the parts clean-

[215] *Ibid.,* pp. 384-387.

ly. All those which were elastic had yielded to its action; the fragile parts were broken or torn; but also the effects of the blow were spread far in such a way as to give a violent jolt to the internal organs, an extremely unfortunate accident which endangers the life of the wounded person, especially when the operation is delayed.

This grenadier was operated on almost immediately after the blow, and in the same manner as the first. The local pain was dispelled; the spasms quieted down. But the pulse remained always weak and contracted; sinister dreams troubled the grenadier's sleep, and he was in a permanent state of restlessness. Suppuration was not abundant, but the wound of the stump was in "good condition" and the doctors had some hope of his recovery "when suddenly new spasms declared themselves with the symptoms of a pernicious fever which caused his death on the tenth day of the accident."

"On opening the corpse" Larrey and his aide "found the viscera of the lower abdomen gorged and weighed down with blackish, fluid blood; the cellular tissue which envelops the semilunar ganglia was choked with a reddish serosity; the ganglia themselves were swollen. The brain was several millimeters distant from the cranium; its vessels were congested. This internal disorder was the result of the concussion which did not occur in the other grenadier. Thus the prognosis of gun-shot wounds must be according to the character of the injury and the manner in which the ball acted."

Among the soldiers of the Guard who had been wounded at Aspern-Essling, complications—chiefly tetanus and nosocomial fever—developed in a great number of cases. Larrey noted that tetanus "attacked by preference the young soldiers who were wounded in the ginglimoid articulations, or deeply in the soft parts with loss of substance."[216]   He also observed that although the essential causes of tetanus were the same, yet it tended to appear in those wounded who had been exposed to extreme changes in temperature. "The wounded," he remarked, "who after the heat of the day were exposed especially during the spring to the cold moist air of the nights when the north north-west winds prevailed readily contracted tetanus."[217]

One of the cases of tetanus which came under Larrey's observation at this time was that of "Charles Yonck,[218] fusilier chasseur, amputated at the right thigh for a huge fracture of the knee caused by a canon-ball." He was attacked by tetanus on the eighth or ninth day after his operation. The irritation or nervous spasm which accompanied the attack "commenced, according to the report of the patient, at the point where the ligature was applied to the vessels. The suppuration of the wound had diminished and become sanious." Larrey and his aides "used epispastic ointment in the dressings, applied warm, oleaginous and camphorated liniments to the entire body, prescribed diaphoretic drinks and strong doses of opiates. All these means, administered with care for three days, scarcely retarded the progress of the disease. Suspecting that one of the principal branches of the crural nerve was included in the ligature of the femoral artery," Larrey "cautiously passed the point of one blade of a pair of scissors down along the grooved probe between the artery and the ligature of thread and cut the latter easily. This little operation seemed to quiet, for a few moments, the tetanic symptoms; but the irritation had spread too far, the symptoms went on increasing, and deglutition (swallowing) was already very difficult." Larrey decided to use his customary method in dealing with tetanus, namely, "to apply a red-hot iron to the surface of the stump.

[216] *Ibid.*, p. 285.   [217] *Ibid.*, pp. 286-287.   [218] *Ibid.*, pp. 297-298.

This application was made the next day." Larrey "burned very deeply, with an iron brought to a white-heat several times, all the area of the wound, a very painful operation but one which the patient endured with courage. Several hours later, to" Larrey's "great surprise, there was a marked improvement. The jaws, before locked, opened at will, and swallowing was less difficult. The rigidity of the muscles disappeared gradually; suppuration was re-established in the wound. The scar grew from the circumference to the center, and before the end of the second month Charles Yonck was completely cured. The use of camphor, opiates, and diaphoretic drinks had not been discontinued."

Another soldier who developed tetanus was François Demaré,[219] a grenadier, struck by a bullet which had carried away "the skin, a part of the spine of the right shoulder-blade, and a portion of the muscles (trapezius, infra and supra spinatus) of that area. On the battlefield the loose flaps of flesh had been trimmed, several loose pieces of bone had likewise been extracted, and the wound" suitably dressed. "The first stages of suppuration passed without unfavorable symptoms, and the wound" had begun "to heal along the circumference, when tetanus declared itself and with the rapidity of an electric spark spread from the wound over the entire nervous system; consequently, in a very few hours, opisthotonos was marked and complete.

"The head was thrown back on the shoulders; the jaws were locked and deglutition (swallowing) was very difficult." Larrey "promptly administered to the patient diaphoretic drinks, and large doses of opiates. Applications of oleaginous camphorated and narcotic lotions were made over the entire body, the dressings of the wound were gentle. In brief, every possible care, every remedy was lavished upon him. Purulent secretion ceased, the healing cicatrice made

[219] *Ibid.*, pp. 299-302.

rapid progress, and in forty-eight hours it covered half the wound. The wounded person then felt a painful pinching in every part of the cicatrice. He told us that the edges of the wound were as painful as if forcibly seized with pincers; and the slightest touch on this very delicate cicatrice, especially with metals such as iron or lead, caused him to utter piercing cries. All the symptoms of tetanus grew sensibly worse; the arms were uncommonly rigid and were twisted backwards; the cervical vertebrae were entirely thrown back, and swallowing no longer occurred. In vain the two incisors had been extracted to introduce the tube of a feeding bottle; not a drop of liquid passed through the esophagus. The mere approach of clear water brought on convulsions; the patient abhorred it as" Larrey "had noticed in several other tetanic cases. The foam formed by saliva increased during these moments of crisis, and all the symptoms became more extreme. Finally, this unfortunate person, who did not have as yet the slightest mental aberration, was nearing the end of his career" when Larrey decided to "employ the cauterizing-iron." For this purpose, he "had four broad and thick irons heated to incandescence and he applied them, one after another, without interruption on the entire area of the wound, in such a manner as to bear strongly on those points of the cicatrice where he suspected that several branches of the spinal nerve were pinched and swollen. This application was extremely painful: however, it was continued until all parts of the wound were deeply and completely burned. Scarcely was it finished than an almost general relaxing took place, preceded by copious perspiration. The patient sat up in bed without assistance and asked for something to drink. The jaws had spontaneously separated." Larrey "gave him a glass of nitrated milk of sweet almond in which" he "had mixed sixty drops of laudanum and several drops of Hoffmann's anodyne liquor." Larrey "had the camphorated narcoctic liniments repeated, and the patient's body wrapped in very warm flannels. Perspiration became abundant: the patient became quite calm, and enjoyed an easy and refreshing sleep for several hours. The next morning," Larrey "found him entirely rid of tetanic symptoms, with the exception of a slight stiffness in the jaws and spine. The dressings were simple and applied gently. The scabs sloughed off between the ninth and tenth days; soon after the cicatrisation recommenced and without pain. The patient improved daily; the cicatrice was finished before the sixtieth day, and this grenadier, being cured, left for France. There remained to him only a degree of stiffness in the movements of the shoulder and arm of the wounded side. This cure," Larrey observes, "is one of the most remarkable in military surgery."

Among those who lay and suffered on the hospital beds of Reneveck, not all were wounded in the arm or leg, or had undergone amputation, nor did all recover. Quite a few had been struck in the abdomen; and since Larrey in discussing their cases generally tells how their wounds had been received, it might be well to mention a few of their cases, without, however, giving an extended account of how each one developed. One of those injured in the abdomen was an infantryman cannoneer,[220] who toward the close of the battle, finding himself exhausted with fatigue, had lain down on the ground in a shallow ditch where he thought he was sheltered from any bullet or cannon ball. But as he was lying there, a cannon ball struck the ground near him, and then passed across his body, tearing a few buttons off his vest, and causing him to feel violent shock in the region of the abdomen. He tried at first to rise, but could not, and had to be carried. Neverthe-

[220] *Ibid.*, pp. 334-336.

less, after a time, he did not find that he was sufficiently injured to ask to be sent to the hospital. He could walk about; his abdomen was tender, it was true, but it was only slightly inflamed; the skin was not broken, and having noticed a bruise in the region of the navel, he contented himself with bathing it with brandy while he remained at the barracks. He remained there for nearly a month, while his trouble grew progressively worse, until he finally decided to seek hospital care. When he arrived at the hospital of Reneveck, his abdomen was "extremely swollen, distended, without perceptible fluctuation"; breathing was difficult, his face was livid and slightly puffed, legs "heavy, painful, difficult to move, the pulse small and rapid." Larrey and his aides did what they could—gave him "diluted laxatives and diuretics," bled him slightly; the cannoneer felt better, but soon he was attacked by a "pernicious fever," and on the fifteenth day after entering the hospital, he died. Upon opening his body the next day, it was discovered that the internal organs—the abdominal viscera, the liver, the spleen, the lungs—were gorged with blood and bathed with a large quantity "of blackish serous fluid, tinged with blood."

A second soldier,[221] a certain René Taillandier, a fusilier-grenadier, had been wounded as he was in the act of putting down his haversack. The cannon ball had struck the ground once or twice and then glanced off his abdomen. The force of the blow, however, had not been severe, and not feeling seriously hurt, he delayed entering the hospital for nearly two months. When he arrived, his abdomen was distended and Larrey deduced that it was filled with bloody fluid which could not be reabsorbed. Larrey, therefore punctured the abdomen twice and each time drained several quarts of "liquid tinged with blood in part coagulated." The patient seemed on the road to recovery, he was walking around the

[221] *Ibid.*, pp. 336-339.

hospital like a well man, when on the fifteenth day after the operation, he was attacked by chills, then fever, which caused him to be sent to the fever ward. A month later "he descended to have his abdomen tapped, a very pronounced and voluminous collection of serous fluid having formed there." Larrey "punctured the cavity and drew off eight to nine quarts of yellowish serous fluid." From this moment, however, Larrey despaired of the recovery of the grenadier.

A third soldier,[222] a grenadier, had been struck in the abdomen by a bullet which was near the end of its course. "The clothes and the skin of the lower abdomen, pressed circularly by this projectile, had due to their elasticity yielded to its impulsion; but the sterno-pubic muscle and the tendons [actually aponeuroses] of the abdominal muscles, being less elastic, had broken." The grenadier was not brought to the hospital until the seventh day after the battle. When he arrived, he had what appeared to be a tumor in the abdomen, "situated three fingers' breadth from the navel, on the right side and the size of a fist. It presented a considerable effusion of blood beneath the surface of the skin, and a point of fluctuation in the center." One of Larrey's colleagues diagnosed the tumor as "a sanguineous effusion" and proposed to the patient an operation. But the patient expressing a wish to see Larrey first, the latter was called in. He perceived that the swelling was formed not by an effusion of blood but by a portion of "the intestine and epiploon"; and he diagnosed the injury as a hernia caused by the blow of the bullet. The patient was put on a regulated regime—rest, camphorated wine, gentle compression, diet—and eventually he was able to leave the hospital. But the hernia still remaining, he was granted a pension from the State, and he retired from active service.

A fourth soldier,[223] like the first we mentioned, was like-

[222] *Ibid.*, pp. 332-334.   [223] *Ibid.*, p. 339.

wise wounded while resting. As he was lying on his back, he saw, but not quite in time, a cannon ball which was about to fall on him on its last bound. Quickly, "he opposed to it the butt of his rifle, but a second too late; the ball" rolled "over his lower abdomen like the wheel of a carriage which passed rapidly." Internal injuries resulted, but after a period of suffering, he was able to return home, incapacitated, however, for further service. A fifth soldier[224] was wounded while he was trying to "fire his gun at an enemy half-company which was approaching the flank" of his battalion. For this purpose his legs were spread apart, when he "was struck from behind by a ball of moderate size shot by one of the batteries of Essling. The ball, whose course directed it toward the interval between the thighs of this soldier, carried away a part of the two buttocks, the margin of the anus with its cutaneous sphincter, the skin of the perineum, the bulbous portion of the urethra, the skin of the scrotum and of the right testicle; the spermatic cord was ruptured, the left testicle was denuded, and the skin of the penis and prepuce torn." The soldier thus horribly wounded was not brought to the ambulance until a day after the battle, and then was evacuated to the hospital at Reneveck. There is no need to go into the details of Larrey's treatment. Suffice to say that after weeks of torment and agony, after weeks of patient care on the part of Larrey and his aides (the wound had to be dressed several times a day), the man finally got well, and toward the end of the fourth month was able to leave the hospital. As Larrey observes, "there remained to this wounded person no other infirmity than that of discharging his urine through an orifice which stayed in the perineum near the beginning of the urethra, whose lower wall had been carried away by the ball."

The concluding case in this section on those who received

[224] *Ibid.*, pp. 342-346.

abdominal injury was a soldier[225] whose abdomen was grazed by a cannon ball which was still in full career. The ball "carried away before it the skin, a portion of the left ilium bone, and the attachments of the large muscles of the lower abdomen, and laid bare a part of the sigmoid curve of the colon." Despite this enormous wound, however, the man recovered and returned to France about four months after the battle. It may finally be noted, as a partial indication of what standing in a cannonade was like, that most of these abdominal wounds were received, it seems, during the long Austrian bombardment which the Guard endured on the afternoon and evening of May 22.

Besides those at the hospital who had suffered amputation or abdominal injury, there were a number of soldiers who had been wounded in the face or head. One of these[226] was a foot-grenadier who had been struck by "a ball in the left temple on a level with the external ear. This projectile had buried itself deeply behind these parts and the crotaphite muscle and had stopped at the base of the mastoid process of the same side. At first the presence of this foreign body was not perceived, and the wound, very trifling in appearance, was simply dressed. In fact, it healed promptly and, on the fifteenth day, this soldier, believing himself cured, asked for his *exeat*. But at the moment when he was about to leave, he was seized with dizziness, heaviness and shooting pains in the head: the hospital attendant was forced to put him back to bed.

"The next morning, on his round of visits," Larrey "explored with care the entire head of the grenadier," and perceived "toward the base of the mastoid process and behind the ear a small red tumor with a point of fluctuation in the center. An ample incision with a bistoury exposed the ball deeply inlaid at the base of this process"; it was ex-

225 *Ibid.*, pp. 339-340.   226 *Ibid.*, pp. 310-311.

tracted "and the wound which resulted from this operation was methodically dressed. The patient experienced temporary relief. However, the symptoms of a disordered brain returned and grew worse; a lethargic fever declared itself and he died in a stupor, after having been stricken with paralysis (hemiplegia) of the right side."

A patient with whom Larrey had more success was a certain Pierre Auger, a fusilier-grenadier,[227] who likewise had been struck by a bullet on his right temple. "After piercing the skin and the crotaphite muscle, the ball fractured the anterior upper (squamous) portion of the temporal bone, and then broke into two pieces, one of which penetrated into the cranium, while the other buried itself under the temporal muscle. Symptoms of concussion and compression of the brain declared themselves at the same time, and threatened the life of the patient." Larrey "hastened to slit open the wound which could not be done without cutting several branches of the temporal artery. Having secured them with a ligature," Larrey "was not stopped by this inconvenience"; he "then exposed to view all the injured part of the cranium, and" soon perceived "in the thickness of the muscle the first fragment of the ball which fell out of itself." He thereupon "by means of an elevator raised a rather large splinter of the cranium and with a pair of dressing forceps was fortunate enough to seize the other fragment of the ball, flattened and deeply sunk between the dura mater and the cranium. Through this accidental opening in the skull, there was discharged a rather large quantity of black fluid blood. The wound was dressed with the customary precautions. From this moment, all the symptoms quieted down and gradually disappeared. The wound suppurated several days; the scaling (exfoliation) along the circumference of the wound took place over a rather ex-

[227] *Ibid.*, pp. 312-314.

tended area, but the space resulting from this loss of substance by degrees diminished; the cicatrisation of the soft parts was completed in a short time; and this fusilier, finding himself completely cured, was discharged before the forty-fifth day. However, one still felt beneath the cicatrix the pulsations of the dura-mater."

This discussion, based upon Larrey, of the treatment of the wounded after the Battle of Aspern-Essling, has dealt with two cases of ordinary amputation, two cases of tetanus, six of injuries to the abdomen, and two of head wounds. For want of space and out of consideration for the reader's feelings, much that is interesting and much that was horrible has been omitted. The cases given convey an idea of what the suffering was like, which went on not only in the hospital of Reneveck, but in the other hospitals at Vienna and Ebersdorf, and not only on the French side but also on the Austrian, for at the Battle of Aspern-Essling—of the French 4,000 were killed, 15,000 were wounded; of the Austrians, 4,012 were killed, 16,020 were wounded. Of the French wounded, 3,000 were only slightly injured and remained with their corps; the remaining 12,000 were hospital cases.

The Battle of Aspern-Essling was a severe check to the French in the heart of the enemy's country. Napoleon, however, maintained a bold countenance; and since the Austrians did not disturb him, he was able during the next month to have constructed three sturdy bridges across the Danube to the Lobau and to turn the Lobau itself into a fortified camp with entrenchments and redoubts. When everything was ready—stores gathered, the forces concentrated—the French Army during the night of July 4-5 in a surprise move crossed from the eastern Lobau to the mainland, thus outflanking the Austrian earthworks which had been erected opposite the northern side of the island. There ensued in the plain beyond the Lobau a long two-day battle (Wagram) in which Napoleon defeated but did not destroy the Austrian Army. The Austrian governing circle, however, was discouraged and sued for an armistice, which was granted. After a three months' truce, a peace was signed on October 14, 1809, by which Austria ceded to Napoleon three and a half million inhabitants and agreed to pay a fairly large indemnity. Thus again Austria was defeated, but only after an effort.

The downward slope for Napoleon led through the Spanish revolt, the Austrian campaign, the difficulties in enforcing the closure of the ports of the Continent to English ships and goods, the disaffection of the subject peoples, the invasion of Russia, the uprising of Germany, and the abdication at Fontainebleau. Upon his return to Paris in the fall of 1809, the Spanish revolt continued; also the war with England. In 1810 he divorced his wife, Josephine, and shortly afterwards married an Austrian archduchess. He and the

Tsar Alexander drifted into war with each other, largely because Russia reopened her ports to English goods if not to English ships, although there were other reasons. In the course of the invasion of and retreat out of Russia in 1812 Napoleon lost an army. In 1813 he raised a new force, defeated Russia and Prussia in the spring campaign, and secured a two months' truce. But in the summer Austria joined the other two powers. "The war was then renewed, and on October 16-19, 1813, at the great battle of Leipzig" the armies of the coalition "completely defeated Napoleon" and drove him out of Germany back across the Rhine. Following him, the allied armies, those of Russia, Prussia, and Austria from the north and northeast, that of England from the south, entered France. Napoleon appealed to the French people, but they, weary of conscription, of taxes, of war, and perhaps of empire, virtually refused to help him. "It was almost with indifference that they watched Napoleon make his last desperate resistance." With the troops at his disposal, he put up a heroic defense but "was driven slowly back along the Marne river towards Paris. Learning too late that the allies had taken Paris from the rear, he retired to the palace of Fontainebleau. The allied armies entered Paris on March 31, 1814,"[1] and on April 11 Napoleon abdicated his throne. The victorious allies allowed him to retain the title of Emperor, and granted him the small island of Elba off the coast of Italy on condition that he would live there and not leave it.

A small island of eighty-six square miles, however, could not contain the energy and ambition of a man who had once controlled Western Europe. Nearly a year after his abdication, on February 26, 1815, Napoleon slipped out from Elba. He crossed the Tyrrhenian Sea and with a small force of seven hundred men landed in southern France at Cannes

---

[1] Carl Becker, *Modern History* (New York, 1933), pp. 300, 301.

to recover a kingdom. The government which the allies had imposed on France, that of the old Bourbon monarchy as represented by the elderly King Louis XVIII, had little support among the great majority of the French people; they merely accepted it. The rank and file of the French Army was still loyal to its old captain, Napoleon. So when Napoleon set out from Cannes for Paris, Louis XVIII received little aid from the people; and the successive army detachments which were sent out to take Napoleon prisoner successively went over to his side. Without firing a shot and without shedding a drop of blood, he was able in a few weeks to reach Paris, to recover France. Louis XVIII fled to Belgium.

Napoleon probably wanted to remain at peace—at least temporarily. But the allies, whose delegates were still at Vienna trying to draft a peace treaty, remained united and began to mobilize a coalition army of eight hundred thousand men along the northern and northeastern frontiers of France in preparation for a grand-scale invasion of that country. Napoleon could either stay on the defensive and await the attack, or take the offensive. He decided on the latter. He would attack the vanguard of the allied forces which was stationed in Belgium—a Prussian Army under Blücher, an English-Allied Army under Wellington. He would shatter these two armies by successive blows and proceed to capture the Belgian capital of Brussels. Perhaps, with the English Army destroyed and the capital of Belgium in his hands, the peace party in England would gain the upper hand, and she would withdraw from the coalition.

WATERLOO

THE BATTLEFIELD of Waterloo lies eleven miles south of Brussels astride one of the two main roads coming up from France to the Belgian capital. In May or the early part of June, 1815, a traveler leaving Brussels by this road would in his cabriolet rattle over the streets of the capital, pass through the Gate of Namur, continue over a paved highroad into open country. After traveling about two miles he would enter the beech-tree Forest of Soignes. Here the road was about forty-five feet broad, the center being paved to the width of fifteen feet, the two sides in dirt of equal width. The forest came down to the road; the trees were high and their branches met overhead; occasionally the sun would break through to gleam on the silver trunks of the beeches. For nearly six miles, with few deviations from the straight line, the road cut its way through the forest; only occasionally a neat white-washed cottage, a woodland crossroad, or openings made by the fellings of timber interrupted the quiet, somewhat somber character of the scenery. After six miles, the road suddenly turned, and at the end in a vista could be seen the tiny-domed church of Waterloo. The road passed through the village of Waterloo—a straggling line of white-washed cottages on both sides—and then began to climb a long, gradual slope. The wood, which had opened at Waterloo, temporarily closed in, though in a straggling and more irregular manner, and then was left behind. The road, continuing its ascent of the long slope but now in open field, after two and a quarter miles from Waterloo passed through the village of Mont St. Jean. After another half mile, still climbing, it reached the crest of what was to be the British position. It cut through the

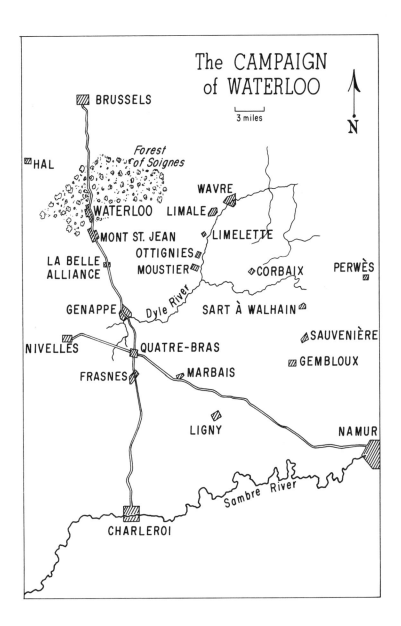

The CAMPAIGN of WATERLOO

3 miles

N

BRUSSELS

HAL

Forest of Soignes

WAVRE

WATERLOO   LIMALE

MONT ST. JEAN

LIMELETTE

OTTIGNIES

LA BELLE
ALLIANCE

MOUSTIER

CORBAIX

PERWÈS

GENAPPE   *Dyle River*   SART À WALHAIN

NIVELLES

SAUVENIÈRE

QUATRE-BRAS

GEMBLOUX

FRASNES   MARBAIS

LIGNY

NAMUR

Sambre River

CHARLEROI

crest at the depth of about five feet before commencing its descent.[1]

If our hypothetical traveler in early June, 1815, had here alighted from his carriage to take in the view (which was unlikely since there was nothing as yet to distinguish this view from many others in Belgium), he would have clambered up the side of the cut and stood on the crest of the ridge. If he stood on the left side of the road facing south, with his back to Brussels, then on his left, to the east, he would notice that the ridge on which he was standing extended for nearly a mile when it expanded into a plateau; to his right, to the west, it continued for about a mile before it dropped into a ravine. Along its crest ran a country crossroad, which for a brief distance when it crossed the Brussels highway was cut down to the latter's depth. In front, to the south, the ground and the Brussels road sloped gently downward to a shallow valley and then rose in gentle slope to another ridge which at a distance of three quarters of a mile paralleled that of the English position, and which was to be occupied by the French. The road descended on the English side perhaps 25 feet in 450 yards, and on the French side rose even more gradually, about 30 feet in 950 yards. In each case, the slope of the road was so gentle that a coach driving up would not slacken pace. The ascent of the ground on both sides was

[1] A description of the road from Brussels to Mont St. Jean and of the character of the scenery along the way may be found in the accounts of English travelers who visited the battlefield of Waterloo in 1815, 1816, 1817. In this connection see Charlotte A. Eaton, *Waterloo Days: The Narrative of an English-woman Resident at Brussels in June, 1815* (London, 1892), pp. 119-126; John Evans, *An Excursion to Windsor in July, 1810, to Which Is Annexed a Journal of a Trip to Paris in the Autumn of 1816* (London, 1817), pp. 510-512; James Simpson, *A Visit to Flanders in July, 1815* (Edinburgh, 1816), pp. 60-65; Seth W. Stevenson, *Journal of a Tour Through Part of France, Flanders, and Holland, Made in the Summer of 1816* (Norwich, 1817), pp. 272-276; also Sergeant-Major E. Cotton, *A Voice from Waterloo* (London, 1849), pp. 165-166; Sir A. S. Frazer, *Letters Written during the Peninsula and Waterloo Campaigns* (London, 1859), p. 544.

equally gradual, although here obstacles would be offered: the long broad slopes were slightly rolling and uneven, they were covered with rye, wheat, and barley, which in some places attained the height of five to six feet, and at some points the English position formed a definite crest.

On the left side of the road, just a short distance down the hill from where our traveler stood, were a knoll and a gravel pit. On the right side of the road, farther down the slope (about 270 yards), was a stone farmhouse, called La Haye Sainte, with a garden and orchard. To the distant right, about 450 yards in front of the right-hand end of the English ridge (so far in front that it was in the valley), was a country estate known as the Château de Hougoumont. It consisted of a substantial stone country house; courtyards to the north and south enclosed by the house, the farm buildings, and a wall; and outside, the farm with walled garden, orchard, and wood. To the far left, in front of where the English ridge expanded into a plateau, were the farms of Ter La Haye and Papelotte, with their houses and enclosures, and the village of Smohain; these, too, were in the valley.[2]

Raising our eyes from the immediate details of the ground, to the rear was the Forest of Soignes, which to the northeast and the northwest blackened the horizon as far

[2] For a description of the battlefield of Waterloo, see the accounts of English travelers and the diaries, journals, and memoirs of participants in the battle: Eaton, *op. cit.,* pp. 126-142; Evans, *op. cit.,* pp. 512-516; Simpson, *op. cit.,* pp. 65-68, 102; Stevenson, *op. cit.,* pp. 276-293; Cotton, *op. cit.,* pp. 26-28, 36; William Hay, *Reminiscences 1808-1815* (London, 1901), pp. 173, 175; Cavalié Mercer, *Journal of the Waterloo Campaign* (London, 1927), pp. 154, 163, 190; General Sir James Shaw Kennedy, *Notes on the Battle of Waterloo* (London, 1865), pp. 59, 84-87, 89-96; "Bericht über den Anteil der hannoverschen Truppen und der Deutschen Legion an der Schlacht bei Belle-Alliance," "Bericht der hannoverschen 4. Infanterie-Brigade, December 10, 1824" (Julius von Pflugk-Hartung, *Belle-Alliance: Berichte und Angaben über die Beteiligung deutscher Truppen an der Armee Wellington an dem Gefechte bei Quatre Bras und der Schlacht bei Belle-Alliance,* Berlin, 1915, pp. 51-52, 84). Pflugk-Hartung's book will hereinafter be referred to as *P-H.*

as the eye could reach. To the east and southeast, several miles distant, the Wood of Frischermont and of Paris bounded the prospect. But otherwise, the eye swinging around from the east to the south to the west saw nothing but rolling open country of minor woods and of fields covered by rye and wheat. Only here and there in the distance, half-concealed by the rolling ground, could be seen villages, on the left Frischermont and Planchenoit, on the right Braine-la-Leud, the spires of the village churches looking down on the peaceful, as yet unaltered, countryside.[3] Across this country the road continued: past the roadside inn of Belle-Alliance at the crest of the French position, through the village of Genappe four and a half miles farther, through the crossroads houses of Quatre-Bras three miles still farther until it finally reached, and we hope our traveler with it, the first large, but still Belgian, town of Charleroi.

In the first two weeks of June, 1815, the allied Prussian and English armies stretched in scattered cantonments along the southern Belgian frontier,[4] the exact intentions of Napoleon being as yet unknown. The headquarters of the Prussian commander, Blücher, were at Namur; those of the English commander, Wellington, at Brussels. A member of the English governing circles by birth, his father an earl, his mother daughter of a viscount, Wellington, the second son, had been a slow starter.[5] Idle at Eton, both at work and games, his mother thought him a fool, destined him for the army, sent him at the age of sixteen to the French military school at Angers. At Angers he was "rather of weak con-

[3] On the general character of the scene: Simpson, *op. cit.*, p. 108; Stevenson, *op. cit.*, pp. 278, 293.

[4] The statement is true, roughly speaking. The forces were arranged in a vast semicircle from Ostend on the coast through Mons and Charleroi around to Liege, with Brussels as a center. The English were to the right (west) of the Brussels-Charleroi road; the Prussians to the left.

[5] The ensuing summary of Wellington's life and character is largely based on Oliver Brett, *Wellington* (London, 1928).

stitution, not very attentive to his studies, lay about a good deal on the sofa and was constantly occupied with a little terrier called 'Vic.'" Through purchase and family influence, he advanced through the grades in the army: ensign at 17, lieutenant at 18, captain at 22, major at 24, lieutenant colonel also at 24 without having much military experience. But then in his twenties he took hold. He participated in the English expedition to the Netherlands in 1793-1794 and showed practical good sense in covering the English retreat. Unlike most aristocrat officers, he studied the details of his profession. In 1796, at the age of twenty-seven (his age was the same as Napoleon's), he went out to India.

There family influence again secured Wellington promotion and command, but he justified the appointment. Studying his opponents with care, he marched from victory to victory over the native states, learned how to handle and supply an army, his constitution becoming wiry and untiring through campaigning under the Indian sun. He returned to England in 1805, a major general, proposing to rise higher. In 1807, placed in command of the English troops dispatched to Portugal, he was soon superseded and returned home. In 1809 he sailed to command the second English expedition to the Spanish Peninsula. For five long years with a small force of about thirty thousand men he advanced, maneuvered, retreated, sniped at the French; handled the politicians at home and the distrustful Spaniards, the latter worthless save for guerrilla warfare. The destruction of Napoleon's Grande Armée in Russia in 1812 enabled Wellington to drive the French out of most of Spain in 1813; the defeat of Napoleon in Germany in 1813 enabled Wellington to invade southern France in 1814. Thus were crowned gloriously five years of patience and sustained brilliance and care.

Wellington was a commander who did everything himself: posted his troops, watched over their supply, handled them on the field of battle.[6] He possessed an infinite capacity for taking pains, plus a vitality and energy which infused it all. In appearance, he was of medium height, five feet nine, a long head and a long nose; blue eyes; brown wavy hair, even in 1815 at forty-six, not yet tinged with grey;[7] wiry, lean, and self-possessed. A strict disciplinarian who praised too little, he did not possess the affection of his soldiers. But he had their admiration and confidence.[8] In Spain "they began to talk of him as 'Arty, the long-nosed ——— that licks the parlez-vous.' At Albuera, for which Wellington was late although he rode 135 miles in three days and killed two horses on the journey, one private turned nervously to another: 'Where's our Arthur?' 'I don't know, I don't see him.' 'Aw wish he woz here.' At Sorauren as he rode along on to the height above the village a cheer went up from the troops, and when the familiar figure on the wiry thoroughbred, dressed neatly in that short frock-coat and small plumeless cocked hat that had already earned him the nickname of the 'Beau,' was seen against the skyline, a corporal is reported to have shouted: 'There goes the little blackguard that whops the French.' "[9] Officers and men both trusted his calm efficiency.

Wellington himself had never met or been opposed to Napoleon. But he respected the French Emperor as a general. When in Spain it was rumored that Napoleon

[6] Wellington to Lord Ellesmere, Sept. 25, 1851 (Egerton, Francis, the first Earl of Ellesmere, *Personal Reminiscences of the Duke of Wellington*, London, 1903, p. 188). The author will hereinafter be referred to as Ellesmere.

[7] Mercer, *op. cit.*, p. 121.

[8] Ellesmere, *op. cit.*, pp. 108, 179; George Robert Gleig, *Personal Reminiscences of the First Duke of Wellington* (New York, 1904), pp. 301-302.

[9] Brett, *op. cit.*, pp. 101-102. The sentence which follows the quotation is also in essentials taken from Brett (p. 102), but slightly changed. Brett's sentence runs: "Both men and officers felt the atmosphere of his calm efficiency."

was coming himself to take charge of operations, Wellington wrote to his second-in-command, that then there would be "hell to pay." But in 1815, in Brussels, Wellington as always was cool, composed, self-confident.[10] At the opening of the Belgian campaign he remarked to one of his attachés that "The French will be devilishly surprised to find out how I can defend a position."[11]

Blücher, the Prussian commander, was a frisky, energetic German of seventy-two, with the simple character of a cavalry hussar (the corps from which he had risen)—that is, always ready to rush into a fight. As Wellington noted, Blücher understood a field of battle, but knew nothing of plans of campaign.[12] Fortunately, Blücher's capable Chief of Staff, Gneisenau, knew how to arrange the movement of troops on march and into battle.[13] Though Napoleon did not realize it, he was facing a dangerous trio.

When, on June 15, Napoleon and his army emerged from behind the screening fortresses of northern France, Wellington concentrated the English Army on its left at Quatre Bras, and Blücher concentrated the Prussian force on its right at Ligny six miles distant.[14] Before the concentration was complete, Napoleon struck. On Friday, June 16, in the late afternoon battle of Ligny, three fourths of the Prussian Army was roughly handled by Napoleon and his main force,

[10] Conversation of Lord Stanhope with Alava and Wellington, Oct. 27, 1838 (Philip Henry, fifth Earl of Stanhope, *Notes of Conversations with the Duke of Wellington (1831-1851)*, London, 1938, p. 121). The author will be hereinafter referred to as Lord Stanhope.

[11] Conversation of Lord Stanhope with Alava and Wellington, Oct. 27, 1838 (*ibid.*, p. 121).

[12] Conversation of Lord Stanhope with Wellington, Oct. 25, 1838 (*ibid.*, pp. 119-120).   [13] *Ibid.*

[14] Duke of Wellington to Earl Bathurst, June 19, 1815 (Wellington, *The Dispatches of Field Marshal, the Duke of Wellington*, London, 1838, XII, 478-479); report of General Gneisenau (Wellington, *Supplementary Dispatches and Memoranda of the Duke of Wellington*, London, 1858-72, X, 502). The two collections will hereinafter be referred to as Wellington, *Dispatches* and *Supplementary Dispatches*.

and retired during the night.[15] In the same afternoon an increasing English force at Quatre Bras had been likewise engaged against another French detachment, but on account of the blunders of Napoleon's lieutenants, Ney (in command) and d'Erlon, and because of Wellington's skill, it had been able to maintain its ground.[16]

Wellington spent the night at Genappe,[17] a few miles back, but was again on the field of Quatre Bras shortly after daylight on June 17.[18] Perceiving through his telescope French outposts on the field of Ligny, he dispatched an aide with half a squadron of cavalry to learn what had become of the Prussians.[19] The aide returned with the report that the Prussians were retreating on roads leading to Brussels through Wavre; at the latter point they would again reassemble.[20] Wellington, thus left alone to face Napoleon and

[15] Duke of Wellington to Earl Bathurst, June 19, 1815 (Wellington, *Dispatches*, XII, 479-480); report of General Gneisenau (Wellington, *Supplementary Dispatches*, X, 502-503); Blücher to his wife, Wavre, June 17, 1815 (Gebhard Lebrecht von Blücher, *Blücher in Briefen aus den Feldzügen 1813-1815*, Stuttgart, 1876, p. 146).

[16] Duke of Wellington to Earl Bathurst, June 19, 1815 (Wellington, *Dispatches*, XII, 479-480); report of General Gneisenau (Wellington, *Supplementary Dispatches*, X, 504); report of Prince of Orange to King of Holland, Nivelles, 2 A.M., June 17, 1815 (*ibid.*, pp. 496-497); William Maynard Gomm, *Letters and Journals of Field-Marshal Sir William Maynard Gomm from 1799 to Waterloo, 1815* (London, 1881), pp. 352-356.

[17] Conversation of Lord Stanhope with Lord Fitzroy, Nov. 7, 1840 (Stanhope, *op. cit.*, p. 251); letter of Sir Hussey Vivian, June 3, 1839 (H. T. Siborne, *Waterloo Letters: A Selection from Original and Hitherto Unpublished Letters Bearing on the Operations of the 16th, 17th, and 18th June, 1815, by Officers Who Served in the Campaign*, London, 1891, p. 153). Siborne's *Waterloo Letters* will hereinafter be referred to as *W. L.*

[18] Letter of Sir Hussey Vivian, June 3, 1839 (*W. L.*, p. 153).

[19] Letter of Sir Hussey Vivian, June 3, 1839 (*ibid.*, p. 154); Wellington to Lord Ellesmere, Sept. 25, 1851 (Ellesmere, *op. cit.*, 185-190); memorandum of the Duke of Wellington, June, 1845 (*ibid.*, p. 201); conversation of Lord Stanhope with Wellington, Oct. 26, 1837 (Stanhope, *op. cit.*, pp. 109-110); Duke of Wellington to Earl Bathurst, June 19, 1815 (Wellington, *Dispatches*, XII, 480); report of Prince of Orange to King of Holland, Nivelles, 2 A.M., June 17, 1815 (Wellington, *Supplementary Dispatches*, X, 496-497; Friedrich Carl von Müffling, *Aus meinem Leben*, Berlin, 1855, p. 207).

[20] Wellington to Lord Ellesmere, Sept. 25, 1851 (Ellesmere, *op. cit.*, p. 187);

his power, could not remain where he was. He decided to fall back on the Charleroi-Brussels road to the ridge in front of Mont St. Jean, which was directly west of Wavre, and to reopen communication with the Prussian staff.[21]

Since on the morning of June 17 the French were strangely inactive in observing both the Prussians and the English, Wellington took the risk of allowing his men to breakfast.[22] While this was proceeding, a Prussian staff officer arrived from Gneisenau and informed the Duke of the intended Prussian concentration at Wavre and asked him if he would be inclined in junction with the Prussians to attack Napoleon. Wellington, sitting on the ground beside an attaché, answered orally that he would accept battle at Mont St. Jean if at least one Prussian Army corps came to his support. Otherwise, he would be forced to retreat to Brussels. With this answer, the aide returned.[23]

About ten o'clock the British, covered by cavalry and still undisturbed by the French, commenced their withdrawal in regular order.[24] The retreat continued into the after-noon.[25] Thus in the afternoon of June 17 the Allied Army was in a broad retrograde movement. In the center Wellington with the main body of the British force was retreat-

memorandum of the Duke of Wellington, June, 1845 (*ibid.*, p. 201); Müffling, *op. cit.*, p. 207; General von Ollech, *Geschichte des Feldzuges von 1815*, Berlin, 1876, p. 179).

[21] Memorandum of the Duke of Wellington, June, 1845 (Ellesmere, *op. cit.*, pp. 203-204); Frazer to his wife, Quatre Bras, June 17, half-past 7 A.M. (Frazer, *op. cit.*, pp. 541-542); Müffling, *op. cit.*, p. 207; Wellington to the Governor of Antwerp, Waterloo, 3 A.M., June 18, 1815 (Wellington, *Dispatches*, XII, 478); Wellington to the Duke of Berri, Waterloo, 3 A.M., June 18, 1815 (*ibid.*, XII, 477); letter of General the Marquess of Anglesey, Malvern, Oct. 18, 1842 (*W. L.*, p. 4). [22] Müffling, *op. cit.*, pp. 207-208.

[23] *Ibid.*, p. 208; report of General Gneisenau (Wellington, *Supplementary Dispatches*, X, 505); Frazer to his wife, Quatre Bras, June 17, 9:30 (Frazer, *op. cit.*, pp. 541-542); Von Ollech, *op. cit.*, p. 180.

[24] Wellington to Lord Ellesmere, Sept. 25, 1851 (Ellesmere, *op. cit.*, p. 187); memorandum of the Duke of Wellington, June, 1845 (*ibid.*, pp. 202-203); letter of General the Marquess of Anglesey, Malvern, Oct. 18, 1842 (*W. L.*, p. 4). [25] Concerning the afternoon retreat see p. 124.

ing down the Charleroi-Brussels road and a converging side road²⁶ to Mont St. Jean. As a rear guard, their cavalry occasionally clashed with the advancing French cavalry. After two o'clock, a heavy, soaking rain favored the British retreat. To the far right, on the other highroad from France to Brussels (the Mons-Brussels road), a separate English detachment of seventeen thousand was falling back to the town of Hal, eight miles west of Mont St. Jean.²⁷ To the left, the Prussians were retreating but in an orderly, organized fashion over various crossroads to Wavre, ten miles east and slightly north of Mont St. Jean.²⁸

In the evening the English in the center bivouacked in the rain along the ridge in front of Mont St. Jean.²⁹ During the evening and then in the early morning Wellington arranged his troops on the ridge and occupied with single detachments the foreposts of the position: the Château of Hougoumont, the farmhouse of La Haye Sainte, the farms of Papelotte and Ter La Haye, and the village of Smohain.³⁰ During the night he also received word from Blücher that he would come to Wellington's support, not only with a single corps, but with his entire army; that the first Prussian corps of thirty thousand would march at dawn, the second would follow, and the third and fourth if possible.³¹

²⁶ The road from Nivelles.
²⁷ Instructions to General Lord Hill for the movement of the army on June 17, 1815 (Wellington, *Dispatches*, XII, 475).
²⁸ Report of Gneisenau, Wavre, 2 P.M., June 17, 1815 (Von Ollech, *op. cit.*, p. 164).
²⁹ Mercer, *op. cit.*, pp. 156-157; Cotton, *op. cit.*, pp. 24-25; "Bericht über den Anteil der hannoverschen Truppen und der Deutschen Legion an der Schlacht bei Belle-Alliance, 1825," "Bericht des hannoverschen Feldbataillons Bremen über seinen Anteil an der Schlacht bei Belle-Alliance, December 4, 1842," "Bericht des hannoverschen Feldbataillons Bremen, December 9, 1824" (*P.-H.*, pp. 51, 127-128, 132).
³⁰ Memorandum of the Duke of Wellington, June, 1845 (Ellesmere, *op. cit.*, pp. 205-206); Duke of Wellington to Earl Bathurst, June 19, 1815 (Wellington, *Dispatches*, XII, 481).
³¹ Duke of Wellington to Earl Bathurst, June 19, 1815 (Wellington, *Dispatches*, XII, 481); Wellington to Sir Charles Stuart, Waterloo, 3 A.M., June

So in the early morning of June 18 this was the situation: at Hal, a detachment of seventeen thousand of Wellington's command; in front of Mont St. Jean, from Hougoumont to Smohain, sixty-seven thousand English, Germans, Belgians, and Dutch and Wellington; around Wavre, one hundred nine thousand Prussians. It was Wellington's calculation that if Napoleon attempted to outflank the English or to draw them away from the Prussians by taking the Mons to Brussels road, the seventeen thousand at Hal would hold him until Wellington with the main force could come to their aid; that if, however, Napoleon with a somewhat superior force attacked the Allied line occupying the ridge in front of Mont St. Jean, that line would hold until Blücher with one or two Prussian corps arrived.[32]

II

Napoleon, at the opening of the campaign, on June 14, issued a proclamation to his army:

Soldiers, today is the anniversary of Marengo and of Friedland, which twice decided the destiny of Europe. Then, as after Austerliz, as after Wagram, we were too generous; we believed the protestations and oaths of the princes whom we left on the throne. Today, however, in coalition against us they begrudge the independence and the most sacred rights of France. They have begun the most unjust of aggressions. Let us march then to the encounter: they and we, are we not the same men as before?

Soldiers, at Jena, against these same Prussians today so arrogant, you were one against three; at Montmirail, one against six.

Let those of you who were prisoners of the English tell of their prison-ships and of the horrors which you suffered. . . .

18, 1815 (*ibid.*, XII, 476); report of General Gneisenau (Wellington, *Supplementary Dispatches*, X, 504); Blücher to Müffling, June 17, 1815 (Von Ollech, *op. cit.*, p. 187).
[32] Wellington to the Duke of Berri, Waterloo, 3 A.M., June 18, 1815 (Wellington, *Dispatches*, XII, 477); Wellington to Major General Colville, June 17, 1815 (*ibid.*, XII, 476); Ellesmere, *op. cit.*, pp. 104-105, 183.

Soldiers, we have forced marches to make, battles to fight, perils to encounter; but with courage, victory will be ours: the rights, the honor and the happiness of our country will be reconquered.

For every Frenchman with heart, the moment has arrived to vanquish or to perish.[33]

Like many of Napoleon's proclamations, this one contained an element of truth. It was true that the French were outnumbered. Napoleon's Army of the North, which he was taking into campaign, numbered 123,000; Wellington's force, 93,000; Blücher's, 121,000. It was also true that the French Army, at least in the rank and file and the officers below the top generals, was superior in quality to the forces opposing it. There were few new French recruits; the bulk of the army consisted of veterans—privates, lieutenants, colonels, generals, who knew their trade. Inasmuch as the army had been shaken together hurriedly, its organization, it is true, was incomplete (but then this was also the case with the opposing forces). In addition, the men distrusted the general officers because many of these had proved turncoats during the first Restoration, transferred allegiance from Napoleon to the Bourbons, then back to Napoleon— who knew that they might not turn traitor again? But whatever their attitude toward their officers, the men were full of confidence in Napoleon, and for him they were ready to fight as before with unexampled admiration and devotion.[34]

In comparison, Blücher's army was likewise composed largely of veterans, of soldiers who had seen service in 1813 or 1814. But they "were certainly not so inured to war as

[33] Napoleon, Proclamation à l'armée, Avesnes, June 14, 1815, No. 22052, in Napoleon Ier, *Correspondance de Napoleon Ier* (Paris, 1869), XXVIII, 281.

[34] Ropes, *The Campaign of Waterloo*, pp. 16-17; conversation of Lord Stanhope with Captain Bridges, Oct. 21, 1839 (Stanhope, *op. cit.*, p. 189).

were those of Napoleon's army, nor were they so well led."[35] Wellington's army, the weakest of the three, was a motley force, consisting of thirty-one thousand British, many of them inexperienced; six thousand members of the Hanoverian Legion (the King of England was also the Elector of Hanover); sixteen thousand Hanoverian militia; seven thousand Brunswickers (youthful, new to the game); three thousand Nassauers (they had formerly fought *for* Napoleon); twenty-nine thousand Dutch-Belgians (of uncertain loyalty to the Allied cause).[36] For stability under fire, only the British and the Hanoverian Legion could be relied on. In some way, Wellington aided by his general officers had to hold that force together. Taken all in all, the French Army, as Napoleon implied, was the best in the field.

But when Napoleon in his proclamation said, "Are we not the same men as before," he overlooked his top generals and himself. As a matter of fact, Napoleon no longer had with him that brilliant coterie of general officers who had helped win his greatest victories by improvising and filling out in execution of his general orders. Of the four corps commanders, Lannes was dead, Davout had been left behind as Minister of War in Paris, Massena was now fifty-seven years old and his infirmities did not permit him to participate in an active campaign;[37] only Ney was with the army—and he, undeniably brave on the field of battle, had been granted a nearly independent command of the left wing, a charge which involved strategical considerations

[35] Ropes, *op. cit.*, p. 33.
[36] The figures are given in round numbers. If the 1,240 engineers are added, they will total 93,000. On the Anglo-Allied force see Ellesmere, *op. cit.*, p. 179; memorandum on the Battle of Waterloo by the Duke of Wellington, Sept. 24, 1842 (Wellington, *Supplementary Dispatches*, X, 517); report of General Pozzo di Borgo, Brussels, June 19, 1815 (*P.-H.*, p. 286); conversation of Lord Stanhope with Wellington, March 18, 1840 (Stanhope, *op. cit.*, p. 221); Gomm, *op. cit.*, p. 364.
[37] Henry Houssaye, *1815: Waterloo* (Paris, 1904), p. 50.

and for which he was inadequate. Of the other older officers, Bessières, commander of the Imperial Guard, had been
killed during the spring campaign in Germany in 1813;
Murat, superb cavalry leader, had lost his kingdom of
Naples, was now in southern France, but Napoleon refused
to use in the French Army a man who had fought against
France the year before;[38] Berthier, chief of staff, had at first
remained loyal to the Bourbons, retired to Belgium and then
to southern Germany, but then had committed suicide when
he discovered he could not return to France.[39] In their
places were Drouot (Guard), Grouchy (Cavalry), Soult
(Chief of Staff), and the five corps commanders, Reille,
d'Erlon, Lobau, Gérard, Vandamme.[40] All of these were
capable men, veterans of years of warfare, but without
brilliance.[41] Furthermore, even though capable and experienced, they were not in all respects equal to their
former selves. Age and the satisfaction of their ambitions
had tempered their youthful audacity. They were more
timid, more careful, and perhaps also, in some cases, less
devoted to Napoleon.[42]

Napoleon himself had changed. Since 1807 he had put
on weight. In 1815 he was a short, fat man of forty-six,
rather bald on top and with a most commanding air.[43] During the same period his energy had decreased, and now he

[38] *Ibid.*, pp. 54-55; H. de Mauduit, *Les derniers jours de la Grande Armée*
(Paris, 1847), II, 501.   [39] Houssaye, *op. cit.*, pp. 57-58.
[40] *Ibid.*, pp. 102-104.   [41] Gérard perhaps an exception.
[42] Napoleon's comment is found in the remarks of June 13, 1816, at St.
Helena reproduced in General Baron Gourgaud, *The St. Helena Journal of
General Baron Gourgaud* (English ed., London, 1932), p. 63; see also Pontécoulant, *Souvenirs militaires: Napoléon à Waterloo ou précis rectifié de la
campagne de 1815* (Paris, 1866), pp. liv-lv, 139; Ropes, *op. cit.*, p. 18.
[43] Letter by an anonymous observer, Plymouth, July 31, 1815, in Near
Observer, *The Battle of Waterloo Containing the Series of Accounts Published
by Authority, British and Foreign, with Circumstantial Details Relative to the
Battle, from a Variety of Authentic and Original Sources* (London, 1816),
pp. 143, 146. Referred to hereinafter as the *Near Observer*.

tired more easily. After several hours of administrative work he would have to stop.[44] After only two days of campaigning he returned to his headquarters, "overwhelmed with fatigue."[45] There was a tendency to chat. At times his energy would return: then "his genius and activity seemed as powerful and as fresh as ever; at other moments he seemed apathetic."[46]

The decline in energy had been accompanied by a decline in mental alertness. Let us not exaggerate, however. The level of his general intelligence remained high. Habit still served him: as a matter of routine he still did much (such as arranging an army before battle) that would have required brilliance from the inexperienced or mediocre. Over and above that basis of routine, when he was given time to meditate, the result was still a product of genius, and flashes of brilliance still occasionally occurred. But there was no longer that rat-tat-tat of swift, successive, brilliant decision. Perceptions and measures did not adjust themselves as quickly as before to the changing situation. Even more serious, in his fatigue one is tempted to say there were perceptions which did not occur, ideas which were not had. Also lacking was that sustained, impatient drive pressing forward immediate execution of his projects. Both in perception and in execution, there was a distinct slowing down. As he said in Paris to Benjamin Constant, "I have aged."[47]

Age, the habit of using the imperative, or giving orders

[44] Mollien, *Mémoires d'un ministre du trésor public: 1780-1815* (Paris, 1845), IV, 198.

[45] Baron Fain to Prince Joseph, Charleroi, 9 P.M., June 15, 1815, No. 22055, in Napoleon, *Correspondance*, XXVIII, 286.

[46] Remark of Marshal Soult to Sir W. Napier (quoted in Ropes, *op. cit.*, p. 24, n. 10); see also *ibid.*, p. 23; F. Martha-Beker, "Relation de la mission du lieutenant-général comte Beker auprès de l'Empereur Napoléon depuis la seconde abdication jusqu'au passage à bord du Bellérophon," published in F. Martha-Beker, *Science, questions diverses, histoire* (Paris, 1876), pp. 242, 260, 279. Referred to hereinafter as Beker.

[47] Pontécoulant, p. 423, n. 1; Beker, *op. cit.*, p. 293; Mauduit, *op. cit.*, II, 361.

and of not suffering contradiction either from men or events, and the early years (until 1812) of great success had also developed a rigidity, an inflexibility in his thinking. On the campaigns of 1812, 1813, 1814, even in the details of reality, he tended to have fixed ideas, and these ideas were fixed on the sanguine side. Thus, during the campaign of 1814, when forming his plans with Marmont, one of his marshals, Napoleon said, "Then Marmont will come with his ten thousand men." Marmont interrupted him to say, "Sire, I have only three thousand." The other nodded and said, "I know"; but soon afterwards again set out with, "Marmont with his ten thousand men." Again did Marmont declare that he had only three thousand—again did Napoleon acquiesce; yet in a little while he once more began to point out and direct what Marmont was to do with his ten thousand men.[48] He constantly tended to overvalue his own resources and also to underrate his opponents and his difficulties. "The habit of Napoleon had been to astonish and deceive mankind; now he had come at last to deceive himself."[49]

To this general condition of Napoleon was added on the Waterloo campaign the special aggravation of hemorrhoidal difficulties. From time to time, for many hours, he was in pain.[50] All this—the decline in energy and in mental alertness and the sanguine quality of his thinking—simply meant that while Napoleon was still a superior commander, he was not the youth of the first Italian campaign, nor even the mature master of Austerlitz and Friedland.

The plan of campaign had been well conceived. He

[48] Conversation of Lord Stanhope with Wellington, May 28, 1837 (Stanhope, op. cit., p. 98).
[49] Wellington, "Memorandum of Napoleon's Russian Campaign" (Gleig, op. cit., p. 388; also p. 392). In addition, on the sanguine quality of his thinking note the observations of General Beker, who in 1815 was, so to speak, Napoleon's warden from Malmaison to Rochefort (Beker, op. cit., pp. 214, 248, 253-254, 259-260, 289).   [50] Beker, op. cit., pp. 279-280.

apparently noted that the Prussian Army, being less scattered than the English, could, therefore, concentrate more rapidly. He apparently proposed, therefore, to assemble his army in relative secrecy behind the French fortresses; to enter Belgium near Charleroi—near the point of junction of the two allied armies; to attack the Prussians first before the English could come to their aid, and then to turn on the British forces. In the course of the maneuver, in brief, he hoped in some way to catch the enemies' armies wide open, to shatter them by successive blows, and to proceed to Brussels.[51]

Everything at first went according to plan. He gathered his army in relative secrecy; he crossed the Belgian frontier near Charleroi, caught the enemy by surprise, and seized the town (June 15); the Prussians did concentrate first, the English more slowly; at Ligny (June 16) he was able to attack the Prussians first, when their concentration was only three-fourths complete and before the English could come to their aid; and the battle itself was on Napoleon's part well conceived and well executed. The Prussians were very roughly handled and retired during the night. The only blur on an otherwise successful day (June 16) was that Ney, in command of the French left wing, in disobedience of Napoleon's orders, had delayed his attack on the small English detachment at Quatre Bras (six miles to Napoleon's left) until much of the British Army had come up or was nearby and it was too late.

The Battle of Ligny against the Prussians, beginning in the midafternoon, was not decided until late and was a hot

---

[51] Ropes, *op. cit.*, p. 4. In support of Ropes's discussion, see also Napoleon to Marshal Ney, Charleroi, June 16, 1815, No. 22058, in Napoleon, *Correspondance*, XXVIII, 289-291; Napoleon to Marshal Grouchy, Charleroi, June 16, 1815, No. 22059, in *ibid.*, pp. 291-292; remarks of Napoleon at St. Helena, Feb. 25, 1817 (General Gourgaud, *Sainte-Hélène: journal inédit*, French ed., Paris, n. d.), I, 502; conversation of Lord Stanhope with Ouvrard and later Wellington, Oct. 31, 1836, Sept. 17, 1839 (Stanhope, *op. cit.*, p. 91).

affair right up to darkness. Napoleon left the battlefield shortly before eleven o'clock, intrusting to Grouchy, commander of the French right wing, the task of making arrangements for the night.[52] Napoleon retired to Fleurus, a mile or so in the rear, where he went to bed weary and suffering.[53] Napoleon used to say that on campaign a good commander after briefly napping arose at three o'clock in the morning to receive reports, to dispatch orders, to get things under way; and this hitherto had been his own practice. But on the morning of June 17 he did not arise until about seven o'clock.

During the night, as we have said, the Prussians retreated in three columns on roads leading north and northeast. Also during the night, Grouchy had dispatched Generals Exelmans and Pajol in pursuit with several divisions of cavalry to observe the direction of the Prussian retreat. But unfortunately, while General Exelmans took the road to the northeast to Gembloux, Pajol took the road to the east to Namur, the line of Prussian communications with Germany. The retreat of two Prussian columns to the north thus remained unobserved. Also unfortunately, Pajol on this road east stumbled across some stray Prussians with artillery and equipment. About dawn, therefore, he reported to Grouchy that he had "set off in pursuit of the enemy" on the road to Namur, that he had then "charged the tail-end of his column, and seized near the village of Mazy eight cannon, and immense quantity of carriages, baggage, forage, etc., from which the horses had been taken."[54] By seven o'clock in the morning this report was communicated to Napoleon,

[52] The exact content of Napoleon's orders to Grouchy is in doubt, if indeed he gave any precise instructions. But he left Grouchy in charge (Marquis Albert de Grouchy, *Mémoires du maréchal de Grouchy*, Paris, 1873, IV, 43, 127; Houssaye, *op. cit.*, p. 218). [53] Grouchy, *op. cit.*, IV, 128, 146.

[54] General Pajol to Grouchy, in front of Mazy, noon, June 17, 1815 (Grouchy, *op. cit.*, IV, 48). This later dispatch summarizes the earlier one of the morning. See also Houssaye, *op. cit.*, p. 219.

and the eight Prussian cannon were in the courtyard of the château where he had slept.[55] With only this report before him, Napoleon naturally assumed that the Prussians were retreating to the right, eastward, on the road to Namur, that he had driven the Prussian and English armies apart.[56]

With the Prussians out of the way, there was no reason why Napoleon should not immediately turn on the English.[57] It had been his intention to attack the English that day;[58] he had at disposal in his own army the Sixth Corps (Lobau) of sixteen thousand men and in Ney's command the First Corps (d'Erlon) of twenty thousand, neither of which had participated in the battles of the preceding day; and the English, as he perceived, were in a singularly vulnerable position—while Ney struck from the front, Napoleon coming from Ligny could appear on their left flank. If the Prussians were driven to the right, there was perhaps no hurry. But time is the essence of a military campaign. As we know, the English did not move off from Quatre Bras until ten o'clock. Instant action on Napoleon's part was required. Instead he dallied.

He dictated a long dispatch to Ney, ordering him to inform Napoleon if the English were still at Quatre Bras: if they were not, Ney was to occupy the position; if they were still there, the two together, Ney and Napoleon, would attack.[59] He dictated another dispatch to the Minister of

[55] Mauduit, *op. cit.*, II, 99; Pontécoulant, *op. cit.*, p. 169.

[56] Major General Soult to Marshal Ney, Fleurus, June 17, 1815 (Grouchy, *op. cit.*, IV, 169-170). The dispatch, ostensibly by Soult, probably reflects Napoleon's ideas.

[57] Later Napoleon noted his error. At St. Helena he remarked: "I ought to have rested on the 16th at Fleurus, beaten the Prussians the same day, the 16th, and then the English on the 17th" (Gourgaud, *St. Helena Journal*, English ed., p. 56).

[58] Napoleon to Marshal Grouchy, June 16, 1815, No. 22059, in Napoleon, *Correspondance*, XXVIII, 292.

[59] Major General Soult to Marshal Ney, Fleurus, June 17, 1815 (Grouchy, *op. cit.*, IV, 170).

War, Davout, recounting the victories of the preceding day. About eight-thirty he left Fleurus for Ligny; since horseback was too painful for him, he proceeded in a carriage.[60] When the way became too difficult, he mounted his horse[61] and rode over the battlefield. As he rode along the lines of troops, which he passed in review, he received their enthusiastic acclamations.[62] After the review, which lasted an hour or so, he dismounted and chatted with his generals about public opinion in Paris, the Legislature, and the Jacobins.[63] During the review and conversation, information began to come in: a report from Ney that the English in front of Quatre Bras displayed eight regiments of infantry and two thousand cavalry—Napoleon's own patrols confirmed the presence of the English force;[64] a dispatch from General Exelmans that he had followed a strong Prussian column of thirty thousand men northeast to Gembloux.[65] This was quite correct; a Prussian column had passed that town on the way to Wavre and Brussels. Finally, about eleven o'clock, Napoleon reached a decision. From little direct evidence, simply from the manner the battle had ended the night before, from the observations of the Prussian prisoners and the fragmentary reports of the cavalry outposts, from the appearance of the battlefield, Napoleon in a sanguine way concluded that he had won a decisive victory at Ligny, that he had shattered the Prussians, and that they were retiring in disorganized defeat.[66] As to the direc-

[60] Mauduit, *op. cit.*, II, 99; Pontécoulant, *op. cit.*, p. 172.

[61] Pontécoulant, *op. cit.*, p. 172.

[62] Mauduit, *op. cit.*, II, 109; Pontécoulant, *op. cit.*, p. 172.

[63] Mauduit, *op. cit.*, II, 110.　　　[64] Houssaye, *op. cit.*, p. 224.

[65] General Exelmans to Grouchy, noon, June 17, 1815 (Grouchy, *op. cit.*, IV, 49). This later dispatch summarizes the earlier one of the morning.

[66] This is apparent from Soult's dispatch to Ney of 7 A.M. that morning, from Soult's report to Davout of 8 A.M. that morning, both of which probably reflected Napoleon's ideas, from Napoleon's oral instructions to Grouchy of 11 A.M. that morning, and from the remarks of Napoleon in the farmhouse of Caillou on the morning of June 18. See Major General Soult to Marshal

tion of their retirement, he with more reason inferred from the reports of the cavalry that they were retiring to the right.[67] He determined, therefore, to leave Grouchy with an independent command of thirty-two thousand men to pursue the Prussians, to attack them, and to keep them under observation. Napoleon himself with the remaining troops would join Ney and attack the English. With this purpose in view, Napoleon ordered the Sixth Corps (Lobau) to move off toward Quatre Bras. About eleven o'clock its infantry, preceded by cavalry, advanced down the road toward the English position. Shortly afterwards the Imperial Guard followed. Napoleon, still at Ligny, then turned to Grouchy. Orally he ordered him to take the Third and Fourth Army Corps, and several other divisions of infantry and cavalry, totaling thirty-two thousand men, and set off in pursuit of the Prussians. "Set out in pursuit of the Prussians," Napoleon said, "attack them as soon as you have joined them, and never lose sight of them. With the troops I am leading I shall join the corps of Marshal Ney and attack the English if they make a stand this side of the Forest of Soignes. You will communicate with me by a paved highway."[68]

Grouchy offered some objection, perhaps noting that the Prussians already had a headstart of twelve hours. But Napoleon impatiently added: "Monsieur le maréchal, proceed toward Namur; because according to all probability, it is toward the Meuse that the Prussians are retreating; it is consequently in that direction that you will find them and

Ney, Fleurus, June 17, 1815 (Grouchy, *op. cit.*, IV, 169-170); Napoleon to Davout, Fleurus, June 17, 1815 (*ibid.*, p. 173; also pp. 44, 128, 244; and pp. 128, 136). Even in his later account of the campaign dictated at Saint-Helena, Napoleon continued to refer to "le desastre de Ligny," to the enormous loss of the Prussians—"on voyait six de leurs cadavres pour un cadavre français" (Napoleon, "Bataille de Mont-Saint-Jean," *Correspondance*, XXXI, 176, 177).
[67] Grouchy, *op. cit.*, IV, 241.   [68] *Ibid.*, IV, 44.

that you should march."[69] Grouchy was silent, obeyed, and left to collect his troops.[70] Shortly afterwards, perhaps half-an-hour later, for some reason as he reflected on the Prussian situation, Napoleon dictated a new set of instructions for Grouchy. As before, the latter was to take thirty-two thousand men. But now Napoleon was no longer so sure that the Prussians had retreated to the east or that he knew Blücher's intentions. He now ordered Grouchy to betake himself to Gembloux:

Proceed to Gembloux with the cavalry of General Pajol, the light cavalry of the 4th corps, the cavalry of General Exelmans . . . and the 3rd and 4th corps of infantry. Reconnoiter in the direction of Namur and Maëstricht and pursue the enemy; send out scouts to observe his march and advise me of his movements so that I can penetrate what he wishes to do. I am taking my headquarters to Quatre-Bras, where the English still were this morning. Our communication will then be directly by the paved high-road of Namur. If the enemy has evacuated Namur, write to the general commanding the 2nd military division at Charlemont to have Namur occupied by several battalions of national guard and several batteries of cannon which he will organize at Charlemont. He will give this command to a marshal of camp.

It is important to penetrate what Blücher and Wellington want to do, and if they propose to unite their armies in order to cover Brussels and Liege, while attempting the fate of a battle. In every case, keep your two corps of infantry together in a single league of ground having several avenues of retreat; station some intermediary detachments of cavalry to communicate with headquarters.[71]

[69] *Ibid.*
[70] For an account of the Napoleon-Grouchy interview, see Grouchy to Napoleon, 10 A.M., June 19, 1815 (*ibid.*, IV, 319; also supplementary evidence on pp. 44-47, 105, 128, 145-146, 243-245).
[71] Napoleon to Grouchy, Ligny, June 17, 1815 (Grouchy, *op. cit.*, IV, 50-51). The time which Grouchy gives for the dispatch, three o'clock in the afternoon, is several hours too late. On the timing of the dispatch see Houssaye, *op. cit.*, p. 229.

Having thus disposed of the Prussian problem, Napoleon apparently dismissed it from his mind and turned to the problems immediately confronting him. In this fashion passed the fugitive hours of the first half of the day.

In accord with his original plan, Napoleon now in the afternoon turned to the English. Over by Quatre Bras, Ney had been unaccountably inactive. Napoleon at Ligny at noon dictated a dispatch peremptorily ordering him to attack the English at once; that a corps of infantry and the Imperial Guard were there to support him; that the Emperor would soon arrive.[72] Napoleon then mounted, with his staff took the road to Quatre Bras, and joined about one o'clock his advance (Lobau's cavalry) at Marbais within view of the Quatre Bras farm.[73] The English had departed, leaving only a rear guard of cavalry and a few guns. When Napoleon arrived, part of the English cavalry was filing down the Brussels-Charleroi road; the remainder was astride the Namur crossroad, facing Napoleon at Marbais.[74] Under Napoleon's supervision the French cavalry took position, the cuirassiers (heavy cavalry) on the right, the light cavalry on the left, the infantry in the second line, and batteries in place.[75] Officers were sent to Ney pressing him to attack Quatre Bras.[76] Lobau, without waiting, immediately made ready to charge.[77]

The morning had been sultry, the sky gradually becom-

[72] Napoleon to Marshal Ney, in front of Ligny, noon, June 17, 1815 (quoted in Pontécoulant, *op. cit.,* p. 237).

[73] Napoleon, "Bataille de Mont-Saint-Jean," *Correspondance,* XXXI, 177; Houssaye, *op. cit.,* p. 232; memorandum by the Marquess of Anglesey (*W. L.,* p. 5).

[74] Hay, *op. cit.,* pp. 167-168; letter of General the Marquess of Anglesey, Malvern, Oct. 18, 1842 (*W. L.,* p. 4); also memorandum by the Marquess of Anglesey (*ibid.,* p. 5).

[75] Napoleon, "Bataille de Mont-Saint-Jean," *Correspondance,* XXXI, 177; Hay, *op. cit.,* p. 169.

[76] Napoleon, "Bataille de Mont-Saint-Jean," *Correspondance,* XXXI, 177.

[77] *Ibid.*

ing overcast.[78] About two o'clock,[79] a storm had developed coming from the northwest. "Large, isolated masses of thundercloud, of the deepest, almost inky black, their lower edges hard and strongly defined, lagging down, as if momentarily about to burst, hung suspended over the English position, involving it in gloomy obscurity,"[80] and bore down on the French, who were still in sunlight. Just as the French were about to charge, an English battery with the rear guard let go its fire. The first gun "seemed to burst the clouds overhead, for its report was instantly followed by an awful clap of thunder and by lightning, whilst the rain came down as if a waterspout had broken over the men. Flash succeeded flash, and the peals of thunder were long and tremendous, whilst, as if in mockery of the elements, the French guns still sent forth their feebler glare and now scarcely audible reports."[81] The English battery limbered up and galloped to the rear; the French cavalry charged into the storm, in headlong pursuit.[82]

Napoleon followed, occupied the farm of Quatre Bras. Despairing of Ney, whose troops had not yet appeared, Napoleon sent orders directly to the corps commanders: d'Erlon and Reille. D'Erlon finally appeared; his corps was given the lead and took over the pursuit of the English rear guard down the road to Brussels. The Second Corps

[78] Hay, *op. cit.*, p. 168.

[79] Houssaye, *op. cit.*, p. 253; memorandum of the Marquess of Anglesey (*W. L.*, p. 5).

[80] Mercer, *op. cit.*, p. 147. The quotation has been changed from the first person to the third, and the last clause somewhat shortened. On the character of the scene see also Hay, *op. cit.*, p. 170.

[81] *Ibid.*, p. 148. The quotation has been slightly shortened and changed from the first to the third person.

[82] *Ibid.*, p. 148. On the weather and the incidence of the storm see also Cotton, *op. cit.*, p. 21; Lieutenant Woodberry, *Journal du Lieutenant Woodberry* (Paris, 1896), p. 308; Napoleon, "Bataille de Mont-Saint-Jean," *Correspondance*, XXXI, 177; Wellington to Ellesmere, Sept. 25, 1851 (Ellesmere, *op. cit.*, p. 187); memorandum of the Duke of Wellington, June, 1845 (*ibid.*, p. 204); Hay, *op. cit.*, pp. 170-171.

(Reille) followed. When Ney appeared, Napoleon expressed his discontent with the Marshal's dilatory conduct. Ney stammered that he thought Wellington and all his army were still at Quatre Bras. The Sixth Corps (Lobau) followed that of Reille, and the Guard marched after. The cuirassiers, heavy cavalry of Milhaud, flanked the march, riding cross-country on the right-hand side of the road.[83]

Napoleon himself, with an apparent return of energy, rode along the column of plodding infantry until he reached the advance guard of cavalry and horse-artillery.[84] "The thunder-cloud, having passed over, left the men in comparative fine weather, although still raining heavily."[85] The infantry marched in water up to their ankles; in the field stood pools of water, and the horses of the cavalry that were riding cross-country sunk up to the knees, and at times nearly up to their girths.[86] Napoleon, again the old master of getting the utmost from men, urged forward his advance guard in pell-mell, steeplechase pursuit.[87] At last he was coming to grips with the troops of his most implacable foe, that nation which for years had clung to him like an old man of the sea. "Mounted on a small Arab horse, he was constantly by the six cannon of the advance, exciting the artillerymen by his presence and his word, and more than once in the midst of the shells and shrapnel which the enemy artillery threw at us, he could be heard shouting to the cannoneers with an accent of anger and hate: 'Fire, fire, those are English.'"[88] The long six-mile chase con-

[83] Napoleon, "Bataille de Mont-Saint-Jean," *Correspondance,* XXXI, 177-178.
[84] *Ibid.,* XXXI, 178.
[85] Mercer, *op. cit.,* p. 150; also Pontécoulant, *op. cit.,* p. 213; Hay, *op. cit.,* p. 171.
[86] Cotton, *op. cit.,* p. 21; Mauduit, *op. cit.,* II, 232; Napoleon, "Bataille de Mont-Saint-Jean," *Correspondance,* XXXI, 178.
[87] Pontécoulant, *op. cit.,* p. 185; Mercer, *op. cit.,* p. 150; MacKenzie MacBride, *With Napoleon at Waterloo* (London, 1911), p. 183.
[88] Pontécoulant, *op. cit.,* pp. 185-186. The quotation has been modified in one respect. In the body of the text, Pontécoulant, who was an eyewitness,

tinued right up to the ridge of Mont St. Jean.[89] There the enemy seemed reinforced. To find out, General Milhaud deployed his cuirassiers and under the protection of the fire from four French batteries, made as if to charge. Sixty British cannon from the ridge thundered in reply.[90] The entire British Army was in presence. It was six o'clock in the evening, too late to begin an attack. The First French Corps (d'Erlon) and the cavalry took position opposite the British Army.[91] The rest of the French force, strung out on the Charleroi road back to Genappe, found quarters where they could. Most of the rank and file bivouacked in the rain, lying in the muddy, water-soaked fields.[92] Napoleon took up quarters at the farm of Caillou, on the road, about a mile and five eighths back from Belle-Alliance, and issued orders that the army be ready for battle early next morning.[93]

On the eve of a general engagement, it might be supposed that Napoleon would concentrate his forces and order Grouchy to pursue the Prussians by roads which approached more closely to Napoleon's present position. This order seemed all the more pertinent since Napoleon had already suggested that the Prussians might join the English before Brussels, and also since by nine o'clock in the evening Napoleon had learned from his flanking cavalry that a fairly

---

speaks of Napoleon's "accent de haine," in the footnote of Napoleon's "accent de colère et de haine." The phrase from the footnote has been used, instead of the phrase from the text.

[89] Napoleon, "Bataille de Mont-Saint-Jean," *Correspondance*, XXXI, 178.

[90] *Ibid.*; Mercer, *op. cit.*, p. 155.

[91] Report of Colonel Van Zuylen von Neyevelt, Oct. 25, 1815 (F. de Bas and J. de Tserclaes de Wommerson, *Campagne de 1815 aux Pays-Bas d'après les rapports officiels*, Brussels, 1908, III, 329).

[92] Mauduit, *op. cit.*, II, 231-234; report of Colonel Van Zuylen von Neyevelt, Oct. 25, 1815 (Wommerson and De Bas, *op. cit.*, III, 329-331); Témoin oculaire, "Relation fidèle et détaillée de la dernière campagne de Buonaparte, terminé par la bataille de Mont Saint-Jean," bound with *Near Observer*, p. 113. This "Relation" will hereinafter be referred to as *Témoin oculaire*. [93] Houssaye, *op. cit.*, p. 276.

strong Prussian column had retreated north from Ligny toward Wavre, and not to the east toward Namur or northeast to Gembloux.[94] Thus already Napoleon was in possession of a fact which would give a clue to the Prussian movements, but he did not absorb the significance of the fact and he dispatched no order. In fact, I doubt if Napoleon was much occupied with the Prussians or Grouchy. The information which he had received concerning the true direction of the withdrawal of a Prussian column, he did not communicate to Grouchy until thirteen hours later (10 A.M., June 18), nor did he answer Grouchy's first report, which was received at 2 A.M. (June 18), until 10 A.M. He probably assumed that the Prussians, disorganized by defeat, were off there to the right retreating north or northeastward, in several columns;[95] that Grouchy also was off there to the right in pursuit. But that the Prussians would turn and descend on his right flank does not seem to have entered Napoleon's mind. He had intended to attack first the Prussians and then the English; he had attacked the Prussians and now he was absorbed in the coming engagement with the English. Sanguine as usual, supremely confident of victory (at one point, he reportedly said: "Ah, I have them at last, these English"),[96] his only fear was that the English would not stand their ground, but would withdraw through the Forest of Soignes during the night.[97]

In the meantime, Grouchy, commanding for the first time a large independent detachment that included both

[94] Napoleon, "Bataille de Mont-Saint-Jean," *Correspondance*, XXXI, 180.

[95] Houssaye, *op. cit.*, p. 273, n. 1.

[96] The remark may be apocryphal (it is apparently based on rumor) and was perhaps uttered at dawn of June 18, rather than the evening of June 17, but it expresses Napoleon's self-confidence during these hours. It is given in *Témoin oculaire*, bound with the *Near Observer*, p. 113.

[97] On Napoleon's optimism in the hours preceding the battle see letter of an interviewer on His Majesty's ship *Northumberland*, Aug. 22, 1815 (*Near Observer*, p. 151); Napoleon, "Bataille de Mont-Saint-Jean," *Correspondance*, XXXI, 182.

infantry and cavalry, had on this afternoon and evening of June 17 made slow progress. The first corps under his command (Vandamme) began to leave the battlefield of Ligny for Gembloux perhaps shortly after noon; it took perhaps an hour and a half for the entire corps to file off.[98] The Second Corps (Gérard) followed an hour later.[99] The storm which had struck Napoleon and the English rear guard at Quatre Bras also caught Grouchy; in fact, it soaked the entire region in which the French, English, and Prussian armies were operating. The rain fell in torrents, and soon the country crossroads over which Grouchy was operating became impracticable.[100] By nightfall his infantry had only reached Gembloux, which was about eight miles from Ligny; his cavalry, slightly in advance, was at the village of Sauvenières. Gembloux was about seventeen miles from the right flank of Napoleon's position in front of Mont St. Jean.[101] If it became necessary for Grouchy to join Napoleon, that distance would have to be covered over country crossroads soaked by an eighteen-hour rain. If summoned by Napoleon, at best Grouchy's detachment of thirty-two thousand, floundering through the mud, could only reach the Belle-Alliance position by midafternoon of June 18.[102]

As serious as Grouchy's slow progress (due to rain and his inability to spur his subordinates) was the circumstance

[98] Ropes, *op. cit.,* p. 211.   [99] *Ibid.*
[100] Grouchy, *op. cit.,* IV, 147; Baron Berthézène, *Souvenirs militaires de la république et de l'empire* (Paris, 1855), II, 390-391.
[101] From calculations based on the map of Ferrari, Kennedy states that "the distance from Gembloux to the centre of Wellington's position behind La Haye Sainte is 20 miles" (Kennedy, *op. cit.,* p. 132). Subtracting the three miles, which would bring Grouchy into effective operation with Napoleon's right wing, would leave seventeen miles.
[102] Over similar roads, on June 18, the leading brigade of the Prussian Army "was eight hours in marching between eight or nine miles" (Kennedy, *op. cit.,* p. 134). If Grouchy's army had left Gembloux at 3 A.M. and encountered similar difficulties, it would certainly have been midafternoon before it floundered to Napoleon's position.

that by singularly culpable negligence, the cavalry General, Exelmans, who on June 17 had been observing the twenty thousand Prussians at Gembloux, had allowed them to retire without pursuing them closely or observing exactly the route of their retreat. By nightfall Exelmans did not know exactly where this corps was or whither it had gone.[103] By nightfall Grouchy was completely out of touch with the Prussians, and for information regarding them was compelled to rely on the reports of the natives and of scattered cavalry patrols.[104]

Weaving this information together the best he could, Grouchy at Gembloux drew up his report to Napoleon at ten o'clock in the evening. The report read:

I have the honor to report that I am occupying Gembloux, and that my cavalry is at Sauvenières. The enemy, about 30,000 strong, continues his movement of retreat; we have seized from him here a park of 400 cattle, stores, and baggage.

It seems according to all reports that upon arriving at Sauvenières, the Prussians divided into two columns: one must have taken the road to Wavre passing by Sart-à-Walhain; the other column seems to have gone towards Perwès.

It may perhaps be inferred that one portion will join Wellington, and that the center which is the army of Blücher is retiring on Liége; another column with artillery having retreated by Namur, General Exelmans has the order to push this evening six squadrons on Sart-à-Walhain, and three squadrons on Perwès. After their report, if the mass of Prussians is retreating on Wavre, I shall follow them in that direction, in order that they may not gain Brussels and to separate them from Wellington.

If, on the contrary, my information proves that the principal Prussian force has marched on Perwès, I shall pursue the enemy by that town.

Generals Thielman and Borstell were a part of the army

[103] Houssaye, op. cit., p. 245.   [104] Ibid., p. 246.

which Your Majesty beat yesterday; they were still here this morning at ten o'clock, and declared that twenty thousand of their men had been disabled. They asked on leaving the distances of Wavre, Perwès, and Hannut. . . .[105]

Being, as the report indicates, still in doubt as to the direction of the Prussian retreat, Grouchy decided "to move at first on Sart-à-Walhain, from which point he could march either on Wavre or on Perwez, according to the information received there."[106] Not realizing the need of dispatch if the Prussians had retreated on Wavre, "he determined to give his troops a good night's rest. . . . Hence, at or soon after 10 P.M. he issued his orders to his corps-commanders to march in the morning to Sart-à-Walhain. Vandamme, whose corps had bivouacked somewhat in advance of Gembloux, was to start at 6 A.M. It was to be preceded in the march by Exelmans' cavalry, the bulk of which was at Sauvenières. Gérard, whose troops were in and about Gembloux, was to follow with his corps at 8 A.M."[107]

During the early morning hours of June 18, however, Grouchy finally received information which "removed his doubts as to the direction of the Prussian retreat."[108] By daybreak, that is, about 3:30 A.M., he wrote to one of his subordinates: ". . . the movement of retreat of Blücher's army appears to me very clearly to be upon Brussels"[109] (by way of Wavre). At 6 A.M. he wrote in his second report to Napoleon:

Sire, all my reports and information confirm that the enemy is retreating on Brussels in order to concentrate there or to offer battle after having united with Wellington. . . . The 1st and

---

[105] Grouchy to Napoleon, Gembloux, 10 P.M., June 17, 1815 (Etienne Maurice Gérard, *Dernières observations sur les opérations de l'aile droite de l'armée française à la bataille de Waterloo, en réponse à M. le marquis de Grouchy*, Paris, 1830, pp. 15-16).

[106] Ropes, *op. cit.*, p. 250.   [107] *Ibid.*, pp. 250-251.
[108] *Ibid.*, p. 251.   [109] *Ibid.*

2nd corps of the army of Blücher seem to be going, the first towards Corbais, the second toward Chaumont. . . . I am leaving immediately for Sart-à-Walhain, from whence I shall proceed to Corbais and Wavre.[110]

It is now generally agreed that as soon as he learned that the Prussians had retreated on Wavre and that Napoleon was threatened by a union of the Anglo-Prussian armies, Grouchy should have marched directly on Napoleon's position. But to Grouchy in the morning of June 18 this was by no means clear. He had received no word from Napoleon since noon, June 17 (he did not even know Napoleon's position), and he was to receive none until 4 P.M., June 18. All Grouchy saw was that now he must march in the direction of Wavre, rather than on Perwès, and he gave orders to that effect. Even in the execution of his new design, he made mistakes. He did not alter the direction given the evening before, although Sart-à-Walhain was to the right of the direct route toward Wavre. He did not put forward the hour of departure: even the hours he had set were not adhered to, for Exelmans "did not start till 7:30 A.M., Vandamme . . . did not move until 8 A.M., and it was not until 9 A.M. that Gérard's corps got through the town of Gembloux."[111] Finally, in proceeding in the direction of Wavre, two routes were open to Grouchy. At Gembloux he was separated from Napoleon by a small stream known as the River Dyle, which there flowed north. Wavre, around which the Prussians were concentrating, was on the west or left bank of the Dyle.[112] If Grouchy marched on Wavre by one route, he would cross the Dyle at the villages of Ottignies and Moustier above (south of) Wavre

---

[110] Grouchy to Napoleon, Gembloux, June 18, 1815 (Grouchy, *op. cit.*, IV, 65-66). Grouchy gives 3 A.M. as the hour of the dispatch; it is probable, however, that it was not composed and sent off until 6 A.M. (see Houssaye, *op. cit.*, p. 286, n. 2). [111] Ropes, *op. cit.*, p. 252. [112] There was a suburb on the right bank.

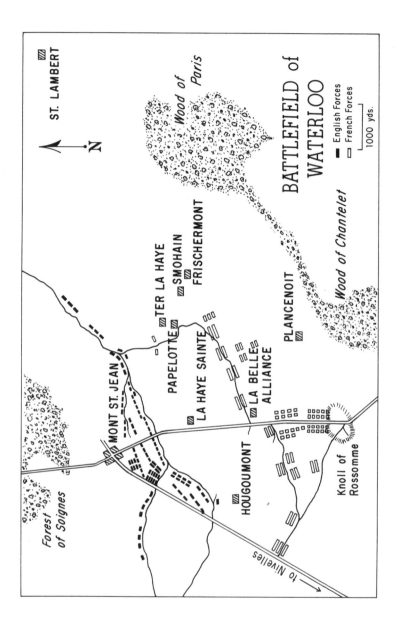

ST. LAMBERT

N

Wood of Paris

Forest of Soignes

MONT ST. JEAN

TER LA HAYE

PAPELOTTE

SMOHAIN

FRISCHERMONT

LA HAYE SAINTE

LA BELLE ALLIANCE

PLANCENOIT

HOUGOUMONT

Wood of Chantelet

Knoll of Rossomme

to Nivelles

BATTLEFIELD of WATERLOO

■ English Forces
☐ French Forces

1000 yds.

and then proceed down the left bank of the river to Wavre. By the other route, he would march directly on Wavre and attempt a crossing there. If he took the first route, he would be closer to Napoleon and, if successful, would be between the Prussians and Napoleon. Only by taking this route would it be possible for him to separate the Prussians from Wellington. If he took the second, he would pursue the Prussians head on with no strategical advantage. In the morning of June 18 Grouchy, a capable cavalry leader but without brilliance, audacity, and apparently without strategical sense,[113] in literal-minded obedience to Napoleon's instructions "to pursue the Prussians and not to let them out of sight," followed the Prussians down their own tracks and took the second route, which crossed the Dyle at Wavre.

Napoleon, if we may credit his own account, in the early morning of June 18 arose at 1 A.M. and, walking along the French outposts, reconnoitered the English position. His intention was "to follow the English army and to attempt to attack it, despite darkness and rain, as soon as it was on march."[114] But the bivouac fires along the English ridge and the silence convinced him that the English were not in retreat.[115] Scouts and spies returning about three-thirty confirmed that the Anglo-Dutch Army was not in motion.[116] Two Belgian deserters brought in shortly afterwards reported that it would offer battle.[117]

Returning to headquarters, the farmhouse of Caillou, Napoleon received and probably read Grouchy's first report

[113] It must be remembered that the situation was by no means so clear to Grouchy as it is to us. He did not know the exact position either of Napoleon, the English, or the Prussians. Nevertheless, inasmuch as he had inferred that the Prussians were retreating on Wavre to join Wellington, a more brilliant man would probably have seen that some maneuver that would bring him closer to Napoleon and yet not lose trace of the Prussians was advisable—the first route to Wavre would answer both requirements.

[114] Napoleon, "Bataille de Mont-Saint-Jean," *Correspondance*, XXXI, 181.
[115] *Ibid.*   [116] *Ibid.*   [117] *Ibid.*

(of 10 P.M., June 17).[118] The phrases of Grouchy's letter, that a column of thirty thousand Prussians had retreated to Sauvenières; that there it had divided—one part proceeding to the left toward Wavre, the other to the right toward Perwès; that it may perhaps be inferred that a portion will join Wellington; that the center, which was Blücher's army, was retreating northeasterly on Liège; that the right had retired through Namur; that at Ligny twenty thousand Prussians had been disabled; that at Gembloux French forces had seized a park of four hundred cattle, stores, and baggage—these phrases probably confirmed Napoleon in his idea that the Prussians had been shattered at Ligny and were retiring in disorganized defeat. The plan of Grouchy—to follow the Prussians to Wavre if the mass were retreating there, or to Perwès if they were retiring in that direction—seemed satisfactory, and Napoleon delayed answering Grouchy until later. Also, on his return to headquarters he issued an order which (perhaps because it was still raining) fixed a later time, nine o'clock, as the hour at which the various French Army corps must be ready for battle.[119]

The day of June 18, which was a Sunday, dawned dismal and dreary.[120] The cold rain (as if in October) continued through the night and into the early morning. Only by seven o'clock did it slacken to a drizzling shower.[121] Shortly after daybreak the two armies began to prepare for battle. Along the English ridge, sixty-seven thousand motley English, Dutch, Belgians, and Germans, along the Brussels highroad, strung out from Belle-Alliance back be-

[118] Houssaye, *op. cit.,* p. 277.

[119] Napoleon to Marshal Ney, June 18 (Pontécoulant, *op. cit.,* p. 339); Houssaye, *op. cit.,* p. 279.

[120] Cotton, *op. cit.,* p. 40; letter of Lieutenant Pratt, March 23, 1835 (*W. L.,* p. 326).

[121] Cotton, *op. cit.,* p. 40; "Bericht der hannoverschen 4. Infanterie-Brigade, December 10, 1824," "Bericht des hannoverschen Feldbataillons Bremen, December 9, 1824" (*P.-H.,* pp. 83, 128).

yond Genappe; seventy-four thousand Frenchmen, stiff and cold, their wet and dirty clothing clinging to them, cleaned their arms, shot out their damp charges, ravaged neighboring farms in search of food, fetched wood and water, and on the French side rallied and began to march into position.[122] The villages and the farms were empty, the peasants having taken refuge in the near-by forests.[123]

Napoleon, short, fat, and optimistic, breakfasted at eight o'clock in the farmhouse of Caillou. "After the meal . . . the maps of Ferrari and Capitain were unfolded on the table." Around Napoleon were the chief of staff Soult, Drouot, and other general officers. "The emperor said: 'The enemy army is superior to ours by more than a fourth. We have nevertheless not less than ninety chances for us, and not ten against us.' Ney, who entered, heard these words. He came from the advance-posts, and he had taken some movements of the English as preparations for retreat; he cried: 'Without a doubt, Sire, if Wellington were simple enough to wait for you. But I inform you that his retreat is decided and that, if you do not hasten to attack him, the enemy will escape you.' 'You have been ill-advised,' replied the emperor. 'There is no longer time. Wellington would expose himself to a certain loss. He has thrown the dice, and they are for us.'

"Soult was anxious. No more than the Emperor did he apprehend the arrival of the Prussians on the battle-field." But he wanted more troops on the field for the attack on

---

[122] Mercer, *op. cit.*, p. 159-160; Cotton, *op. cit.*, pp. 40-41; Mauduit, *op. cit.*, II, 236-237; letter of Lieutenant Pratt, March 23, 1836 (*W. L.*, p. 326); "Bericht der hannoverschen 4. Infanterie-Brigade, December 10, 1824," "Bericht der hannoverschen 4. Infanterie-Brigade, December 10, 1824," "Bericht des hannoverschen Feldbataillons Bremen, December 9, 1824" (*P.-H.*, pp. 76, 83, 128); report of Colonel Van Zuylen von Neyevelt, Oct. 25, 1815 (Wommerson and De Bas, *op. cit.*, III, 331).

[123] Simpson, *op. cit.*, pp. 48, 87; letter of Lieutenant Ingilby, April 25, 1838 (*W. L.*, p. 197).

the English. "As chief of staff of Lefebvre, Soult had carried by assault, on July 9, 1794, this same plateau of Mont-Saint-Jean and had thrown the Imperial Austrian infantry back from the Forest of Soignes into Brussels." But Soult had led the French against Wellington in Spain. "He knew the English infantry to be quite otherwise unyielding than the Austrian infantry. Hence, on the preceding evening he had already advised the emperor to recall a part of the troops placed under the orders of Grouchy. This morning he reiterated his advice. Napoleon, impatient, answered him brutally. 'Because you have been beaten by Wellington, you consider him as a great general. And I, I tell you that Wellington is a bad general, that the English are bad troops, and that it will be the matter of a luncheon.' 'I hope so,' said Soult."[124]

At one point in the conversation Jerome, brother of Napoleon, entered and communicated to him "a conversation heard the day before in the inn of the *Roi-d'Espagne* at Genappe. The waiter who had served him supper, after having served Wellington at luncheon, recounted that an aide-de-camp of the Duke had spoken of a planned reunion of the English and Prussian armies at the entrance to the Forest of Soignes. This Belgian, who seemed well-informed, had even added that the Prussians would arrive by way of Wavre. The Emperor dismissed that as idle talk. 'After a battle like that of Ligny,' he said, 'the junction of the English and the Prussians is impossible two days hence; besides the Prussians have Grouchy on their heels.' "[125]

By nine o'clock the weather had somewhat cleared. The drizzling shower had ceased, the warming sun came out briefly, and a moderate, drying wind blew over the countryside.[126] Some artillery officers "who had surveyed the

---

[124] Houssaye, *op. cit.*, pp. 309-311.   [125] *Ibid.*, pp. 314-315.
[126] Cotton, *op. cit.*, p. 40; report of Colonel Van Zuylen von Neyevelt, Oct.

ground" reported that soon it would be firm enough for the guns to be maneuvered.[127] Napoleon left the farmhouse of Caillou and rode along a column of French infantry marching up the Brussels road into position. Advancing somewhat beyond Belle-Alliance, the roadside village at the crest of the French ridge, he descended nearly to the line of French sharpshooters and peered at the English line about nine hundred yards distant along the opposite ridge and the English center forepost of La Haye Sainte. He "ordered General Haxo of the engineers to approach closer in order to make sure if any redoubts or entrenchments had been raised. The general returned, promptly reported that there was no sign of any fortification."[128]

While Napoleon was reconnoitering, three divisions of the First Corps (d'Erlon) were already in position along the French ridge to the right of the Brussels road, but the head of the column of the Second Corps (Reille) was just coming into view at Belle-Alliance; behind it were the troops of the Sixth Corps (Lobau), the Imperial Guard, the cuirassiers of Kellermann, the division Durutte of d'Erlon's corps, still coming up. Napoleon reflected a quarter of an hour (doubtless on the English position, the troops at his disposal, his plan of attack) and dictated orders assigning places to the advancing infantry and cavalry divisions.[129] Then, while this order was being executed, he retired three fourths of a mile behind Belle-Alliance to a knoll on the farm of Rossomme, which commanded a broad view over the country.[130] "From the farm was brought a chair and

25, 1815 (Wommerson and De Bas, *op. cit.*, III, 333); Hay, *op. cit.*, p. 176; "Bericht der hannoverschen 1. Infanterie-Brigade," "Bericht des hannoverschen Feldbataillons Bremen über seinen Anteil an der Schlacht bei Belle-Alliance, December 4, 1842" (*P.-H.*, pp. 76, 133).

[127] Napoleon, "Bataille de Mont-Saint-Jean," *Correspondance*, XXXI, 183.
[128] *Ibid.*   [129] *Ibid.*, pp. 183-184.
[130] La Coste's account in Stephen Weston, *Two Sketches of France, Belgium, and Spa, in Two Tours, during the Summers of 1771 and 1816* (London, 1817), p. 135.

a small table, on which were unfolded his maps."[131]   On the knoll the Emperor was seen "to walk up and down, his hands behind his back, to stop, to place his elbows on the table, then to resume his walk."[132]   Here he finally found time to dictate a reply to Grouchy's report of the night before which had been received at imperial headquarters at 2 A.M., had probably been read by Napoleon at 4 A.M., and was answered at 10 A.M.

The answer reveals by inference the sanguine misconceptions under which Napoleon was operating that morning.   The dispatch as drafted by the Chief of Staff Soult read:

Marshal Grouchy:

The Emperor has received your last report, dated from Gembloux.   You speak to his Majesty of only two Prussian columns, which have passed at Sauvenières and Sart-à-Walhain. Nevertheless, reports say that a third column, which was a pretty strong one, has passed by Gery and Gentinnes, directed on Wavre.

The Emperor instructs me to tell you that at this moment his Majesty is going to attack the English army, which has taken position at Waterloo, near the Forest of Soignes; therefore his Majesty desires that you will direct your movements on Wavre, in order to approach us, to put yourself in the sphere of our operations, and to establish communications with us, pushing before you those portions of the Prussian army which have taken this direction and which may have stopped at Wavre, where you ought to arrive as soon as possible.

You will follow the enemy's columns which are on your right by some light troops, in order to observe their movements and pick up stragglers.   Instruct me immediately as to your dispositions and your march, as also as to the news which you have of the enemy; and do not neglect to keep up your com-

[131] Houssaye, *op. cit.*, p. 314.   [132] *Ibid*.

munications with us. The Emperor desires to have news from you very often.[133]

Thus Napoleon had no conception of the Prussians dropping down on his right flank. But in view of the battle impending with the English and perhaps of later maneuvers he asked Grouchy to come closer, to come within the sphere of his (Napoleon's) operations by marching for Wavre, instead of trekking off to the right, and to re-establish communications. On his part, Napoleon dispatched our friend Marbot, now Colonel Marbot, with a cavalry regiment and an infantry battalion to set out two series of cavalry posts—one from the field of battle northeast to Saint-Lambert, and another from the battlefield east to the River Dyle at the bridges of Moustier and Ottignies—to establish contact with Grouchy's forces whether they crossed by Wavre or Moustier.[134] But from the delay in framing this reply to Grouchy, from the general, almost casual character of the orders the reply contained, apparently Napoleon believed he had plenty of time.

In the meanwhile the other French troops continued to march into position. As we have seen, the French and English positions were about three quarters of a mile apart with a shallow valley between and the Charleroi-Brussels road running through the center of both. From the French side the land sloped gently downward to the valley and

[133] Napoleon to Grouchy, in front of the farm of Caillou, 10 A.M., June 18, 1815 (Grouchy, *op. cit.*, IV, 175-176).

[134] The assertion that Colonel Marbot was dispatched with a cavalry regiment and an infantry battalion to the flank of the army to establish contact with Grouchy rests on a letter of Marbot written from Laon, June 26, 1815, and published in General Marbot, *Mémoires du général Baron de Marbot* (Paris, 1891), III, 403. The other details of Marbot's activities on that day are known to us, however, through a letter Marbot wrote to Grouchy in 1830. This latter letter, however, seems worthy of credence since each step of Marbot's activity on that day as he relates it dovetails with the other known facts of the activities of Napoleon and of the Prussians. See Marbot to Grouchy, 1830 (*ibid.*, p. 405).

then rose in gentle slope to the English position. Both slopes were somewhat rolling. Back of the English summit the land again sloped downward toward the Forest of Soignes. Wellington, as we have indicated, had occupied with troops the foreposts of the position: the farmhouse of La Haye Sainte in the center about one third of the way down the English slope, of Hougoumont in the valley opposite the right-hand end of the English line, and of Ter la Haye and Papelotte also in the valley opposite the left-hand end of the English position. During the night the farmhouse of Hougoumont and the outbuildings had been placed in a stage of defense. "Workmen and tools were sent to it; an additional supply of ammunition was placed in it; and the work of loopholing the walls had been carried on with energy."[135] But with the farmhouse of La Haye Sainte little had been done. The garrison was insufficient, the workmen and tools had been withdrawn; the ordinary precautions of throwing out the hay (in case of fire), of barricading the gates and doors, or piercing the walls with loopholes had not been taken.[136] Along the summit of the two-mile English ridge Wellington had placed most of his field guns, from whence they could sweep the forward slope and the valley below,[137] and had arranged some of his infantry, whose line of somber red uniforms was visible to the French three fourths of a mile away. But at this moment the

---

[135] Kennedy, *op. cit.,* p. 72. Certain phrases have been omitted, and the tense of the last clause has been altered to fit the quotation into this paragraph. The complete passage reads: ". . . the workmen and tools from La Haye Sainte were sent to it; an additional supply of ammunition was placed in it; and the works of loopholing and preparing platforms were carried on with energy." See also letter of Colonel Woodford, Jan. 14, 1838 (*W. L.,* p. 265); dispatch of General Alava to Don Cevallos, June 20, 1815 (*Near Observer,* p. 191); Woodberry, *op. cit.,* p. 311.

[136] Kennedy, *op. cit.,* pp. 71, 176; letter of Lieutenant Graeme, Dec. 6, 1842 (*W. L.,* p. 407); "Bericht über den Anteil der hannoverschen Truppen und der Deutschen Legion an der Schlacht bei Belle-Alliance" (*P.-H.,* p. 52).

[137] Cotton, *op. cit.,* p. 27; letter of Lieutenant Pratt, March 23, 1835 (*W. L.,* p. 327).

greater proportion of the English-Allied infantry and cavalry was behind the crest, all along the backward slope, concealed from the French.[138] Although Napoleon was probably aware he had the full Anglo-Dutch force before him, he could not be sure of the disposition of its strength. As a matter of fact, the English position was strongly maintained on its right, rather vulnerable in the center, and lightly held on its left. With the occupation of the farmhouses, the English line formed a re-entering curve; that is, its ends enclosed the French attack. But in view of the length of the line—over two miles—that circumstance, while an advantage, was not necessarily decisive.

Napoleon's arrangement of his army reveals his intent. The infantry of the First Corps (d'Erlon) and of the Second Corps (Reille), forming the first line, occupied the crest of the French ridge at the height of Belle-Alliance: the three divisions of Reille extended from the Nivelles road on the left to the Brussels road on the right, the four divisions of d'Erlon from the Brussels road on the left to opposite Papelotte on the right. Behind the first line in the center was the infantry of the Sixth Corps (Lobau) massed to the left of the Brussels highway and the cavalry of Domon and Subervie situated to the right of the road. Still in the second line, the cuirassiers of Kellermann were to the left of Lobau, those of Milhaud to the right of Subervie. In the third line in the center in reserve was the infantry of the Imperial Guard, massed to the left and right of the Brussels highway. On the wings of the Guard, back of the cavalry of Kellermann, was that of Guyot; back of the cavalry of Milhaud, that of Lefebvre-Desnoëttes.[139] Seventy-

[138] Kennedy states that all the cavalry was concealed. It is apparent from a study of the arrangement of the English reserves that much of the infantry was likewise hidden (Kennedy, *op. cit.*, p. 66). Also letter of Lieutenant Pratt, March 23, 1835 (*W. L.*, p. 327).

[139] Mauduit, *op. cit.*, II, 242-244.

four thousand men in all, 266 guns,[140] with the strength concentrated in the center. It was Napoleon's plan that while the Second Corps would keep the English occupied at the left, the four divisions of d'Erlon, preceded by a violent artillery bombardment, supported and followed if necessary by the infantry of the Sixth Corps (Lobau), by the cavalry of Domon, Subervie, Kellermann, and Milhaud, and by the Guard, would advance and smash through the English left center, seize at the summit the crossroads of the Brussels-Wavre highways and half-a-mile back of it the village of Mont St. Jean, cut off the English retreat through the Forest of Soignes, split the English Army in two, throw it into utter disorder, confusion, defeat.[141] It would be the affair of a luncheon.

Either because the saturated ground was still too muddy and slippery for artillery to maneuver easily (throughout the day the weather was dull and wet, shadow and rain at intervals with only occasional sunshine)[142] or because all the French Army was not entirely in place, Napoleon postponed the main attack until one o'clock.[143] In the meantime, about eleven o'clock, with his staff he rode along the partly assembled array and received the plaudits of his army. "His troops hailed him with repeated shouts of *Vive l'Empereur!* the infantry raising their caps upon their bayonets, and the cavalry their casques or helmets upon their swords and lances."[144] He returned to the knoll of Rossomme and dictated a brief, preliminary general order for Ney, who was to be in charge of the major central thrust:

[140] Houssaye, *op. cit.*, p. 322.

[141] Gourgau, *Sainte-Hélène: Journal inédit* (French ed.), I, 544.

[142] Remarks of Wellington, Nov. 12, 1831, and Nov. 4, 1840 (Stanhope, *op. cit.*, pp. 19, 245); letter of Lieutenant Ingilby, Nov. 20, 1834 (*W. L.*, p. 199); report of Colonel Van Zuylen von Neyevelt, Oct. 25, 1815 (Wommerson and De Bas, III, 333); *Témoin oculaire*, bound with *Near Observer*, p. 114; "Bericht des Nassauischen 1. Regiments" (*P.-H.*, p. 197).

[143] See also letter of Sir Hussey Vivian, June 3, 1839 (*W. L.*, p. 158).

[144] Houssaye, *op. cit.*, p. 323.

Once all the army is ranged in battle-order, about one o'clock, at the moment when the Emperor will give the order to Marshal Ney, the attack will begin by seizing the village of Mont-Saint-Jean, where the intersection of the Nivelles and Brussels roads is located. For that purpose the batteries of twelve of the 2nd corps and those of the 6th corps will be united to those of the 1st corps. These twenty-four cannon will fire on the troops of Mont-Saint-Jean, and the Comte d'Erlon will begin the attack by advancing his left-hand division and supporting it, according to circumstances, by the other divisions of the 1st corps.

The Second Corps will advance on the left to keep pace with that of Erlon.

The companies of sappers of the First Corps will be ready to barricade themselves immediately at Mont-Saint-Jean.[145]

The order reveals that Napoleon expected that d'Erlon's single corps of itself would be sufficient to sweep the English center off the plateau, to occupy Mont-Saint-Jean, and to barricade itself therein; presumably the infantry of Lobau, the cavalry, the Guard would follow to complete the English discomfiture.

As a preliminary diversion against Wellington's right, about eleven-fifteen, Napoleon ordered Reille (Second Corps) to occupy the approaches to Hougoumont. He probably meant the woods and the grounds on the French side of the Hougoumont group of structures.[146] Reille commissioned Jerome's division to undertake the attack. The French infantry deployed into a swarm of skirmishers supported by columns and after some trouble cleared the woods of the enemy.[147] But on approaching the buildings they

[145] Ordre à chaque commandant de corps d'armée, 11 A.M., June 18, 1815, No. 22060, in Napoleon, *Correspondance*, XXVIII, 292.

[146] The exact nature of Napoleon's order is in doubt. See Houssaye, *op. cit.*, p. 327 and n.

[147] Kennedy, *op. cit.*, p. 103; Napoleon, "Bulletin de l'armée," Laon [*sic*], June 20 [*sic*], 1815, No. 22061, in *Correspondance*, XXVIII, 296; Mauduit, *op. cit.*, II, 282.

were shot down by the English from behind the hedges, the stone walls, the loopholes in the house.[148] The French commanders, contrary to Napoleon's intentions, moved to take possession of the buildings, fed in more and more infantry. It was a bloody waste. The capture of the Hougoumont forepost was not vital to Napoleon's plan; if seizure of the buildings was necessary, a few heavy guns could have knocked in and demolished the doors and the stone walls which furnished the English protection. Nevertheless, Reille eventually employed not only Jerome's division of infantry but also part of Foy's—six to ten thousand men in all.[149] Through several hours this attack (which had been intended as a diversion) and the stubborn defense of the buildings and grounds simmered, rose and fell in fury, the participants of both sides absorbed in their work, unaware of what was passing on the broader field.[150]

While this conflict over on the left continued, Napoleon built up a concentration of eighty guns in front of d'Erlon's corps, well down the slope of the French position, nearly to the flat valley, far advanced toward the English line.[151] He also received[152] and read Grouchy's second report dated Gembloux, 6 A.M., that morning, in which Grouchy had said: "Sire, all my reports and information confirm that the

[148] Kennedy, *op. cit.*, p. 104; Mauduit, *op. cit.*, II, 283; dispatch of General Alava to Don Cevallos, June 20, 1815 (*Near Observer*, p. 191).

[149] Letter of Colonel Woodford, Jan. 14, 1848 (*W. L.*, p. 262); Kennedy, *op. cit.*, p. 103; Mauduit, *op. cit.*, II, 283.

[150] Kennedy, *op. cit.*, p. 104; Mauduit, *op. cit.*, II, 283; Ellesmere, *op. cit.*, pp. 105-106; letter of Colonel Hepburn, Nov. 22, 1834 (*W. L.*, p. 267).

[151] Kennedy, *op. cit.*, 106-107; letter of Lord Saltoun, Jan. 29, 1838 (*W. L.*, p. 246); report of Prince William of Orange, June 22, 1815 (Wellington, *Supplementary Dispatches*, X, 555-556).

[152] The exact time that Grouchy's second report was received is uncertain. But from the fact that Napoleon's first dispatch to Grouchy does not refer to the news contained in Grouchy's second report, it may be assumed that the latter was received after Napoleon's first dispatch was written—that is, after 10 A.M. On the other hand, Napoleon's reply to Grouchy's second report was timed at 1 P.M. It is obvious, therefore, that Grouchy's second report was received sometime between 10 A.M. and 1 P.M.

enemy [that is, the entire Prussian Army] is retreating on Brussels in order to concentrate there or to offer battle after having united with Wellington. . . . I am leaving . . . for Corbais and Wavre." This information was serious—that the Prussian Army was no longer retreating in scattered columns to the north and northeastward but was concentrating on Brussels, and Napoleon foresaw at last, somewhat tardily, that a Prussian corps might insert itself between him and Grouchy. He dictated, therefore (shortly before one o'clock), a dispatch to Grouchy:

Marshal: You wrote to the Emperor at 2 o'clock this morning, that you would march on Sart-lez-Walhain; your plan then is to proceed to Corbaix or to Wavre. This movement is conformable to his Majesty's arrangements which have been communicated to you. Nevertheless, the Emperor directs me to tell you that you ought always to maneuver in our direction. It is for you to see the place where we are, to govern yourself accordingly, and to connect our communications, so as to be always prepared to fall upon any of the enemy's troops which may endeavor to annoy our right, and to destroy them. At this moment the battle is in progress on the line of Waterloo. The enemy's center is at Mont St. Jean; maneuver, therefore, to join our right.[153]

In the meantime Marbot had extended his two series of cavalry posts to the northeast toward Saint-Lambert and to the east to the villages of Moustier and Ottignies. The leader of the detachment to the last two villages, Captain Eloy, discovered none of Grouchy's troops there, but the natives mistakenly assured him that the French contingent east of the Dyle (that is, Grouchy's command) was crossing the river farther down at Limal, Limelette, and Wavre. This information was carried by relays to Marbot and then to Napoleon.[154] To the latter the news seemed plausible,

[153] Ropes, *op. cit.*, pp. 271-272.
[154] Marbot to Grouchy, 1830 (Marbot, *op. cit.*, III, 405-406). In regard

since if Grouchy in accord with his second report had left Gembloux for Wavre he must by now as late as one o'clock be in that neighborhood.[155] Napoleon, therefore, dispatched a staff-officer to Marbot with instructions to push his patrols beyond Saint-Lambert in the directions of Limal, Limelette, and Wavre.[156]

As these events were occurring—the dictation of the letter to Grouchy, the arrival of Marbot's messenger—the central bombardment and the central attack of the English position was about to begin. Napoleon on the knoll of Rossomme took his telescope for a last general survey before the smoke of battle obscured the valley and the landscape. Far off to the northeast nearly five miles over the rolling countryside he perceived a cloud, a cloud of men emerging from the Forest of Saint-Lambert. He turned to his chief of staff Soult: "Marshal, what do you see on the heights of Saint-Lambert?" "I think I see," answered Soult, "five or six thousand men. It is probably a detachment of Grouchy." Other members of the staff turned their glasses to that point. The air was rather hazy. Some said there were no troops, but trees; others that there were columns in posi-

---

to the time that Captain Eloy reached the Dyle, Marbot wrote: "Il me serait impossible, après un laps de temps de quinze années, de fixer au juste l'heure à laquelle le détachement dirigé vers Moustier parvint sur ce point . . . Mais en remarquant qu'il partit à onze heures du champ de bataille, et n'avait plus de deux lieues à parcourir, on doit présumer qu'il les fut en deux heures, ce qui fixerait son arrivée à Moustier à une heure de l'après-midi" (*ibid.*, pp. 405-406). But the events which he describes—the dispatch of Captain Eloy's detachment, its arrival at Moustier, the transmission of Captain Eloy's note to Marbot and then to Napoleon, Napoleon's counter-order—all by Marbot's account occurred before Marbot's Saint-Lambert detachment captured a Prussian who was taken to Napoleon. Now it is known that this Prussian prisoner was brought before Napoleon shortly after one o'clock. Consequently, the events which Marbot is describing—including the presentation of Captain Eloy's note to Napoleon— must have occurred before one o'clock and probably before Napoleon's perception of the Prussians on the height of Saint-Lambert.

[155] This is surmised from the nature of the information Napoleon received and from the instructions he gave.

[156] Marbot to Grouchy, 1830 (Marbot, *op. cit.*, III, 406).

tion; several that they were troops on the march. In this uncertainty, Napoleon ordered the cavalry of Domon and Subervie (three thousand men) which was in the second line, to wheel to right, betake itself to the heights of Saint-Lambert, to reconnoiter the troops there; if they were those of Marshal Grouchy, whom Napoleon assumed to be near, to join them; if they were those of the enemy, to hold them in check.[157] The cavalry moved off and took up a position to the right of the army.[158]

About a quarter of an hour later one of Marbot's officers brought to Napoleon a Prussian courier whom Marbot's men had captured.[159] The courier bore a letter to Wellington, and he was quizzed orally. Yes, the column on Saint-Lambert was the advance guard of the Prussian General Bülow, who was arriving with thirty thousand men; it was the Prussian Fourth Corps which had not fought at Ligny. He (the courier) had been at Wavre that morning; the other three Prussian corps were camped there. He had not seen the French detachment (that is, Grouchy) in pursuit, and supposed that this detachment was making for the French right at Belle-Alliance.[160] This latter statement would tend to confirm Napoleon's view that Grouchy was close by. So to the dispatch to Grouchy, which had not yet been sent, he dictated a postscript: "A letter, which has just been intercepted, says that General Bülow is about to attack our right flank; we believe that we see this corps on the height of St. Lambert. So lose not an instant in drawing near and joining us, in order to crush Bülow, whom you will catch wide open."[161] Napoleon also dispatched a messenger to

[157] Napoleon, "Bataille de Mont-Saint-Jean," *Correspondance*, XXXI, 188-189.
[158] *Ibid.*, p. 189.
[159] *Ibid.*; Marbot to Grouchy, 1830 (Marbot, *op. cit.*, III, 406).
[160] Napoleon, "Bataille de Mont-Saint-Jean," *Correspondance*, XXXI, 189.
[161] Soult to Grouchy, 1 P.M., June 18, quoted in Houssaye, *op. cit.*, pp. 335-336; Ropes, *op. cit.*, p. 271.

Marbot: since Grouchy was not crossing to the northeast through Wavre and Saint-Lambert, he must be crossing to east by Moustier and Ottignies; look for him there.[162] Finally, with a Prussian advance impending, Napoleon ordered Lobau, commander of the Sixth Corps of ten thousand infantry which was in the second line to the left of the Brussels highway, to face his corps to the right, to cross the highway, and to place himself off to the right of the French Army in an intermediary position where with ten thousand men he could check thirty thousand if that became necessary; to attack energetically the Prussians as soon as he heard the cannon of Grouchy in their rear.[163]

But Napoleon did not take the arrival of the Prussians too seriously.[164] They were still distant. He thought that he had to deal with only an isolated corps.[165] He did not know, and the Prussian courier (whether from ignorance or design) did not inform him, that back of Bülow's corps

[162] Marbot to Grouchy, 1830 (Marbot, *op. cit.*, III, 407). The exact time of the order to Marbot is uncertain. But from Marbot's account it is clear that it was given after the capture of the Prussian hussar at one o'clock or one-fifteen, and from its nature it is apparent that it was probably issued before Napoleon learned for certain that Grouchy was still miles away. Napoleon learned this about two-thirty o'clock upon the arrival of Grouchy's third messenger, Major La Fresnaye. It is probable, therefore, that the order to Marbot was given sometime between one-thirty and two-thirty o'clock. It is possible, however, that it was given after the order to Lobau, although that cannot be determined.

[163] Napoleon, "Bataille de Mont-Saint-Jean," *Correspondance*, XXXI, 190.

[164] Later, in August, 1815, when in the hands of the English, Napoleon reportedly said " 'that he knew of the advance of the Prussians, but that he did not regard it of much consequence' " (letter of an interviewer on His Majesty's ship *Northumberland*, Aug. 22, 1815, in *Near Observer*, p. 151).

[165] The official communique or bulletin concerning the battle was dictated by Napoleon in Paris on June 21. This bulletin, though inaccurate, sometimes seems to reflect the ideas which Napoleon had at the battle itself: "On estimait les forces de l'armée anglaise à 80,000 hommes; on supposait que le corps prussien, qui pouvait être en mesure vers le soir, pouvait etre de 15,000 hommes" (Napoleon, "Bulletin de l'armée," Laon [*sic*], June 20 [*sic*], 1815, No. 22061, in *Correspondance*, XXVIII, 295). The order to Lobau that he should prepare to check thirty thousand men would also seem to indicate that Napoleon thought he had to deal with only a single Prussian corps.

was Pirch's with twenty thousand men, and back of Pirch's but approaching on another road was Ziethen's corps of another twenty thousand.[166] Besides, in Napoleon's view, Grouchy was probably near.[167] In fact, at this moment the mind of Napoleon presents an interesting psychological study. Through June 17 and the morning of June 18 his fundamental illusion had been that he had decisively defeated the Prussians at Ligny, that they were retiring in disorganized defeat. Even the information that one Prussian column was retreating by way of Wavre did not disturb this conception. Doubtless in this disorganization there were various retreating columns. But the second report of Grouchy that the entire Prussian Army was retreating by Wavre—and not dispersed to east and west in various columns—forced him to foresee the possible arrival of a Prussian corps between him and Grouchy, and he ordered Grouchy to him. When the Prussian corps appeared it confirmed his foresight, but did not upset his fundamental illusion of the condition of the Prussian Army—the corps was that which had not fought at Ligny; the others, doubtless harshly handled at that battle, were still at Wavre and were still not his concern. Marbot's first report, furthermore, that the inhabitants of Moustier and Ottignies assured that Grouchy's contingent was crossing the Dyle at Limal, Limelette, and Wavre and Grouchy's second report of 6 A.M. that he intended to leave for Wavre also led Napoleon not unreasonably to assume that Grouchy was

[166] Mauduit, *op. cit.*, II, 376; Kennedy, *op. cit.*, p. 134; Report of General Von Ziethen (Wommerson and De Bas, *op. cit.*, II, 501); Rapport des General Leutnant von Bülow, Paris, July 10, 1815 (*ibid.*, pp. 520-524).

[167] The remark of Soult—that the troops on the height of Saint-Lambert were probably a detachment of Grouchy, Napoleon's instructions to Domon and Subervie—to join the Saint-Lambert detachment if they were Grouchy's troops, the instructions to Lobau—to attack the Prussians as soon as he heard Grouchy's cannon in their rear, the instructions to Marbot—Grouchy must be crossing by Moustier and Ottignies, look for him there would all seem to indicate that Napoleon thought Grouchy was near.

near, for if Grouchy had left Gembloux early as every general should and marched for Wavre, he would be by now somewhere not very far to the right in the valley of the Dyle. The arrival of the Prussians at Saint-Lambert and the statement of the Prussian prisoner that he had not seen Grouchy's troops but assumed they were marching for Belle-Alliance proved in Napoleon's mind that the natives of Moustier and Ottignies were mistaken—Grouchy was not crossing by Limal, Limelette, and Wavre, but did not destroy his new illusion of the proximity of Grouchy—if Grouchy was not crossing by Wavre, he must be crossing by Moustier and Ottignies, and he instructed Marbot to look for him there. But always a fancy-filling mind, actively reworking new material to form sanguine illusions, instead of a harsh, realistic appraisal of the situation as it might be at its worst. The tendency, barely observable at Aspern-Essling, toward a blanking out of the harsher phases of reality and of possibility had become exaggerated. Then, in addition to these two ideas—concerning the single Prussian corps and the nearness of Grouchy, there was added a third: that the English line was weak and could be easily overwhelmed.[168]

In the meanwhile, Grouchy off to the right was committing his final error. Arriving at Sart-à-Walhain, he dispatched about eleven o'clock by a Major La Fresnaye his third report to Napoleon: that the Prussian columns were marching for Brussels, that they intended to join the English Army, that he (Grouchy) would mass his own forces at Wavre; and he requested further orders that he might maneuver "tomorrow."[169] While Grouchy then remained

[168] Incidentally, the Prussians had encountered such difficulty in traversing the muddy defile of Saint-Lambert that a few thousand Frenchmen placed across their path would have barred them from the battle; but Napoleon, who had thought of the Prussians as retiring off to the right in disorganized defeat, had not possessed the foresight to take that precaution.

[169] Marshal Grouchy to Napoleon, Sart-à-Walhain, 11 A.M., June 18, 1815 (Grouchy, *Mémoires*, IV, 71-72).

at Sart-à-Walhain for lunch, he heard the distant roar of the fusillade and cannonade of the opening conflict around Hougoumont. By noon he was convinced that a great battle was in progress to the left. His immediate subordinate, General Gérard, urged, begged, insisted that Grouchy march toward the firing. But Grouchy, in literal-minded execution of Napoleon's instructions to pursue the Prussians and fearful perhaps of disobeying, refused[170] and followed the Prussians down their tracks to Wavre, where he met their rear guard.[171] He did not receive Napoleon's dispatch of 10 A.M. enjoining him to enter Napoleon's sphere of operations until 4 P.M.; or the second dispatch ordering him to march on Belle-Alliance until 7 P.M.[172] Through the afternoon he was to the east of the River Dyle.

III

FROM THE TIME the Prussians appeared within the field of observation Napoleon was fighting two battles, an offensive one against Wellington, a defensive one against Blücher.[173] He stationed himself in the center on the Brussels road about four hundred and fifty yards back of Belle-Alliance on a height[174] from which he could watch the general development of the struggle both against the English and the Prussians, although unable to supervise all the details.[175] Since

---

[170] On Grouchy's experiences around noon and the Grouchy-Gérard interview see Grouchy to Napoleon, June 19-20, 1815 (*ibid.*, pp. 318-320); Marshal Grouchy, *Fragments historiques relatifs à la campagne de 1815* (Paris, 1829), pp. 12, 26; Marshal Grouchy, *Observations sur la relation de la campagne de 1815* (Philadelphia, 1818), p. 15; Houssaye, *op. cit.*, pp. 293-297.

[171] Grouchy to Napoleon, June 19-20, 1815 (Grouchy, *Mémoires*, IV, 319, 321-322).

[172] Grouchy to Napoleon, June 19-20, 1815 (*ibid.*, p. 317); Grouchy to Napoleon, June 20, 1815 (*ibid.*, p. 331).

[173] Blücher was with Bülow.

[174] Houssaye, *op. cit.*, p. 314 and n. 3.

[175] At Saint Helena Napoleon said to General Gourgaud: "Je n'ai pas pu bien voir la bataille; je veux faire, comme à Montmirail, une attaque perpendiculaire et la conduire moi-même, mais l'arrivée de Bulow m'a forcé de rester dans une position centrale; Ney n'a pas pu comprendre cette attaque" (Gourgaud,

he was still a quarter of a mile back of Belle-Alliance (which marked the position of the French first line), more than half-a-mile from the valley, and a full mile from the English crest, he of necessity left Ney in immediate charge of the operations against the English. But in regard to Wellington, Napoleon, governed by his previous intentions and his illusions, retained his original plan of a perpendicular attack on the English center, though he no longer had at his disposal all the troops he had probably intended to employ to complete the attack.

About one-thirty he ordered Ney to begin. On the right of the Brussels road, French skirmishers had already been pushed forward into the valley.[176] The advanced battery of eighty guns, some of large caliber, bombarded the English position east of the Brussels road, causing destruction on that portion of the English plateau.[177] To the bombardment, the English artillery replied.[178]

While the cannonade was in progress, Napoleon reorganized his line at one point.[179] He became aware of the

---

Sainte-Hélène: Journal inédit, French ed., I, 544; I have changed the passage from the third person in which it is written to the first person).

[176] Letter of Private Cruickshank, Sept., 1839 (*W. L.*, p. 361).

[177] Letter of Lieutenant Pratt, March 23, 1835 (*ibid.*, pp. 327-328; Pontécoulant, *op. cit.*, p. 266).

[178] Houssaye, *op. cit.*, p. 338.

[179] While the general outline of the Battle of Waterloo is clear and beyond dispute, the details of the sequence and timing of events and of responsibility for certain orders have been a subject of controversy among historians. In part this disagreement has arisen from national bias and from the varying attitudes of admiration or antipathy with which writers have regarded Napoleon. In part the controversy arose from the absence of good contemporary reports: in the confusion of rout and change of government no one on the French side insisted on and obtained reports from the French generals, the contemporary English reports were vague and general, only the reports of the German troops (both Prussian and in the English-Allied Army) presented a detailed picture of what actually occurred in their areas of activity. In the controversial details I have referred not only to the sources but also to the works of Kennedy, Ropes, and Houssaye. All three authors make mistakes, but all three give plausible, intelligent accounts, stimulating by their disagreement.

The problem which now faces us is the sequence of events from one-thirty in

severe conflict raging around Hougoumont nearly a mile to his left,[180] which had become prolonged beyond his intention. Where his subordinates had vainly used infantry to beat against the English forepost, Napoleon from a

the afternoon to three o'clock. It is generally agreed that the cannonade preceding d'Erlon's grand attack opened at one-thirty o'clock, that the infantry moved off at two o'clock, that it reached the crest of the English position about two-thirty, that it was repulsed and then was back in the valley by three o'clock. The problems are: where do Napoleon's order to use howitzers to set fire to the Hougoumont buildings and the arrival of Grouchy's messenger, Major La Fresnaye, fit in? To solve the second problem, which is the easier, first: Grouchy's third report from Sart-à-Walhain was dated June 18, 11 A.M. Major La Fresnaye, the courier who bore the message, wrote Grouchy on December 17, 1829, that after receiving Grouchy's dispatch "Je partis sur-le-champ, et au moment de mon départ, une cannonade, qui n'avait pas l'air d'un engagement général, se fit entendre; je me dirigeai au bruit du canon, et après avoir marché *deur grandes heures et demie au trot et au galop*, je trouvai Napoléon sur le champ de bataille de Waterloo" (Grouchy, *Fragments historiques relatifs à la campagne de 1815*, p. 41). The cannonade which he heard was probably the opening fire by Hougoumont, which began at eleven-thirty. Since he reached Napoleon after two hours and a half, he arrived sometime between two o'clock and two-thirty, just as the cannonade preceding d'Erlon's grand attack had ceased and the infantry advance was under way. In other words, in all probability the news of Grouchy's position reached Napoleon while d'Erlon's attack was still moving off, before its fate had been decided. He had the news in mind when the repulse occurred. Hence, for convenience, the arrival of Grouchy's messenger can be placed just before the attack started.

In regard to the French bombardment of Hougoumont, the French apparently opened fire about two-thirty o'clock and set fire to the buildings. English guns were then detached and they silenced the French battery by about three o'clock or some time thereafter (letter of Lieutenant Sharpin, Dec. 6, 1834, in *W. L.*, p. 228; "Bericht über den Anteil der hannoverschene Truppen und der Deutschen Legion" and "Bericht des hannoverschen Feldbataillons Bremen, December 4, 1842," in *P.-H.*, pp. 54, 134). Since it naturally took some time to transmit Napoleon's order (the battery was along the Nivelles road about one and one-eighth miles from Napoleon's position (J.-B. A. Charras, *Histoire de la campagne de 1815, Waterloo*, Brussels, 1869, II, 46) and for the battery to make ready, it may be assumed that Napoleon's order was given shortly before or shortly after two o'clock, that is, while the half-hour cannonade of the English position was still in progress or had just ceased. In any case the order was given before d'Erlon's attack had been repulsed and consequently was part of the general situation in Napoleon's mind when the repulse occurred. Hence, although the Hougoumont bombardment overlaps with the d'Erlon attack, it is logical to discuss it first.

[180] Seven eighths of a mile to be exact, from the height back of Belle-Alliance to the buildings of Hougoumont.

distance ordered in a battery of eight howitzers to set fire to the buildings.[181] The howitzer shells soon set aflame the great barn, and "the smoke and flames bursting out in a terrific manner communicated with rapidity to the other outbuildings" of the Hougoumont position.[182] The English wounded had been carried into these buildings, the barn and the stables. The English officers attempted to save them, but could not penetrate the conflagration. The wounded perished in the flames and smoke. An eyewitness says their writhings and cries in the flames were those of the damned in Hell.[183] The fire spread to the little chapel of the estate. The flames consumed the chapel door, burned across the floor to the inside entrance, but miraculously stopped at the foot of the crucifix, which was gazing down upon the scene.[184] In the meanwhile, the English themselves brought up a battery which destroyed the howitzers. Thereafter the fight around Hougoumont settled down to a vigorous sharpshooter-skirmisher exchange. But the buildings remained in the British grasp.[185]

Shortly after the Hougoumont order, Napoleon received Major La Fresnaye, who delivered Grouchy's third report, dispatched that morning shortly after eleven o'clock. Napoleon read the report: that the Prussians were marching for Brussels; that they would join the English; that he (Grouchy) would mass at Wavre; that from thence he would maneuver "tomorrow." Napoleon asked the Major

[181] Napoleon, "Bataille de Mont-Saint-Jean," *Correspondance*, XXI, 188.

[182] Quotation from the letter of Colonel Woodford, Jan. 14, 1838 (*W. L.*, p. 264). Woodford's passage, which has been slightly modified to fit into my sentence, actually reads: ". . . the smoke and flames burst out in a most terrific manner, and communicated with rapidity and fury to the other outbuildings."

[183] *Ibid.*, pp. 262, 264; Mercer, *op. cit.*, p. 190; Stevenson, *op. cit.*, p. 287; Pontécoulant, *op. cit.*, pp. 302-303.

[184] Letter of Colonel Woodford, Jan. 14, 1838, and of Ensign Standen, no date (*W. L.*, pp. 264, 269); Stevenson, *op. cit.*, p. 288; Eaton, *op. cit.*, pp. 141-142.

[185] Kennedy, *op. cit.*, p. 106; "Bericht über den Anteil der hannoverschen Truppen und der Deutschen Legion an der Schlacht bei Belle-Alliance" (*P.-H.*, p. 54).

where Grouchy was when he left him. "Sart-à-Walhain," was the reply, and Napoleon requested the Major to remain near him.[186] At last Napoleon knew that Grouchy at eleven o'clock that morning was still twelve to fourteen miles[187] from the battlefield, that he intended to maneuver "tomorrow." Napoleon still retained the hope, however, that Grouchy in response to previously dispatched messengers or perhaps to the sound of firing would yet appear.[188]

In the meantime the bombardment in front of Napoleon had continued. After half-an-hour of cannonading, the

[186] La Fresnaye to Grouchy, Dec. 17, 1829 (Grouchy, *Fragments historiques*, p. 42).

[187] The distance is estimated. General Gérard, who was with Grouchy and became his enemy, later visited the possible route of march from Sart-à-Walhain to the right flank of Napoleon's army at Frischermont. From information thus collected on the spot he concluded that the distance was no more than four leagues. If he were using the modern French league that would be ten miles; if some other league, perhaps twelve miles. But by Ferrari's map of Belgium reproduced in the rear of Ropes's book, the air-line distance from Sart-à-Walhain to Frischermont is thirteen miles; it would be longer over country crossroads. Pontécoulant, a friend of Gérard, walked the distance from Sart-à-Walhain to Couture, which was in the rear of the Wood of Frischermont, in three hours and forty minutes. Assuming that he was walking at the rate of three miles an hour, the distance would be a little over eleven miles. Assuming that he was walking at the rate of four miles an hour, the distance would be fifteen miles. Kennedy gives the distance from Gembloux to Mont-Saint-Jean as twenty miles. But Grouchy was at Sart-à-Walhain, not at Gembloux; and Napoleon's right flank was at Frischermont, not a Mont-Saint-Jean. Subtracting the distances from Gembloux to Sart-à-Walhain and from Mont-Saint-Jean to Frischermont, measured by country crossroads, we arrive at about thirteen and a half to fourteen miles as the distance from Sart-à-Walhain to Frischermont (Pontécoulant, *op. cit.*, pp. 363-364 and nn.; Kennedy, *op. cit.*, p. 132). Whether Napoleon knew the exact distance is doubtful, but he had the map of Ferrari before him, and he probably had a rough notion of the distance Grouchy had to cover.

[188] Wellington was later informed by someone and Colonel Gurwood of the English Army was told by Flahault, Napoleon's aide-de-camp, that at one stage of the battle, probably in the afternoon after one o'clock, Napoleon turned to Soult, his Chief of Staff, and asked him if he had sent for Grouchy (presumably the one o'clock message). "Soult answered that he had despatched an officer at a particular hour. '*Un officer!* exclaimed Napoleon, turning round to his suite, *un officier! Ah! mon pauvre Berthier! S'il avait été ici il en aurait envoyé vingt*" (Stanhope, *op. cit.*, pp. 65, 249). The story would seem to indicate that even later on in the afternoon Napoleon still hoped Grouchy might appear.

French first line to the right of the Brussels road, the infantry of d'Erlon's corps numbering about sixteen thousand divided into four divisions of approximately equal size, descended the French forward slope. The French guns temporarily ceased fire to allow the infantry to pass forward between them, and then resumed once it had passed ahead. The French grand attack moved forward on the broad front of about one and a quarter miles. To the left of the Brussels highway a brigade of heavy cavalry (cuirassiers) advanced toward the English right center. To the right of the highway, three divisions of infantry, Alix's, Donzelot's, and Marcognet's, advanced toward the English left center. Farther to the right, Durutte's division was told off to occupy the farmhouses of Ter la Haye and Papelotte and the hamlet of Smohain. The formation of the infantry was unfortunate. While Alix's division was apparently divided into two brigades, Donzelot's and Marcognet's divisions had each been formed into a heavy, thick, unwieldly column, 160 to 200 men broad and 24 ranks deep.[189] Throughout the battle the common French soldier and the common English, Scotch, and German soldier fought with unexampled devotion and fury. Only the Dutch and Belgians proved untrustworthy. In this case, the French infantry moved off alertly, echelonned from their left, that is, Alix's division forward first, then Donzelot's, then Marcognet's, and finally Durutte's. Alix's left-hand brigade marched across the fields and up the highway toward the English forepost of the farm of La Haye Sainte, which lay on the left side of the road. Upon surmounting the last, local rise of ground which had hid their advance from the defenders, the French brigade stormed the post, drove the defenders who were in the orchard into the barn, those who were in the garden into the house, and surrounded the buildings.[190] When

[189] Houssaye, *op. cit.*, p. 338.
[190] Letter of Lieutenant Graeme, Dec. 6, 1842 (*W. L.*, pp. 406, 407);

Wellington dispatched to the defenders' aid two infantry battalions, the advancing French cavalry on the left met the reinforcement, rode it down, cut it to pieces, and then charged up onto the English ridge.[191] In the meanwhile to the right, Alix's right-hand brigade, Donzelot's and Marcognet's huge columns slowly ascended the long slope, drove in the English skirmishers, braved the English musket and artillery fire, gained the crest of the ridge.[192] Far off to the right, Durutte's division had won possession of the farm of Papelotte.[193] To the circle of officers around Napoleon who had watched the descent of the French infantry and then its rise on the English forward slope, the total operation occupying about half-an-hour, everything was going marvelously ("toute va à merveille")[194] and victory seemed within their grasp.[195]

Yet in a few minutes all was over. Napoleon's hammer-blow was parried by the wrist and thrust of an opponent superior to any he had hitherto encountered. Wellington had kept most of his infantry and cavalry concealed on the reverse slope of the English position. During the cannonade he even had the infantry lie flat on the ground to reduce the

Editor's note (*ibid.*, p. 404); "Bericht des 2. Leichten Bataillons der Deutschen Legion" (*P.-H.*, p. 107).

[191] "Bericht der hannoverschen 1. Infanterie-Brigade" and "Bericht des 2. Leichten Bataillons der Deutschen Legion" (*P.-H.*, pp. 77, 107); Lieutenant General Alten to Wellington, June 19, 1815 (Wellington, *Supplementary Dispatches*, X, 534); letters of Major General Somerset, April 4, 1835, and of Private Cruickshank, Sept., 1839 (*W. L.*, pp. 40, 361).

[192] Letters of Captain Seymour, Nov. 30, 1842, of Major Sir de Lacy Evans, Sept. 1, 1839, of Major General Kempt, of Private Cruickshank, Sept., 1839, of Lieutenant Colonel Leach, of Captain Kincaid, May 2, 1839 (*W. L.*, pp. 21-22, 63, 347, 361, 364, 367); Editor's note (*ibid.*, p. 345); "Bericht der hannoverschen 1. Neunpfunder-Batterie, December 6, 1824," and "Bericht der hannoverschen 2. Neunpfunder-Batterie" (*P.-H.*, pp. 183, 187-188).

[193] Kennedy, *op. cit.*, p. 109.   [194] Houssaye, *op. cit.*, p. 341.

[195] The next day Soult wrote to Davout: "Monsieur le maréchal, hier j'ai eu l'honneur de vous écrire du champ de bataille de Waterloo, à deux heures et demie, alors que la bataille était très bien engagée et donnait l'espoir d'un grand succès" (Soult to Davout, June 19, 1815, in Grouchy, *Mémoires*, IV, 303-304).

casualties caused by the bombardment. Wellington himself stood "under a great elm which grew a little to the west of the Brussels highway, at the intersection of the road with the one from Wavre."[196] When Alix's right-hand brigade attained or nearly attained the top of the English position, it stopped to deploy into line.[197] In front of it, out of sight on the backward slope was one of these English brigades of infantry which had hitherto lain on the ground. Now, on the order of its commander, Kempt, it stood up, marched quickly to one of the hedges that ran along the crest, and at forty paces fired a volley into the deploying French column.[198] The leading French soldiers, caught in a moment of formation and somewhat startled, naturally displayed hesitation.[199] Seizing the psychological moment, Kempt ordered his brigade to charge, and it drove the French down the hill.[200]

Farther to the right as the French columns of Donzelot and Marcognet had ascended the forward slope of the English position, the English cavalry leader, Lord Anglesea, organized a brigade of heavy cavalry of one thousand men,[201] and under the direction of its commander, Ponsonby, it advanced gradually up the backward slope of the English position, toward the summit of the ridge opposite where

[196] Houssaye, *op. cit.*, p. 340; also Wellington to Sir Walter Scott, Aug. 17, 1815 (Wellington, *Dispatches*, XII, 610).

[197] Letters of Lieutenant Shelton, Sept. 29, 1839, of Ensign Mounsteven, Aug. 19, 1829, of Private Cruickshank, Sept., 1839 (*W. L.,* pp. 349, 350, 361); Editor's note (*ibid.,* p. 346).

[198] Letters of Lieutenant Shelton, Sept. 29, 1839, of Ensign Mounsteven, Aug. 19, 1829 (*W. L.,* pp. 349, 350); Editor's note (*ibid.,* p. 345).

[199] Kennedy, *op. cit.,* p. 109.

[200] Letters of Major General Kempt, of Lieutenant Shelton, Sept. 29, 1839, of Ensign Mounsteven, Aug. 19, 1839, of Private Cruickshank, Sept., 1839 (*W. L.,* pp. 347, 349, 350, 361-362); Editor's note (*ibid.,* p. 345).

[201] Letters of Lord Anglesea, Nov. 8, 1839, of Captain Kennedy, June 18, 1839 (*ibid.,* pp. 8, 70). Lord Anglesea did not lead this charge, but returned to organize Somerset's brigade and led it. On the effective number in Ponsonby's brigade see letter of Captain Kennedy, Oct. 28, 1839 (*ibid.,* pp. 77-78).

the French columns would emerge.[202]   The advance of the
French columns was apparent to the English leaders who
stood on the summit of the position;[203] the advance of the
British cavalry was unknown to the French. Donzelot's and
Marcognet's huge columns reached the top of the ridge,[204]
forced aside the British infantry along the summit, crossed
the hedge which ran along one side of the Wavre crossroad,
crossed the slightly sunken road, reached and in some places
crossed the hedge that ran along the other side, and then
saw the line of British cavalry about one hundred yards distant.[205]   Again among the French front ranks, already somewhat disordered by the crossing of the road and the flank
fire of the British infantry, a moment of hesitation; the
columns began to crumble inward.[206]   The British cavalry
charged the front of the columns, overlapped their flanks,

[202] Letters of Major Sir de Lacy Evans (ibid., pp. 61, 63-64).

[203] Ponsonby and his aide-de-camp were on the summit; also probably
Picton (letters of Major Sir de Lacy Evans, of Colonel Muter, June 17, 1839,
in ibid., pp. 63-64, 85).

[204] Donzelot's columns had taken longer to ascend the slope than had
Marcognet's. Hence, although echelonned from the left, the two columns
reached the crest at about the same time. Marcognet's division did not stop
to deploy and passed ahead. They were struck by English cavalry almost
simultaneously and were driven down the hill as a single mass. In details
of action along the crest their experiences differed, but in general what caused
their defeat was the same. I have given a general description of what occurred.
For a detailed account, one may read Kennedy, op. cit., pp. 108-109, and the
Editor's (Siborne's) notes in Waterloo Letters. Houssaye's account of the repulse, it seems to me, is entirely inaccurate, for he has Alix's right-hand brigade
repulsed by cavalry, Donzelot's division by the infantry of Kempt's brigade. A
glance at the arrangement of the English line would show that Kempt's brigade
was opposite the advance of Alix's right-hand brigade, that Donzelot's division
was roughly speaking opposite the interval between Kempt's and Pack's
brigades.

[205] Letters of Lord Anglesea, Nov. 8, 1839, of Major Sir de Lacy Evans,
Sept. 1, 1839, of Captain Kennedy, June 18 and July 27, 1839, of Colonel
Muter, June 17, 1839, of Lieutenant Colonel Miller, June 18, 1839, of Lieutenant
Winchester (W. L., pp. 9, 60-61, 69-70, 72, 85, 89, 383); Editor's note (ibid.,
pp. 345-346); report of Colonel Van Zuylen von Nyevelt, Oct. 25, 1815
(Wommerson and De Bas, op. cit., III, 341-342).

[206] Letters of Major Sir de Lacy Evans, Sept. 1, 1839, and Aug. 23, 1842,
of Captain Kennedy, June 18, 1839, of Colonel Muter, June 17, 1839, of
Lieutenant Colonel Miller, June 18, 1839 (W. L., pp. 61, 64, 70, 85, 89).

and pressed them backwards down the hill.[207] The cavalry
was Scotch; likewise at this point a section of the British
infantry. In the exhilaration of the moment the infantrymen joined in with the cavalry, running at the stirrups shouting "Scotland for ever."[208] Back down the hill the Frenchmen streamed like a flock of sheep, the British horsemen
hacking almost at will among the French masses, rounding
up two thousand prisoners.[209]

Then, as this was proceeding, back on the summit of
the English position, the English cavalry leader, Lord Anglesea, having organized the Ponsonby attack, crossed the
highway and organized another brigade of heavy cavalry
(Somerset's) of twelve hundred. He led it against the
brigade of French cuirassiers who had gained the ridge west
of the highway.[210] The English went after that French
brigade, hammered on the cuirasses until it sounded as if
a thousand tinkers were at work, drove it down the hill,
and (after passing La Haye Sainte) across the road where
the French rode down some of their own retreating infantry,
and in brief pursued the cuirassiers to the foot of the French
position and then returned.[211]

On the forward slope of the English position were now
strewed accoutrements, standards, wounded men, some

[207] Letters of Major Sir de Lacy Evans, Sept. 1, 1839, of Captain Kennedy,
June 18, 1839, of Lieutenant Wyndham, 1839, of Colonel Muter, June 17,
1839, of Lieutenant Colonel Miller, June 18, 1839, of Major General Kempt, of
Lieutenant Winchester, Nov. 24, 1834 (*W. L.,* pp. 61, 71, 72-73, 78-79, 85-86,
89, 347, 383).

[208] Letters of Captain Kennedy, Oct. 28, 1839, of Lieutenant Winchester,
Nov. 28, 1834 (*W. L.,* pp. 77, 383).

[209] Letters of Major Sir de Lacy Evans, Sept. 1, 1839, of Captain Kennedy,
June 18, 1839, of Colonel Muter, June 17, 1839, of Lieutenant Winchester,
Nov. 24, 1834, of Lieutenant Graeme, Dec. 6, 1842 (*W. L.,* pp. 61, 71, 86,
383, 406).

[210] Letter of Lord Anglesea, Nov. 8, 1839 (*W. L.,* p. 8).

[211] Letters of Major General Somerset, April 4, 1835, of Private Cruickshank, Sept., 1839 (*ibid.,* pp. 40, 361); Major General Somerset to Wellington,
June 24, 1815 (Wellington, *Supplementary Dispatches,* X, 577). Some of the
regiments even ascended the French slope.

individuals in solitary devotion shouting "Vive l'empereur," and one Frenchman with both legs shattered trying to take his life.[212] In the meanwhile Napoleon, back on the height, seeing his columns rolled back, displayed considerable agitation, took frequent pinches of snuff and threw them away, yet could not restrain his admiration for the English cavalry, reportedly saying: "Regardez ces chevaux gris! Qui sont ces beaux cavaliers? Ce sont de braves troupes."[213] But as he watched, the English cavalrymen of Ponsonby's troop, carried away by the momentum and excitement of a successful charge, passed through the broken French infantry, swept up into the French position, rode among the battery of eighty guns, sabered the gunners and decommissioned some of the guns.[214] Napoleon rode over to his second line, General Milhaud's cuirassiers, and dispatched a brigade.[215] With it, went a regiment of French lancers.[216] They descended on the English cavalrymen. The latter, without formation, their horses blown, unsupported by a second line, were massacred. Only a few, as individuals, or as twos or threes, escaped to the English lines.[217] But this sharp counterblow could not alter the fact that the first French grand attack had failed. Even the enclosures around La Haye Sainte were not retained, for in the general French rout these had to be abandoned,[218] while far off to the right Durutte was forced to relinquish Papelotte.[219] As a consequence of the French

[212] Letters of Lieutenant Winchester, Nov. 24, 1834, of Lieutenant Graeme, Dec. 6, 1842 (*W. L.*, pp. 383, 406-407).

[213] Based on the testimony of Lacoste, the Belgian guide who was beside Napoleon throughout the day (Simpson, *op. cit.*, pp. 111-112; *Near Observer*, pp. 135-136). On the probable value of Lacoste's evidence see pp. 183-184, n. 297.

[214] Letters of Lord Anglesea, Nov. 8, 1839, of Major Sir de Lacy Evans, Sept. 1, 1839, of Lieutenant Wyndham, 1839 (*W. L.*, pp. 8-9, 61-62, 79).

[215] Mauduit, *op. cit.*, II, 299.

[216] Major Sir de Lacy Evans, Sept. 1, 1839 (*W. L.*, p. 62).

[217] Letters of Major Sir de Lacy Evans, Sept. 1, 1839, of Captain Kennedy, June 18, 1839, of Lieutenant Wyndam, 1839 (*W. L.*, pp. 62, 71, 79).

[218] Kennedy, *op. cit.*, p. 111; Editor's note (*W. L.*, p. 404).

[219] Mauduit, *op. cit.*, II, 307-314; Kennedy, *op. cit.*, p. 111; letter of Captain Barton, Nov. 3, 1834 (*W. L.*, pp. 114-115).

attack, which had started so brilliantly, the English had suffered losses; but the French had been checked, their troops were back in the valley, and it was now three o'clock. There was then an interlude while both contestants reorganized their forces.[220]

With the defeat of the initial attack on the English, with the Prussians present off to the right, with the knowledge that Grouchy was probably nowhere near, other commanders, probably even Napoleon in earlier years, would have stood on the defensive and retired during the night. Perhaps he did consider momentarily alterations of plan. But probably failing to realize fully the desperateness of the situation, under the illusion that he had to deal with only a single Prussian corps, Napoleon was still sanguine.[221] He clung, furthermore, to his original plan of a perpendicular attack on the English center. His intentions were now somewhat as follows. The advance guard of Bülow's Prussian

[220] Houssaye, *op. cit.*, p. 349; Mauduit, *op. cit.*, II, 304.

[221] Napoleon, in his own account of the battle, said that after the appearance of the Prussian corps he turned to Soult and remarked: "Nous avions ce matin quatre-vingt-dix chances pour nous, l'arrivée de Bülow nous en fait perdre trente, mais nous avons encore soixante contre quarante. Et si Grouchy répare l'horrible faute qu'il a commise en s'amusant à Gembloux et marche avec rapidité, la victoire en sera plus décisive, car le corps de Bülow sera entièrement détruit" (Napoleon, "Bataille de Mont-Saint-Jean," *Correspondance,* XXXI, 190). Thus at one-thirty or two o'clock, Napoleon, taking into consideration the presence of the single Prussian corps and discounting the nonappearance of Grouchy, still thought the chances were for him. That was probably before the repulse of d'Erlon's attack. But the repulse of the attack, although it caused losses and lost time, did not change the essential situation: the single Prussian corps was present, Grouchy had not appeared, Napoleon retained the bulk of his reserve for a hammer blow against the English. It was likely that he still thought the chances were for him at three o'clock in the afternoon. Shortly after four o'clock, furthermore, when he perceived that Ney had launched a cavalry attack unwisely and prematurely, he remarked according to Flahault, his aide-de-camp: "Voilà Ney qui d'une affaire sûre fait une affaire incertaine" (Houssaye, *op. cit.,* p. 364, n. 4). This remark would suggest that as late as four o'clock, and hence also at three o'clock since the essential situation as he knew it had not altered in that hour, he thought the chances of winning the battle were in his favor. It is well, perhaps, to observe that they probably were under the circumstances he imagined himself to be with a single Prussian corps, and an orderly, powerful attack on the English center.

corps, after remaining on the height of Saint-Lambert for nearly an hour, had begun about two o'clock to move forward toward the Wood of Paris, which was two thirds of a mile east and slightly in the rear of the French right flank. By three-thirty o'clock, the leading Prussian contingents were approaching the Wood. Before launching another major attack against the English, Napoleon would await the result of the Prussian maneuver. He would hold the Imperial Guard in reserve until it became apparent that the Prussians were not going to advance from the Wood of Paris or that they had been checked by Lobau, who with the Sixth Corps was on the French side of the Wood.[222] Meanwhile, Napoleon would seize La Haye Sainte[223] and under the protection of this key forepost throw forward a

[222] In the bulletin of the battle Napoleon said: "Il était trois heures après midi. L'Empereur fit avancer la Garde pour la placer dans la plaine, sur le terrain qu'avait occupé le Ier corps au commencement de l'action, ce corps se trouvant déjà en avant. La division prussienne, dont on avait prévu le mouvement, commença alors à s'engager avec les tirailleurs du comte Lobau, en plongeant son feu sur tout notre flanc droit. Il était convenable, avant de rien entreprendre ailleurs, d'attendre l'issue qu'aurait cette attaque. A cet effet, tous les moyens de la réserve étaient près à se porter au secours du comte Lobau et à écraser le corps prussien lorsqu'il se serait avancé.

"Cela fait, l'Empereur avait le projet de mener une attaque par le village de Mont-Saint-Jean, dont on espérait un succès décisif; mais par un mouvement d'impatience si fréquent dans nos annales militaires, et qui nous a été souvent si funeste, la cavalerie de réserve, s'étant aperçue d'un mouvement rétrograde que faisaient les Anglais pour se mettre à l'abri de nos batteries, dont ils avaient déjà tant souffert, couronna les hauteurs de Mont-Saint-Jean et chargea l'infanterie. Ce mouvement, qui, fait à temps et soutenu par les réserves, devait décider de la journée, fait isolément et avant que les affaires de la droite fussent terminées, devint funeste" ("Bulletin de l'armée, June 20, 1815," in Napoleon, *Correspondance*, XXVIII, 296). General Gourgaud, in his account written under Napoleon's dictation, said that before the attack on Mont-Saint-Jean would be resumed "il fallait 'voir l'issue de la manoeuvre des Prussiens'" (quoted in Houssaye, *op. cit.*, p. 357, n. 2). It seems fairly clear that Napoleon intended to await the issue of the Prussian maneuver before launching his second grand attack; that the presence of the Prussians was the reason for delaying the main attack.

[223] Gourgaud wrote: "L'empereur avait ordonné au maréchal Ney de se maintenir dans la Haye-Sainte en la crenelant et en y établissant plusieurs bataillons, mais de ne faire aucun mouvement. . ." (quoted in Houssaye, *op. cit.*, p. 353, n. 3).

long line of skirmishers to within 100 yards of the English crest to preoccupy and devastate the British center.[224] Then, with the Prussian corps checked and held at a distance, he would bully the English with an artillery cannonade, throw the mass of his cavalry reserve (ten thousand) to occupy the English plateau, follow with the disposable infantry division of d'Erlon's and Reille's corps and with the infantry reserve (eleven thousand) of the Imperial Guard, secure the plateau and break the English line.[225] It would be a care-

[224] This is inference. That is, Napoleon did intend to use La Haye Sainte as a point of support for the main attack on the British center. That he would use it in the specific manner indicated is likely, especially since that is the way La Haye Sainte was employed after it was captured.

[225] As to the nature of the projected attack, Napoleon had said that morning at the farmhouse of Caillou: " 'Je ferai jouer ma nombreuse artillerie, je ferai charger ma cavalerie, et je marcherai avec ma vieille garde' " (Notes journalières of General Foy, quoted in Houssaye, op. cit., p. 356, n. 3). The remarks of Napoleon at eight to nine o'clock in the morning are not necessarily good evidence as to his intentions at three o'clock in the afternoon. But there is other evidence, and it is possible to analyze more closely. The preliminary artillery bombardment may be taken as a matter of course. Then would follow cavalry supported by the infantry of the first two corps (d'Erlon and Reille) and the infantry of the reserve, that is, the Guard. In support of this view, it may be noted that Napoleon in the bulletin of the battle said: "Ce mouvement de cavalerie qui fait à tempts et *soutenu par les réserves,* devait décider de la journée" (Napoleon, "Bulletin de l'armée, June 20, 1815," *Correspondance,* XXVIII, 296). The cavalry was thus to attack first, supported by reserves. But the only reserves would then be the infantry of the Guard. Jerome, who was with Napoleon at this stage of the battle, wrote a month later: "L'empereur ordonna au maréchal Ney de se porter avec une grande partie de la cavalerie, deux corps d'infanterie et la garde sur le centre de l'ennemi pour donner le coup de massue, et certes c'en serait fait de l'armée anglaise, si le maréchal eût exécuté les ordres de l'empereur; mais emporté par son ardeur, il attaqua trois quarts d'heure trop tôt" (quoted in Houssaye, op. cit., p. 356, n. 3). Then, too, Napoleon in his account dictated at Saint-Helena said: "L'intention de l'empereur était d'ordonner cette attaque de cavalerie, mais une heure plus tard, et de la faire soutenir par l'infanterie de la garde' " (quoted in *ibid.,* p. 353, n. 3). Finally, it may be noted that Napoleon never blamed Ney for making the cavalry charge, or for making it in advance of infantry, but for launching it prematurely before it could be supported by infantry. The statement therefore that Napoleon planned to follow the artillery bombardment with cavalry in turn supported by the infantry of the Guard would thus seem fairly well sustained by the evidence; the statement that the infantry support would also include the disposable divisions of d'Erlon's and Reille's corps rests only on the letter of Jerome—but that these corps would be employed seems

fully timed attack. For this purpose he advanced his Guard from the third to the second line, to the position vacated by Lobau's corps.[226] But, as before, he intrusted the details of the operation to Ney.

The latter, however, was no longer the master tactician of Friedland, or even of the Russian retreat, who with inspired coolness in the presence of danger arranged his artillery, infantry, cavalry for almost incredible effects. He was still brave beyond reproach. But worn by an active life and perhaps by dissipation, he was now erratic, possessed by a febrile impatience. Apparently his only idea today was to fling his troops in loosely co-ordinated assaults against the English.[227]

At about three-thirty, after d'Erlon had reformed his infantry in the valley, Ney threw some of them for a second attack against the forepost of La Haye Sainte. Only slightly supported by artillery, again bare French infantry were flung against the stone walls of what was in effect a fortified position, and were repelled.[228]

While this attack was proceeding, the French artillery along the line resumed its bombardment of the English plateau. To this the English replied. Never, said the English officers, was heard so deafening a cannonade.[229] To

likely. Not in proof but simply as supporting material, it may be observed that Wellington, who was a good judge of his opponent, likewise thought this was Napoleon's plan. Arbuthnot in quoting Wellington said: "I have heard the Duke say that Napoleon tried to gain the victory of Waterloo in the same way he gained other victories by moving immense bodies of cavalry at a slow pace, and then following up the advantages gained by furious attacks of infantry" (Arbuthnot to Lord Ellesmere, June 17, 1845, in Ellesmere, *op. cit.,* p. 240; also see pp. 98-99).

[226] Mauduit, *op. cit.,* II, 290-292; Napoleon, "Bulletin de l'armée, June 20, 1815," *Correspondance,* XXXVIII, 296.

[227] On Ney see Gourgaud, *Sainte-Hélène: journal inédit* (French ed.), I, 502, 544; Charles A. Thoumas, *Les grands cavaliers du premier empire: Première série* (Paris and Nancy, 1890), p. 102.

[228] "Bericht des 2. Leichten Bataillons" (*P.-H.,* p. 108).

[229] Houssaye, *op. cit.,* pp. 354-355; Cotton, *op. cit.,* p. 74.

protect some of his troops, Wellington withdrew in the center some of his forward artillery and infantry to the reverse slope of the position. Ney, peering through the smoke up at the English ridge, mistaking this movement of withdrawal for a movement of retreat, thought the decisive moment was at hand. Riding over to the right of the French second line, he ordered the cuirassiers (heavy cavalry) of General Milhaud to charge. The cavalry leaders made some objections, but were overruled, and the body (of three thousand) moved off. Without orders, merely because in leaving General Milhaud said to a colleague, General Lefebvre-Desnoëttes, "I am about to charge; support me," the lancers (light cavalry) of the Guard (two thousand in number) of the latter general followed.[230] In grand order, the cuirassiers and the lancers five thousand strong obliqued across the highway in a slow, deliberate charge up the slope toward the center of the British right wing under the hail of British shrapnel and shell.[231]

Ney pointed his charge between Hougoumont and La Haye Sainte toward a portion of the British line that had not yet been attacked; he was employing cavalry alone against a line of infantry supported by artillery and cavalry— before the key center forepost of La Haye Sainte had been captured—on the basis of a hasty hazardous guess that the British were in retreat and in violation of any well-considered plan. The British leaders on the summit had uneasily wondered what the terrific artillery bombardment portended; they were relieved when they saw the cavalry ascend the slope.[232]

Wellington's purpose was to hold the position until the Prussians arrived. He commanded, therefore, that the infantry of the right wing west of the Brussels highway form squares along the English plateau. That is, in accord with

[230] Houssaye, *op. cit.*, pp. 355-356; Thoumas, *op. cit.*, p. 222.
[231] Kennedy, *op. cit.*, pp. 115-116.   [232] *Ibid.*, pp. 114, 116.

the custom of the day, to receive cavalry, each battalion of infantry formed a hollow square usually with each side three ranks deep. The first rank kneeling on the right knee, the butt of their muskets resting on the ground, would present their bayonets at an angle. The second and third ranks standing erect would likewise present their bayonets. On four sides, the square bristled with bayonets.[233] Although the cavalry cuirassiers wore a helmet and virtually a coat (cuirass) of iron, they were well horsed,[234] and towered over the kneeling and standing infantrymen; nevertheless, in the balance of offense and defense of the day an infantry square of steady troops was impregnable to cavalry alone. In this instance along the plateau, the squares were formed in checkerboard fashion; that is, the first line of infantry alternated spaces and squares; the squares of the second line were opposite the spaces of the first; twenty to twenty-three squares in all covering a front of about three fourths of a mile. Opposite the forward corners of the first-line squares was artillery. The artillery horses and limbers were sent to the rear. Wellington's orders were that the guns should be fired at the last possible moment, but that then, when cavalry was close, the gunners should take refuge within the adjacent squares. Back of the English infantry, on the reverse slope, was the cavalry in reserve.[235]

Milhaud's cuirassiers and the accompanying lancers of the Guard were formed in squadrons. As they ascended the slope, "the French batteries ceased firing and the English batteries accelerated their fire. Their pieces had double charge: cannon ball and grape-shot or double-headed bar-shot. A storm of iron. The horses mounted the long slope at a trot, rather slowly, on this soft ground into which they sometimes sank to the knee, in the midst of the tall rye which swept their harness. By hastening the fire, the bat-

[233] Cotton, op. cit., p. 75.   [234] Near Observer, p. 34, n. #.
[235] Gomm, op. cit., p. 373; Cotton, op. cit., p. 75.

teries could make several discharges. A last volley, at forty paces, from the batteries of Lloyd and Cleeves . . . half mowed down the front squadrons. The survivors stopped a few seconds, seeming to hesitate. The charge sounded more vibrant; there were shouts of *Vive l'empereur!* The cuirassiers rushed upon the cannon. All the batteries were taken in turn. A superb feat, but an illusive prize." The English gunners had taken refuge in the nearest square, and the French "lacked the teams of horses to lead the pieces away, the spikes to put them out of service. . . .

"The cannon were silent, but the musket fire (from the English squares) rolled and crackled. The bullets struck and ricocheted on the cuirasses with the noise of hail on a slate roof. Cuirassiers and lancers, their ranks already broken by the fire, by the ascent, by the passage itself of this hedge of cannon, darted upon the squares."[236] They swarmed around the squares, trying to break them open. They "assailed them on all four sides, charged against the corners, hacked at the bayonets with their swords, punched holes in breasts with their lances, fired their pistols at the distance of a few paces."[237] But the English-Allied squares, presenting their bayonets or firing their muskets on order, stood firm, immobile, though surrounded by cavalry which towered over them. "A few breaches were made which were at once closed. Despite their blows with their spurs and with their swords, despite their valor and their rage, the horsemen could not pierce these walls of men."[238]

In the course of this mêlée between the infantry squares and the French horsemen, Lord Anglesea, leader of the English cavalry, saw his opportunity. The French horsemen on the summit were now without formation. Two thirds of the English-Allied cavalry had not been used. Lord Anglesea organized a fresh force of five thousand cavalry-

[236] Houssaye, *op. cit.*, pp. 360-362.
[237] *Ibid.*, p. 362. [238] *Ibid.*

men and charged up the backward slope to the summit. The Frenchmen, in disorder, abandoned the plateau.[239] The English gunners "ran back to their pieces; all along the crest, the line of fire of the English batteries was re-kindled.

"Hardly had they reached the bottom of the valley than the soldiers of Milhaud and Lefebvre-Desnoëttes turned, reformed, and resumed the charge. Again, they ascended under a hail of grape-shot the muddy slopes of Mont-Saint-Jean, seized the cannon, crowned the heights, darted on the infantry,"[240] and again were driven off by a charge of the English cavalry.

Back on the height of Belle-Alliance, Napoleon, per-ceiving in the distance Milhaud's cuirassiers on the summit of the English position was surprised and discontented that cavalry should have been used so soon and inopportunely.[241] According to various witnesses, Napoleon said different things: to Soult, "There is a premature movement which can have fatal results on this day"; to Jerome, speaking of Ney, "The wretched fool! this is the second time since day before yesterday that he has compromised the destiny of France"; according to Flahault: "There goes Ney who makes of a sure thing an uncertain affair."[242] But they agree that Napoleon considered the cavalry charges prema-ture by at least three quarters of an hour[243]—that is, before the artillery bombardment had had time to exercise its ravages; before La Haye Sainte had been captured; before the Prussian problem had been solved and Napoleon was free to use his Guard to hold what the cavalry had gained.

[239] Houssaye, *op. cit.*, pp. 362-363; Kennedy, *op. cit.*, p. 117; Major General Lord Somerset to Wellington, June 24, 1815 (Wellington, *Supplementary Dispatches*, X, 578). [240] Houssaye, *op. cit.*, p. 363. [241] *Ibid.*, p. 364. [242] *Ibid.*, p. 364 and nn. [243] In his own account written at St. Helena, Napoleon said that he remarked in regard to the cavalry charges: " 'C'est trop tôt d'une heure; cependant il faut soutenir ce qui est fait' " (Napoleon, "Bataille de Mont-Saint-Jean," *Corre-spondance*, XXXI, 194).

He added, however: ". . . but now that the movement has begun there is nothing else to do but to support it," and he ordered Kellermann's cuirassiers (three thousand) and the heavy cavalry of the Guard (two thousand) commanded by Guyot to support Milhaud.[244] In a kind of madness Ney, attempting to break the British line with cavalry alone, now swept the entire French reserve of cavalry into these slow, deliberate, reiterated charges of the British right wing; ordered in the cuirassiers of Kellermann and followed them with the heavy cavalry of Guyot, the cuirassiers of Milhaud, the lancers of Lefebvre-Desnoëttes; and then, when these were forced to withdraw after forty-five minutes' occupation of the plateau, added the eight hundred carabineers which Kellermann had left in reserve, and ordered the cavalry to charge again and again.[245]   In each charge the routine was the same: the French artillery would bombard the English plateau, the French cavalry would begin the ascent, the French cannonade would cease, the English guns would pour in a decimating hail, the cavalry would reach the crest, the gunners would take refuge in the squares, the cavalry would swarm around the squares, a mêlée during which the cavalrymen in trying vainly to break open the squares with their saber blows would suffer from the English musket fire, and, finally, the cavalry would be charged and forced to retire by the English horsemen or would voluntarily withdraw to reform, the mutual, destructive cannonade would resume, both sides—the French cavalry and the English cavalry and infantry—being steadily weakened and diminished.[246]

[244] Houssaye, *op. cit.*, pp. 364-365.

[245] *Ibid.*, pp. 371-376; Kennedy, *op. cit.*, pp. 117-119; Charras, *op. cit.*, II, 59-60.

[246] For various descriptions of the cavalry attacks and their repulse, see Cotton, *op. cit.*, pp. 74-77, 84-87; Simpson, *op, cit.*, p. 96; Lieutenant General Alten to Wellington, June 19, 1815 (Wellington, *Supplementary Dispatches,* X, 534); Hay, *op. cit.*, p. 184; Report of Major General Trip (Wommerson

How these charges appeared to a spectator we learn
from Captain Mercer of the English horse artillery, who
wrote a full account of his experiences.[247] At the time
of the first cavalry charges, Mercer's battery was in reserve
in the rear of the British right wing rather far down the
reverse slope. From that position, the squares with guns
between them stood out as dark masses against "the grey
smoke which seemed to fill the valley beyond and to rise
high in the air above the hill."[248] "The roar of cannon and
musketry in the main position never slackened. Occasionally, from time to time, was to be seen still more dense
columns of smoke rising straight into the air like a great
pillar, then spreading out a mushroom-head. These arose
from the explosions of ammunition wagons, which were
continually taking place, although the noise which filled
the whole atmosphere was too overpowering to allow them
to be heard."[249]

As Mercer stood in the rear conversing with a Colonel
Gould, bodies of French cavalry "swept over the summit
between the squares and dispersing on the reverse slope of

and De Bas, *op. cit.*, III, 403-405); letters of Lord Anglesea, of Major General
Somerset, April 4, 1835, of Lieutenant Colonel Thackwell for Major General
Grant, July 9, 1835, of Captain Walcott, Jan. 18, 1835 (*W. L.*, pp. 11-12, 41,
126, 193-194); Editor's note (*ibid.*, p. 38); "Bericht der Fuss-Batterie des
Captain-Cleeves Königlich Deutsche Legion, 1825," "Bericht der hannoverschen
1. Infanterie-Brigade," "Bericht der 3. Gemischten Kavallerie-Brigade," November
12, 1824, Journal des 1. Linien Bataillons der Deutschen Legion," "Journal
des 8. Linien bataillons der Deutschen Legion," "Bericht des hannoverschen
Feldbataillons Bremen, December 4, 1842," "Bericht des 1. Leichten Dragoner-
Regiments der Deutschen Legion" (*P.-H.*, pp. 70, 77-78, 102-103, 111, 126,
134-137, 151).

[247] As an artillery officer Mercer kept a journal. But during the three days
of the Quatre-Bras-Waterloo campaign he was apparently too busy to post his
diary, and the date of composition of these three passages is uncertain. ("I
think I have already mentioned that it was not until some days afterwards
that I was able to resume my regular journal, consequently that everything
relative to these three days is written from memory"—Mercer, *op. cit.*, pp.
165-166.) Nevertheless, in these passages he proves himself to be, when
checked with other writers, a careful, accurate reporter.

[248] *Ibid.*, p. 164.   [249] *Ibid.*, p. 167.

the position vanished again. Several avalanches of this sort had already occurred when suddenly a huge, dark mass of cavalry appeared for the instant on the main ridge, and then came sweeping down the slope in swarms among the squares, reminding Mercer of an enormous surf, a mountainous wave breaking against the isolated rocks on a rocky coast, and running hissing and foaming up the beach. In a twinkling the space between and behind the infantry was covered with horsemen, crossing, turning, and riding about in all directions. There were lancers amongst them, hussars, and dragoons—it was a complete mêlée. On the main ridge no squares were to be seen; the only objects were a few guns standing in a confused manner, with muzzles in the air, and not one artilleryman. . . . For a moment an awful silence pervaded that part of the position to which Mercer and Gould anxiously turned their eyes. 'I fear all is over,' said Colonel Gould. Mercer could not withhold assent, and prepared his battery to resist attack."[250] But at this moment he was distracted for a few minutes by an incident on his right. When his attention returned to the ridge, the French cavalry had vanished, like the backwash of a wave, while the squares and the guns remained, like isolated rocks.

Shortly afterwards Sir Augustus Frazer, commander of the English Horse Artillery, galloped up to conduct Mercer's battery to a position on the summit of the ridge. The battery limbered up and moved off like a flash. "Frazer's face was black as a chimney's sweep, and the jacket-sleeve of his right arm was torn open by a musket-ball or case-shot, which had merely grazed his flesh. As he and Mercer rode up the reverse slope, Frazer explained that a mass of heavy cavalry was about to attack the point to which he was leading the battery. As the men ascended the slope toward the

[250] Pieced together from *ibid.*, p. 168, and from Mercer's letter (Nov. 26, 1834) in Siborne, *The Waterloo Letters*, p. 216. Changed from first to third person.

ridge, Mercer breathed a new atmosphere—the air was suffocatingly hot, resembling that issuing from an oven. He was enveloped in a thick smoke. Despite the incessant roar of cannon and musketry, in the smoke he could distinctly hear around him a mysterious humming noise, like that which one hears of a summer's evening proceeding from myriads of black-beetles—the whine and hum of bullets; cannon shot, too, ploughed the ground in all directions, and so thick was the hail of balls and bullets that it seemed dangerous to extend the arm lest it should be torn off."[251]

Amidst this storm the battery gained the summit, strangely enough, without a casualty. It unlimbered before the forward angles of its allotted two infantry squares. No need to detail Mercer's activity. From that position, his battery poured into the advancing French cavalry, time and again, a murderous fire until the dead were heaped before the guns. What was passing to the right and left he did not know. The smoke confined his vision to a small compass, so that his battle was restricted to the two squares and his own battery. In that small circle, as for every other common soldier on both sides, incidents passed like a stream; the first casualty—Gunner Butterworth, wounded by his own gun, "he was No. 7 (the man who sponged, etc.), he had just finished ramming down the shot and was stepping back outside the wheel, when his foot stuck in the miry soil, as a man naturally does when falling he threw out both his arms, they were blown off at the elbows, he raised himself a little on his two stumps, and looked most piteously in Mercer's face";[252] the advance of the French cavalry seen through the smoke less than one hundred yards distant; the opening fire, and so on. Each person was absorbed in his little world. The spirit of the battle, the fury, the concern, the immobility under fire penetrated every participant; they were immersed in it.

[251] Partly quoted, partly paraphrased from Mercer, *Journal*, pp. 169-170.
[252] *Ibid.*, pp. 172-173, *passim.*

The battle itself on that somber day increased in intensity and scope and roared to a climax whose end no one could foresee. While the grand cuirassier charges were in progress, the Prussians to the right entered the conflict. Throughout the day, while Napoleon and Grouchy worked at cross-purposes, Blücher and Wellington had co-operated closely. Between the two commanders there had been a constant interchange of couriers, who informed Wellington of the approach and arrival of the Prussians and Blücher of the course and sway of the battle.[253] By one o'clock, as we have said, the advance guard of Bülow's corps appeared on the heights of Saint-Lambert, five miles northeast of Napoleon at Belle-Alliance. By four o'clock, unopposed by the French, it had advanced to occupy the Wood of Paris only two miles east of Belle-Alliance. The mere presence of the Prussians within the field of observation had already paralyzed a portion of Napoleon's reserves—first, the cavalry of Domon and Subervie; then, the Sixth Corps of Lobau; finally, the Imperial Guard. Blücher at first determined to remain in the Wood of Paris to wait for the remainder of Bülow's corps to come up to the advance guard, but receiving alarming reports from the Prussian representative (Müffling) near Wellington and perceiving the cuirassiers in occupation of the English plateau, he decided to enter the conflict at once with the troops at his disposal "to give Wellington air."[254] The Prussians, therefore, about four-thirty, debouched from the Wood of Paris, not far from the French right wing.[255]

They were opposed by the cavalry of Domon and the

[253] Müffling, *op. cit.*, p. 213; "Bericht des 1. Husaren-Regiments der Deutschen Legion" (*P.-H.*, p. 161).

[254] "Rapport des General Leutnant von Bülow, July 10, 1815" (Wommerson and De Bas, *op. cit.*, III, 524-526); Report of Gneisenau (Wellington, *Supplementary Dispatches*, X, 505); Müffling, *op. cit.*, pp. 213-214; Kennedy, *op. cit.*, p. 136.

[255] "Rapport des General Leutnant von Bülow, July 10, 1815" (Wommerson and De Bas, *op. cit.*, III, 524-526); Hay, *op. cit.*, p. 185.

infantry of Lobau, who were formed in a line parallel to the Brussels highway and perpendicular to and behind the French right wing, and who maintained their ground until about five-thirty.[256] Blücher sent some troops to occupy the villages of Frischermont and Smohain and thus tied his left flank with Wellington's left wing.[257] Then, as the other brigades of Bülow's corps arrived, he extended his line south, formed the brigades to Lobau's right, and advanced.[258] Lobau, outnumbered (thirty thousand to ten thousand) and fearful of being outflanked, was forced to retreat toward the Brussels highway until the French-Prussian line formed an acute angle with the French-British position and reached from Smohain to about Planchenoit.[259] The shells from the advancing Prussian artillery fell on the Brussels highway and on the height back of Belle-Alliance, where Napoleon and his Guard were standing.[260] By six, Bülow's corps, steadily outflanking Lobau, threatened to take the village of Planchenoit, which was in the right rear of Napoleon and whose fall would endanger the French retreat. Napoleon now undertook from back of Belle-Alliance the personal supervision of this defensive battle against the Prussians.

In the meantime, on the original English battlefront, the charges of the cuirassiers had gradually slowed down and petered out, and came to an end about six o'clock.[261]

[256] Letters of Sir Hussey Vivian, Major Taylor, Nov., 1829, of Lieutenant Ingilby, Nov. 20, 1834 (*W. L.*, pp. 160-161, 171, 200); Napoleon, "Bataille de Mont-Saint-Jean," *Correspondance*, XXXI, 192.

[257] Letter of Major Taylor, Nov., 1829 (*W. L.*, p. 171); "Rapport des General Leutnant von Bülow, July 10, 1815" (Wommerson and De Bas, *op. cit.*, III, 526).

[258] Letter of Major Taylor, Nov., 1829 (*W. L.*, p. 171); "Rapport des General Leutnant von Bülow, July 10, 1815" (Wommerson and De Bas, *op. cit.*, III, 526-532).

[259] Letter of Major Taylor, Nov., 1829 (*W. L.*, p. 171); "Rapport des General Leutnant von Bülow, July 10, 1815" (Wommerson and De Bas, *op. cit.*, III, 530-532); Napoleon, "Bataille de Mont-Saint-Jean," *Correspondance*, XXXI, 192.

[260] Mauduit, *op. cit.*, II, 390-391; Napoleon, "Bataille de Mont-Saint-Jean," *Correspondance*, XXXI, 192-193.   [261] Kennedy, *op. cit.*, pp. 121-122.

Napoleon's and Ney's attempt to break the English line with cavalry alone had failed. The entire French cavalry was by now sadly reduced—perhaps one third to one half killed or wounded, the remaining men and horses utterly weary, unfit for any great effort during the rest of the day. The English cavalry was likewise diminished and exhausted, but possessed a reserve of twenty-two hundred men in Vivian's and Vandeleur's brigades on the far left flank. The English infantry-squares had been worn thin, but retained occupation of the plateau. The battle—its first stage being the diversion against Hougoumont, the second d'Erlon's infantry attack, the third the cuirassier charges (to the participants all these must have seemed long ago)—now graded imperceptibly into its next stage. While the cuirassier charges were yet in progress, the French, better supported by artillery, assailed once again (about five o'clock) La Haye Sainte, but again the attack broke and failed on an active defense.[262] The successive French attacks, however, had exhausted the defenders' ammunition. By an oversight, the English-Allied garrison had not been furnished with enough ammunition for a day's fight, and on account of the confusion in English supply, the pleas of the post's commander for cartridges remained unanswered.[263] To the fourth French attack, the garrison could oppose only their bayonets, and the French quickly captured this key center-forepost, shortly before or after six o'clock.[264]

The French swiftly made use of their prize. The stone farmhouse of La Haye Sainte was about three hundred yards down from the summit of the British position. The

[262] "Bericht des 2. Liechten Bataillons der Deutschen Legion" (P.-H., p. 108).

[263] Letter of Lieutenant Cathcart, April 13, 1835 (W. L., p. 33); Editor's note (W. L., pp. 404-405); Kennedy, op. cit., pp. 122-123.

[264] Kennedy, op. cit., p. 122. It was probably captured just before the cuirassier attacks came to an end (Major General Kempt to Wellington, June 19, 1815, in Wellington, Supplementary Dispatches, X, 536).

French now filled the house to the roof with sharp-shooters.[265] Under the protection of their fire, additional skirmishers occupied a knoll on the right of the road about one hundred yards from the crest of the English position.[266] The second-story of the house and the knoll were on a level with the summit of the English plateau. A battery of light guns was brought around the house to fire on the English position.[267] For some distance, running out from both sides of the road, a long, thick line of skirmishers was established just below the top of the English ridge.[268] Skirmishers from the house, from the knoll, from under the crest, the light guns poured in a withering, destructive fire which swept this portion of the plateau and which more than decimated the English troops stationed in the center.[269] East of the highway, Lambert's Brigade, which had not entered the action until three o'clock, suffered so severely that in the course of a few minutes one regiment lost half its number.[270] Picton's Division—the infantry which had repelled d'Erlon's attack—which had entered the action with four thousand, now due to cumulative losses from cannonade and attack, and from this fierce musketry counted only five hundred. It could no longer cover effectually its front.[271] West of the highway the two cavalry brigades

[265] Letter of Major Leach, Nov. 22, 1840 (*W. L.*, p. 365); Wellington in conversation, March 18, 1840 (Stanhope, *op. cit.*, p. 221).

[266] Letters of Major Leach, Nov. 22, 1840, of Major Browne, May 6, 1835 (*W. L.*, pp. 365, 399); Gomm, *op. cit.*, p. 361; Kennedy, *op. cit.*, p. 127.

[267] Lieutenant General Alten to Wellington, June 19, 1815 (Wellington, *Supplementary Dispatches*, X, 534); "Bericht der hannoverschen 1. Infanterie-Brigade," "Tagebuch des nassauischen 1. Regiments" (*P.-H.*, pp. 73, 78, 198).

[268] Letter of Major Leach, Nov. 22, 1840 (*W. L.*, pp. 365-366); Editor's note (*W. L.*, p. 390).

[269] Editor's note (*ibid.*, p. 346); Kennedy, *op. cit.*, p. 124; Gomm, *op. cit.*, p. 360.

[270] Editor's note (*W. L.*, p. 390); Major General Kempt to Wellington, June 19, 1815 (Wellington, *Supplementary Dispatches*, X, 536); "Bericht der Fuss-Batterie des Captain Braun, 1825" (*P.-H.*, p. 71).

[271] Woodberry, *op. cit.*, p. 313.

(Ponsonby's and Somerset's) which had helped to repel d'Erlon's first attack and had numbered twenty-two hundred now, as a result of cumulative losses and this musketry, counted only two hundred. They were arranged in a single line near the crest to make a show of force.[272] Around them, two brigades of Allied infantry (German) had retreated to Mont-Saint-Jean, and the few remaining squares were greatly thinned.[273] In front of them, most of the guns were dismounted, or for lack of ammunition had been withdrawn.[274] By six-thirty to seven, an "air of ruin and desolation" pervaded the English center. "The pavement of the Brussels road was torn up and scattered. . . . The ground was strewed with wounded. . . . Wounded or mutilated horses wandered or turned in circles. . . . The noise was deafening" and the smoke obscure.[275] West of the

[272] Letters of Captain Seymour, Nov. 21, 1842, Major General Somerset, April 4, 1835, Captain Kennedy, June 18, 1839, of Sir Hussey Vivian, June 23, 1815, of Lieutenant Colonel Murray, Jan., 1835 (*W. L.*, pp. 20, 42, 74, 149, 179); Editor's note (*ibid.*, p. 39).

[273] Lieutenant General Alten to Wellington, June 19, 1815 (Wellington, *Supplementary Dispatches*, X, 534); Report of General Hügel, June 19, 1815 (Albert Pfister, *Aus den Lager der Verbündeten*, Stuttgart and Leipzig, 1897, p. 370); letter of Sir Hussey Vivian, June 23, 1815 (*W. L.*, p. 149); "Journal des 8. Linien Bataillons der Deutschen Legion," "Bericht des hannoverschen Feldbataillons Bremen, December 9, 1824" (*P.-H.*, pp. 73, 126, 128 ff.).

[274] "Bericht der hannoverschen 1. Infanterie-Brigade," "Bericht des Oberstleutnant der Artillerie des Deutschen Legion, October 28, 1824," "Bericht des hannoverschen Feldbataillons Bremen, December 4, 1842," "Bericht der 4. Batterie der Deutschen Legion," "Tagebuch des nassauischen 1. Regiments," "Bericht des nassauischen 1. Regiments, June 21, 1815" (*P.-H.*, pp. 78, 105, 137, 178, 198, 201).

[275] These phrases are taken from Lieutenant Colonel Murray's description of the English right center as he saw it between seven o'clock and seven-thirty. Murray belonged to General Vivian's cavalry, which was transferred from the English left about seven o'clock and reached the English right center probably a short time before seven-thirty. But the situation between six-thirty to seven was even more serious than it was between seven and seven-thirty, because in the intervening period Wellington had had the opportunity to reinforce the right center. I assume that the phrases which Murray used to describe the situation shortly before seven-thirty and which I have quoted, also apply to the situation at six-thirty to seven (letter of Lieutenant Colonel Murray, Jan., 1835, in *W. L.*, p. 179).

highway for half a mile, the English plateau was practically empty of troops.[276] Far off to the French right, furthermore, Durutte's French division finally conquered the positions of Ter la Haye and of Smohain.[277]

Ney was not unaware of the plight of the English center. But with the troops at his disposal he was unable to take advantage of it. His cavalry was diminished and physically utterly spent. His infantry from an afternoon of attack was likewise reduced in number and extenuated with fatigue. From the remnants of the First and Second Corps (d'Erlon and Reille), he could send forward swarms of skirmishers, but he could no longer form a decisive column of attack. He needed fresh troops—the Imperial Guard, as yet unemployed. He dispatched, therefore, his aide, a Colonel Heymès, to ask Napoleon for infantry. But at that moment, sometime between six-thirty and seven o'clock, Napoleon was preoccupied with the Prussian danger as yet unsolved. His only reserve, now that the cavalry was exhausted, was the infantry of the Guard. He might need it against the Prussians. In any case, in his view it was not safe to dispose of his last reserve while the Prussian attack on Plancenoit— the rear of the army—was still developing.[278] He refused, therefore, Ney's request, responding irritably to Heymès: "Some troops! Where do you want me to get them? Do you want me to make them?"[279]

Of the seventy-four thousand with which Napoleon had entered the battle, and who did not now lie killed,

[276] Kennedy, op. cit., pp. 124-127; Major General Edward Somerset, April 4, 1835 (W. L., p. 42).

[277] "Bericht des 3. Bataillons des nassauischen 2. Regiments, December 28, 1835" (P.-H., p. 211).

[278] Napoleon in the bulletin of the battle said: "Il était impossible de disposer de nos reserves d'infanterie jusqu'à ce qu'on eût repoussé l'attaque de flanc du corps prussien" (Napoleon, "Bulletin de l'armée, June 20, 1815," Correspondance, XXVIII, 297). The statement made in the bulletin, I am inclined to believe, was also Napoleon's idea in the battle.

[279] Houssaye, op. cit., p. 382.

wounded, or were fighting on a far-flung, encircling line from Hougoumont to La Haye Sainte to Ter la Haye to Smohain around to Planchenoit, Napoleon had left with him on the height of Belle-Alliance a compact reserve of eleven thousand—the infantry (twenty-two battalions)[280] of the Old, the Middle, and the Young Imperial Guard. The Young Guard was a new organization, but the Middle and the Old Guard were the élite of the army.[281] In dealing with the Prussian menace, Napoleon, wishing to retain as large a force as possible for the final attack on the English which he still intended, doled out detachments from his reserve with skill and parsimony. Perceiving Lobau outflanked, about six o'clock he dispatched the eight battalions of the Young Guard (forty-two hundred men, twenty-four guns) under General Duhesme to occupy the ground east of Planchenoit.[282] The Prussian masses, however, outflanking the Young Guard on both sides, forced it to retire into the town.[283] The Prussians, gathering their strength, stormed the village through a gulf of fire. The Young Guard held.[284] But the Prussians rallied, collected fourteen battalions, nearly eight thousand men, renewed the attack, expelled the Young Guard, and seized the village.[285] Napoleon ordered in two battalions of the old Guard—eleven hundred men.[286] He entered one of the battalion squares

[280] While the Guard usually consisted of twelve regiments of two battalions each (Kennedy, *op. cit.*, p. 121) and each battalion numbered about five and fifty men, nevertheless in the battle of Ligny two regiments had suffered so severely as in effect to be reduced to a single battalion each (Mauduit, *op. cit.*, II, 397-398; Houssaye, *op. cit.*, p. 389, n. 1) leaving twenty-two battalions, while the number in the whole Guard had been diminished to about eleven thousand.

[281] In the following narrative, the distinction between the Middle and Old Guard will be ignored, although as a matter of fact the eight battalions of the Old Guard were, so to speak, the élite of the élite.

[282] Mauduit, *op. cit.*, II, 385.   [283] *Ibid.*, II, 393-394.

[284] *Ibid.*, II, 398-399; "Rapport des General Leutnant von Bülow, July 10, 1815" (Wommerson and De Bas, *op. cit.*, p. 534).

[285] Mauduit, *op. cit.*, II, 399. Mauduit says ten thousand men (*ibid.*, II, 403); "Rapport des General Leutnant von Bülow, July 10, 1815" (Wommerson and De Bas, *op. cit.*, II, 534).   [286] Mauduit, *op. cit.*, II, 394, 400.

before it moved off, and personally instructed its members not to stop to load and fire but to use only the bayonet. In accord with these directions, these eleven hundred veterans of years of warfare in a fury of determination in twenty minutes ferociously cleared with the bayonet the village of Prussians and swept on to the heights beyond.[287] It was the achievement of giants. The Young Guard in support reoccupied Planchenoit; Lobau recovered ground.[288] Bülow, stupefied, thought he had to do with all the Imperial Guard, drew off his attacking force, ceased his attacks; and activity along this front, by seven o'clock, quieted down.[289]

Thus apparently the Prussians with skill and economy of means had been contained; the Prussian danger had been resolved. As a matter of fact, however, directly behind the center of Bülow's corps was formed three fourths of Pirch's corps, fifteen thousand men, and portions of this corps were already in support by Plancenoit.[290] Off to the northeast, furthermore, coming on at a forced pace toward Papelotte was Von Ziethen's corps of twenty thousand, whose advance guard was now perhaps less than a mile from the battlefield.[291] But these facts Napoleon did not know. In accord with his fixed illusions, he had checked and fought to a standstill the single corps (Bülow's) that

[287] *Ibid.*, II, 400-403.
[288] Napoleon, "Bataille de Mont-Saint-Jean," *Correspondance*, XXXI, 193.
[289] *Ibid.*, XXXI, 193; Mauduit, *op. cit.*, II, 404, n. a; letter of Lieutenant Ingilby, Nov. 20, 1834 (*W. L.*, p. 201); von Bülow in his report speaks as if he had to deal with the entire Imperial Guard and with overwhelming numbers ("Rapport des General Leutnant von Bülow, July 10, 1815," Wommerson and De Bas, *op. cit.*, III, 532-534).
[290] Von Bülow said in his report: "The Second Army Corps [Von Pirch] during this time had also arrived and formed behind our center." Von Pirch, however, in his report indicates that of the four brigades of his corps, the Fifth, Sixth, and Seventh had arrived but the Eighth had been delayed. The corps had suffered severely at Ligny but assuming all brigades had suffered equally we may say that three fourths of the corps had arrived ("Rapport des General Leutnant von Bülow, July 10, 1815," and "Bericht von General Major von Pirch," Wommerson and De Bas, *op. cit.*, III, 506-508, 534).
[291] Müffling, *op. cit.*, p. 214.

he knew was near the field. Having accomplished that, he now turned for one last blow against the English.[292]

The rain had ceased, the clouds had dispersed, and in weather it was now a fine afternoon.[293] In preparation for the final thrust to be delivered by the Guard, Napoleon took certain precautions which probably would have been adequate under the circumstances in which he imagined himself to be. Two battalions of the Guard were already at Planchenoit. To assure that they would not be outflanked, that Bülow's corps would remain checked, he dispatched another battalion south of Planchenoit to the Wood of Cantelet.[294] Since he was descending into the valley with his reserve, he left two additional battalions of the Guard on the Brussels-Charleroi road on the knoll of Rossomme to serve as a center of rally in case of retreat.[295] He instructed General Drouot to assemble the remaining nine battalions of the Guard for entrance into battle, and he himself made ready to accompany them.

As the Guard descended the slope of the French position along the left side of the highway, Müffling, the Prussian representative to the English Army, was standing a mile or so away on the extreme left of the English line over by Papelotte. He perceived the descent of the Imperial Guard toward the English center. Looking behind him, he de-

---

[292] Napoleon in the bulletin of the battle said: "L'ennemi [the Prussians] fut contenu, fut repoussé et recula; il avait epuisé ses forces et l'on n'en avait plus rien à craindre. C'est ce moment qui était celui indiqué pour une attaque sur le centre de l'ennemi" (Napoleon, "Bulletin de l'armée, June 20, 1815," No. 22061, *Correspondance,* XXVIII, 297). The statement in the bulletin, it seems to me, also reflected Napoleon's idea in the battle.

[293] Letter of Lieutenant Ingilby, Nov. 20, 1834 (*W. L.,* p. 201).

[294] Mauduit, *op. cit.,* II, 396-397.

[295] *Ibid.,* II, 395-396. The two battalions had been placed there while the Prussian attack of Planchenoit was still underway. They were apparently left there, however, to cover a retreat should it occur. Napoleon's bulletin of the battle says: ". . . the remainder of the guard was placed in reserve . . . in part on the plateau which in rear of the battle field formed our position of retreat" (Napoleon, "Bulletin de l'armée, June 20, 1815," No. 22061, *Correspondance,* XXVIII, 297).

scried the advance guard of General Von Ziethen, the Prussian reinforcements, on the nearest height. On his own authority, therefore, as the Prussian First Corps was coming up, Müffling ordered the English cavalry reserve of Generals Vivian and Vandeleur of twenty-two hundred horsemen on the English left wing to betake itself to the English center where it would be needed[296]—a swift, smooth action symbolic of the English-Prussian co-operation on that day.

Just before leaving Belle-Alliance to descend into the valley with his Guard, Napoleon took his telescope for one last survey. He, too, through the glass, perceived approaching Papelotte the fresh Prussian troops whom he had thought miles away and on whose presence he had not counted.[297] Brute fact had finally burst in on a plan of battle

[296] Müffling, op. cit., p. 214. It would seem, however, that a like order from Wellington arrived almost simultaneously: see letter of Captain Seymour, Nov. 21, 1842 (W. L., p. 20).

[297] There are two critical problems involved: (1) when and from what point did Napoleon perceive the arrival of the Prussians; (2) how did he perceive them. In regard to the first question, I have followed Napoleon's own account confirmed by Lacoste. According to Napoleon the sequence of events was as follows: he ordered General Drouot to assemble the remaining battalions of the Guard in front of Belle-Alliance; other members of the French Army perceived the arrival of fresh Prussian contingents and hesitated; presumably either just before, during, or just after this hesitation Napoleon perceives the Prussians; he leads the first four battalions of the Guard from Belle-Alliance toward La Haye Sainte (Napoleon, "Bataille de Mont-Saint-Jean," Correspondance, XXXI, 197-198). Thus he knew of the Prussian arrival before he left Belle-Alliance. Also Lacoste, the Belgian guide who was beside Napoleon throughout the day, said: "At four he mounted his horse . . . and preceded his staff . . . to a small eminence nearer the Belle Alliance, where they remained till seven o'clock. Previously to leaving this place, Bonaparte, looking through his glass, exclaimed, 'Je crois que je vois le drapeau Prussien.' Bertrand then looked through his glass and replied, 'Je crois que oui.' Upon which Bonaparte shook his head and turned quite pale. . . . At seven, with shouts as before of Vive l'Empereur, Bonaparte and his staff went towards the farm of La Haye Sainte, about a quarter of a mile from La Belle Alliance, in the direction of Waterloo, and there remained in a hollow of the road till past eight (Weston, op. cit., p. 136). In regard to the second question, how he perceived the Prussians, I have followed Lacoste. This, in turn, raises the problem of the reliability of the testimony of Lacoste. The latter was a man in the early fifties who kept a small, obscure tavern on the high road between the farm of Rossomme and Belle-Alliance. On the day of the battle he was used by

and a set of mind founded on illusion. The drama of a battle lies not merely in the array of troops, the deeds of valor, the heroic charges, however stirring these may seem; the true drama lies in the minds of the commanders—their intentions and failure, their intentions and success. Apparently Napoleon realized the significance of what he had seen. Lacoste, the Belgian guide who was beside Napoleon throughout the day, says that Napoleon displayed a calm countenance and confidence until evening. But upon perceiving the Prussian contingent he "shook his head and turned quite pale."[298] Other members of the French Army had likewise espied the arriving Prussians, had displayed hesitation, and some regiments had even fallen back.[299] Napoleon later said that at this point, when the Prussians appeared in such numbers, he should perhaps have fought a rear-guard action and retreated.[300] We do not know if in

---

Napoleon as a native guide, and was by the side of the Emperor from about eight o'clock in the morning until late at night. He had full, free, uninterrupted opportunity for observation of Napoleon. The day of the battle was the great event in Lacoste's life. To English travelers who visited his tavern in 1815 and 1816 he told the story, always the same story, of what he had witnessed of the conduct of Napoleon. In his story he told of literal-minded details—Napoleon taking snuff, Napoleon's change of position, Napoleon's remarks on the English cavalry, but he reported nothing of maneuvers, reports, counter-orders, and to-and-fro of staff officers. From his story I judge that since he was ignorant of military affairs and perhaps not too bright he fundamentally did not know what the activity around Napoleon was all about; but as a literal-minded person he perceived, understood, and probably reported accurately literal-minded details. Hence, it may be assumed that if he said Napoleon perceived the Prussians through his telescope, the fact is probably correct. On Napoleon's perception of the Prussians while still on the height of Belle-Alliance, see also the anonymous "Journal of Napoleon's aide-de-camp" (MacBride, *op. cit.*, p. 189).

[298] Weston, *op. cit.*, p. 136.

[299] Napoleon, "Bataille de Mont-Saint-Jean," *Correspondance*, XXXI, 197.

[300] Speaking at St. Helena to General Gourgaud, he said: "J'aurais peut-être dû, en voyant l'immense supériorité des Prussiens, battre plus tôt en retraite. J'aurais perdu alors cinquante ou soixante pièces de canon. Mon plan avait réussi: J'avais surpris les Prussiens et les Anglais" (Gourgaud, *Sainte-Hélène: Journal inédit*, I, 504). The problem is to what period of the battle was Napoleon referring: when the first Prussians appeared at one o'clock, or when Prussian reinforcements appeared at seven o'clock. It would seem

the battle he even considered this more cautious alternative. All we know is that, drawn by the hope that his line to the right would hold until he could smash the English center, drawn by the hope and desperation of the hour, he only precipitated his action.

Without waiting for all the Guard to assemble, he placed himself at the head of several battalions and led them into the heat, roar, and smoke of the valley back of La Haye Sainte.[301] On the march of about three quarters of a mile, to hold his army in control until the new attack could be launched, he dispatched aides-de-camp to spread along the line the fabrication that Grouchy had arrived to the right, that he had attacked the English and Prussian left, and that with a little constancy victory would be theirs. This fiction, in fact, reanimated the weary troops.[302] At the same time "he had the order carried to the batteries to accelerate their fire, to d'Erlon, to Reille, and to the commanders of the cavalry to second on their respective fronts the attack of the Guard."[303] Upon arriving in the valley, he personally conducted and stationed a single battalion halfway between the highway and Hougoumont, in case the English attempted an offensive from that forepost.[304] Returning to the other battalions, he led them to a position back of La Haye Sainte. Meeting Ney, he expressed the wish to renew the attack and to penetrate the English center with these troops, and ordered Ney to lead them on.[305] Ney mar-

---

that he was referring to the second hour: the Prussians did not arrive with "immense superiority" at one o'clock, but at seven; if he had retreated at seven o'clock Napoleon would perhaps have lost "fifty to sixty cannon," but retreating at one o'clock he would probably have lost none; at one o'clock he had not yet "surprised the English"; by seven o'clock in a sense he had.

[301] Napoleon "Bataille de Mont-Saint-Jean," *Correspondance*, XXXI, 197-198; Ney to Fouché, June 26, 1815 (Cotton, *op. cit.*, p. 251); Lacoste narrative (Weston, *op. cit.*, p. 136).

[302] Ney to Fouché, June 26, 1815 (Cotton, *op. cit.*, p. 251); Napoleon, "Bataille de Mont-Saint-Jean," *Correspondance*, XXXI, 198.

[303] Houssaye, *op. cit.*, p. 390.   [304] Mauduit, *op. cit.*, II, 418.

[305] Ney to Fouché, June 26, 1815 (Cotton, *op. cit.*, p. 252).

shaled the five battalions that had arrived (not quite three thousand men),[306] arranged them for attack, and then, riding at the head of one of the squares, led them up the slope toward the English right wing. Napoleon retired to the highway back of La Haye Sainte near two batteries of the Guard whose cannoneers were being decimated by English canister. In the twilight Napoleon was somber and absolutely livid.[307]

The details of the attack of the Guard in the smoke and gathering dusk[308] are still a subject of dispute among French and among English historians and between the two groups, but the general outlines of what occurred are clear. Throughout the battle Wellington on his side of the position had been omnipresent—near Hougoumont when Jerome's diversionary attack opened,[309] in the center when d'Erlon's corps advanced,[310] in an infantry square during one of the cuirassier attacks,[311] an observer of Mercer's battery as it galloped into action,[312] on the crest of the center at the critical moment when La Haye Sainte was captured and the French sharpshooters were creeping around the building to the garden on the English side.[313] Through it all, through the fury Wellington had ridden calm and com-

---

[306] According to Houssaye, the attack was made by (1) the First Battalion of the Third Grenadiers, (2) the two battalions of the Fourth Grenadiers united into a single battalion by reason of losses sustained at Ligny, (3) the first and second battalions of the Third Chasseurs, and (4) the two battalions of the Fourth Chasseurs reduced to a single battalion (Houssaye, op. cit., p. 392). According to Mauduit, these now numbered approximately: (1) 550; (2) 500; (3) 1,028; (4) 841, totaling 2,919 (Mauduit, op. cit., II, 397-398).

[307] Pontécoulant, op. cit., p. 324, n. 1.

[308] Letters of Lieutenant Cathcart, Dec. 24, 1835, of Major Lautour, Feb. 28, 1835, of Major General Sir Hussey Vivian, June 23, 1815, of Major Kelly, Nov. 26, 1834 (W. L., pp. 34, 100, 149, 340, 341).

[309] Ellesmere, op. cit., pp. 105-106.

[310] Wellington to Sir Walter Scott, Paris, Aug. 17, 1815 (Wellington, Dispatches, XII, 610).

[311] Letter of Major Kelly, Nov. 26, 1834 (W. L., p. 339).

[312] Mercer, Journal, p. 171, n. 1.

[313] Letter of Lieutenant Cathcart, April 13, 1835 (W. L., p. 33).

posed in absorbed concentration. Though almost all his aides were killed or wounded either beside him or on mission, he remained unscathed. Except for the blunder of failing to appreciate the importance of La Haye Sainte and to provide adequately for its defense, in all his proceeding he had exhibited cool, steady, measured understanding, restraint, and sagacity.[314]

His battle had been formed on the deliberate calculation that the British-Allied line would hold until the Prussians arrived. Although he had been informed of the arrival of Bülow's crops within the field of observation, only about six o'clock, when he heard Blücher's guns by Planchenoit, did he become aware that the Prussians had actually entered the conflict.[315] The respite afforded him by the cessation of the cuirassier attacks (although skirmishing and cannonade continued) and by Blücher's occupation of Napoleon's attention and of the French reserves enabled Wellington to reorganize his lines. With several thousand troops which he had hitherto held in reserve he rounded out and thickened his right wing—that portion which had been worn thin by the cuirassier charges. In addition, he extended three brigades of infantry from the right-hand end of the British plateau down to Hougoumont so that they would be able to flank any French attack that came up toward the right wing again.[316] As he anticipated an attack by infantry and cavalry combined, he formed his troops neither in squares, which were vulnerable to infantry, nor in an ordi-

---

[314] In general on Wellington's conduct: Cotton, *op. cit.*, pp. 101, 254-255; Kennedy, *op. cit.*, pp. 174-177; Stanhope, *op. cit.*, p. 183; Captain S. Rudyard, Jan. 6, 1835 (*W. L.*, p. 234).

[315] "Memorandum on the Battle of Waterloo, written by the Duke of Wellington after reading the statements of General Clausewitz, September 24, 1842" (Wellington, *Supplementary Dispatches*, X, 528-529); Pfister, *op. cit.*, p. 370; letter of Lieutenant Ingilby, Nov. 20, 1834 (*W. L.*, pp. 197, 202); Ellesmere, *op. cit.*, p. 210; "Bericht des 1. Husaren-Regiments der Deutschen Legion" (*P.-H.*, p. 161).

[316] Kennedy, *op. cit.*, pp. 125-126.

nary line of two deep, vulnerable to cavalry, but ordered his brigades along the summit to form a line four deep.[317]

While he was completing these arrangements on the right, an aide brought him the astounding intelligence of the huge gap in the English right center—for nearly half a mile west of the highway, the English line was practically empty of troops.[318] Wellington received this "very startling information" with coolness, and in perfect command of the situation "replied in an instant with precision and energy. . . . 'I shall order the Brunswick troops to the spot, and other troops besides; go you and get all the German (Allied) troops of the division to the spot that you can, and all the guns that you can find.' "[319] The aide departed to bring back into position those squares of Allied infantry which had retreated.[320] Artillery officers did their utmost to strengthen this vulnerable sector.[321] Wellington, exposing himself to the close and deadly fire the French skirmishers were pouring into the center of the position, personally led the Brunswick reserve into line.[322] He also at the same time dispatched orders to General Vivian to shift his brigade of cavalry from the left wing to the center.[323] As we have seen, on this point Wellington had been anticipated by Müffling, and General Vivian's cavalry arrived

[317] Ellesmere, *op. cit.,* p. 209; letters of Major General Maitland, Nov. 24, 1834, of Major General Adam, of Captain Budgen, Dec., 1834, of Corporal Aldridge, Dec., 1834, (*W. L.,* pp. 244, 254, 276, 299-300, 302); journal of Captain Powell (*ibid.,* p. 254).

[318] Kennedy, *op. cit.,* pp. 23-25, 127-128.

[319] *Ibid.,* p. 128.   [320] *Ibid.*

[321] "Bericht des Generals Hartmann" (*P.-H.* p. 105); Kennedy, *op. cit.,* pp. 128-129.

[322] Kennedy, *op. cit.,* p. 124.   Vincke's brigade of Hanoverian infantry was also transferred from left to right center. On its arrival one battalion of the brigade was placed in position under the personal direction of Wellington ("Bericht der hannoverschen 5. Infanterie-Brigade, January 7, 1825," "Bericht des hannoverschen Landwehr-bataillons Hameln, November 10, 1824" (*P.-H.* pp. 97, 146).

[323] Letter of Captain Seymour, Nov. 21, 1842 (*W. L.,* p. 20).

perhaps even sooner than it was expected.[324] It was placed in the right center in the rear of those squares of Allied infantry which still exhibited hesitation.[325] Thus the huge gap in the English center was in part repaired.

As a consequence of these arrangements, west of the highway the Allied-English brigades of infantry (by names of commanders) were stretched along the plateau in a mile-long concave line in the following order—beginning at the highway: Ompteda's Brigade (German Legion); Kielman-segge (Hanoverian); Kruse (Nassau); Vincke (Hanover-ian);[326] Brunswick troops; C. Halkett (British); Maitland (British Guards); Byng (British); then curving down to Hougoumont, Adam (British); Du Plat (German); W. Halkett (Hanoverian). The brigades near the highway—Ompteda, Kielmansegge, Kruse—had been worn to tatters by the French cannonade and musketry; they were only shreds and fragments.[327] Back of them, moreover, there was no second line of infantry, but only Vivian's brigade of cavalry. Behind the Brunswickers and the brigades of C. Halkett and Maitland, there was a second line of infan-try—a Dutch-Belgian division numbering over six thou-sand. Behind these was General Vandeleur's cavalry bri-gade. The English right center (near the highway) was thus weakly held, more with a display of force than with actual, sufficient power; it was on the English right that the line was thickest.

[324] Cotton, *op. cit.*, p. 104; "Bericht des 1. Husaren-Regiments der Deutschen Legion" (*P.-H.*, p. 162).

[325] Cotton, *op. cit.*, p. 104; letters of Sir Hussey Vivian, June 23, 1815, Jan. 18, 1830 (*W. L.*, pp. 149, 159).

[326] In strict accuracy one battalion of Vincke's brigade was to the left of the Nassau troops of Kruse, the other battalions to the right ("Bericht der hannoverschen 5. Infanterie-Brigade, January 7, 1825," "Bericht des Hanover-schen Landwehr-bataillons Hameln, November 10, 1824," *P.-H.*, pp. 97, 146).

[327] "Bericht der hannoverschen 1. Infanterie-Brigade," "Journal des 8. Linien bataillons der Deutschen Legion," "Bericht des hannoverschen Feldbataillons Bremen, December 4, 1842," "Tagebuch des nassauischen 1. Regiments,"

Sometime while these dispositions were being made, a French deserter, a cavalry captain, with his sword in its scabbard, his right hand in the air, galloped into the English lines shouting "Vive le Roi." He added: "That son of a bitch Napoleon is down there with his Guard. You will be attacked within half an hour." This information was carried to Wellington.[328] So to the English leader the plans of Napoleon were not unknown, the attack of the Imperial Guard was not unexpected. Since he had already received word of the approach of Von Ziethen's Prussians, and it was now seven-thirty, Wellington knew that all he had to do was to hold an hour longer.

By all accounts Napoleon's evening attack was hurriedly thrown together. Napoleon later said that four battalions of the Guard were sent up the slope without waiting for the others to come up;[329] General Petit, who was present and who later collected testimony from other witnesses, concluded five were advanced before the others arrived.[330] Napoleon had said in the morning at the farm of Caillou: "I shall have my numerous artillery play, I shall have my cavalry charge, and I shall march with my Guard."[331] But most of his Guard was now strewed in critical positions over the battlefield; the Guard was marching, but it was only a fragment, just as only a fragment of Napoleon's grand plan remained.

"Bericht des nassauischen 1. Regiments, June 21, 1815" (*P.-H.*, pp. 78-79, 126, 137, 198-199, 202).

[328] Houssaye, *op. cit.*, pp. 390-391; letters of Major General Adam, of Major Blair, Nov. 29, 1835, of Colonel Colborne (*W. L.*, p. 283). The Frenchman was obscene, but no eyewitness quotes his obscenity, merely using dashes. I have inserted a possible phrase.

[329] Napoleon, "Bulletin de l'armée, June 20, 1815," No. 22061, *Correspondance*, XXVIII, p. 297; Napoleon, "Bataille de Mont-Saint-Jean," *ibid.*, XXXI, 198.

[330] Houssaye, *op. cit.*, pp. 389, n. 1, 392, n. 2. Mauduit said that six battalions were advanced, but he counted the regiment of the Fourth Chasseurs, which had been reduced to 841 men, as two battalions, while General Petit counted the regiment thus reduced as a single battalion (Mauduit, *op. cit.*, II, 398).

[331] Houssaye, *op. cit.*, p. 353, n. 3.

In the formation of the Guard for attack, a similar haste or carelessness was revealed. "Instead of forming the Guard into a single column, sufficiently strong to pierce the English line,"[332] it was left in the formation in which it arrived; namely, divided into squares of a battalion (550 men) each, and the squares were advanced echelonned from the right—that is, the right-hand square in advance, then the next square a little to the left and a little behind, the next square a little to the left of the second and a little behind, and so on. "Between each echelon, the cannoneers of the Guard's horse-artillery led two eight-pounders, to total a complete battery commanded by Colonel Duchand."[333] But the entire formation tended to diffuse the strength of the five battalions over a long line.

Nor was the direction given to the Guard wisely selected. Napoleon, who in the afternoon had been distant from the battle line and in the evening preoccupied with the Prussians and who had just arrived, was probably ignorant of the local situation. In any case, he probably intrusted the direction to Ney. The latter could not in the smoke know where Wellington had or had not reinforced his line. But Ney was doubtless aware that in the center on both sides of the highway the French skirmish line was within sixty yards of the crest of the English position. Under the protection of La Haye Sainte and of the skirmishers he could have brought the Guard up close, and then sprung it on the English right center.[334] Instead of taking advantage of the prize (La Haye Sainte) for which the French had fought all afternoon, he sent the Guard on a bias "up the slopes which had been climbed by the cuirassiers in their first charge,"[335] toward the brigades of Brunswick, C. Halkett, and Maitland, where the English line was thickest and where on the left the Guard could be flanked by the English line curving

[332] *Ibid.*, p. 392.   [333] *Ibid.*
[334] Kennedy, *op. cit.*, p. 167.   [335] Houssaye, *op. cit.*, p. 392.

down to Hougoumont. But then in the swift stream of combat, some things are not always clear to the participants, and it is not always possible to make a wise decision. It was probably Napoleon's intention that Bachelu's and Foy's divisions of infantry and some cavalry would flank the Guard on its left and shield it from the English extreme right.[336] But the Guard was sent off while these troops were still in the process of formation in the valley.[337]

The advance of the Guard was preceded by violent artillery fire[338] and accompanied by a general infantry assault on the entire English line. To the far left Jerome's division with renewed vigor assailed Hougoumont. To the far right, Durutte's division struggled for Papelotte, and Marcognet's division gained a portion of the English plateau. To the immediate right of the highway, Alix's division occupied the attention of Kempt's and Pack's brigades.[339] But the burden of attack, including that of the Guard, fell on the English line west of the highway around *to* Hougoumont. Here Donzelot's division of d'Erlon's corps attacked the English right center. It rather quickly overthrew and drove back the remnants of the brigades of Ompteda, Kielmansegge, and Kruse, and perhaps of Vincke. These brigades reformed in front of Vivian's cavalry, but did not re-advance. The French brought up artillery and occupied this sector of the plateau, so that their center was now in the rear of the English right.[340]

[336] Ropes, *op. cit.*, p. 318.

[337] Houssaye, *op. cit.*, pp. 393, 398.

[338] Journal of Captain Powell (*W. L.*, p. 254).

[339] Letters of Major Calvert, April 19, 1835, of Major Browne, May 6, 1835 (*W. L.*, pp. 352-353, 398).

[340] Letter of Lieutenant Colonel Murray, Jan., 1835 (*W. L.*, p. 180); "Bericht der hannoverschen 1. Infanterie-Brigade," "Bericht des 2. Leichten Bataillons der Deutschen Legion," "Bericht des hannoverschen Feldbataillons Bremen," "Tagebuch des nassauischen 1. Regiments," "Bericht des nassauischen 1. Regiments, June 21, 1815" (*P.-H.*, pp. 79, 109, 137-138, 199, 202). In regard to Vincke's brigade, all its report vaguely says is: "worauf wir ein Quarree formirten und, den Bewegungen der Linie folgend, mehrermale rück-

To the left of Donzelot's division were the five battalions of the Guard. To quote Houssaye:[341] "They marched *l'arme au bras,* aligned as at a review at the Tuileries, superb and impassible. All their officers were at the head, the first to come to blows. Generals Friant and Porret de Morvan commanded the battalion of 3rd grenadiers; General Harlet, the battalion of 4th grenadiers; General Michel, the first battalion of the 3d chasseurs; Colonel Mallet, a faithful follower of the island of Elba, the 2d battalion; General Henrion, the battalion of 4th chasseurs. Ney rolled to earth with his horse, the fifth killed under him. He disengaged himself, stood up and marched on foot, sword in hand, beside Friant. The English artillery, arranged in a long concave line from the Brussels highway to the heights above Hougoumont . . . fired with double charge of grape-shot beginning at a distance of two hundred yards. The Guard was struck from the front and from the flank. Each volley opened a breach. The grenadiers closed their ranks, contracted their squares, and continued to mount at the same pace crying: 'Vive l'empereur.'

"The 1st battalion of the 3d grenadiers (right échelon) routed the Brunswick troops, seized the batteries of Lloyd and Cleeves which the cannoneers abandoned," occupied that sector of the summit, and "by a slight conversion proceeded toward the left of the brigade of C. Halkett. The 30th and 73d English regiments fell back in disorder. Friant, wounded, left the field of battle believing in the imminence of victory." But General Chassé, the commander of the Dutch-Belgian division in the English second line,

---

warts und vorwarts ruckten" ("Bericht der hannoverschen 5. Infanterie-Brigade, January 7, 1825," *P.-H.,* p. 98).

[341] Houssaye, *op. cit.,* pp. 394-398. Houssaye's account of the attack of the Guard seems to me reasonably accurate. I have, however, disagreed with some of his details, and this disagreement is indicated either by omission or by the following footnotes. The account has also been changed from the historical present to the past.

"had Van der Smissen's battery advance to the right of the 30th and 73d regiments, and subject the assailants to a flank fire. Then he deliberately brought up to the left the Belgian brigade of Ditmer, 3,000 strong, and launched it in a bayonet charge against the weak square, broke the square, disrupted it, crushed it under mass, and drove the debris to the foot of the slope.

"The battalion of 4th grenadiers (second echelon) during this time had engaged the right of the brigade of C. Halkett. Under the grape-shot of the two guns of Duchand and the musket fire of the grenadiers, the debris of the 33d and 69th English regiments gave way. General Halkett seized the flag of the 33d regiment, stopped while waving it, and by his example checked his men. 'Look at the general!' someone cried, 'he is between two fires; he cannot escape!' In fact, he fell severely wounded. But the English rallied, they stood firm. An old soldier biting his cartridge said: 'It is to whomever can stand the killing longest.' "

The 1st and 2d battalions of the 3d chasseurs (third echelon) almost reached the summit without encountering any infantry. Suddenly, just when they were within reach of the crest, there arose before them at fifty or sixty paces "a red wall. This was the 2,000 British Guards of Maitland, arranged four deep. They had been waiting, lying" for protection from the cannonade in the grain and in the ditch and behind the bank of a cart-road that ran along the ridge.[342] At the command to stand up,[343] they arose. They made ready, aimed, and fired. "Their first discharge mowed down 300 men, nearly half of the two battalions already decimated by artillery. General Michel fell dead. The

[342] Journal of Captain Powell (*W. L.*, p. 254).
[343] The famous order attributed to Wellington "Up Guards and at them," which Houssaye quotes, is probably apocryphal (letter of Major General Saltoun, Jan. 29, 1838, in *W. L.*, p. 248).

French stopped, their ranks broken, their march obstructed by corpses. Instead of hurling them instantly in a bayonet charge without bothering about the disorder in which they found themselves, the officers tried to form them into line to answer fire with fire. The confusion increased. The deployment took place badly and slowly. During" several[344] "minutes, the chasseurs remained on the spot under the musket fire of Maitland's brigade of guards and the grape-shot of the batteries of Bolton and Ramsay which took them in the flank." The English leaders,[345] perceiving the French confusion, finally ordered the brigade to charge. "The 2,000 English rushed head down on this handful of soldiers, broke up their formation," and drove the remnants of these two battalions of the 3d chasseurs part way down the slope. At the same time the 4th grenadiers in front of C. Halkett's right likewise retreated.

But in the course of the pursuit, the front of Maitland's guards passed the front of the last French square (battalion of 4th chasseurs) coming up on Maitland's right.[346] Fearful of being outflanked, Maitland's brigade in some confusion halted, turned, and regained the ridge. The remnants of the French battalions which had retreated with the fresh French square "followed it closely, ascending the hill under volleys of grape." But upon approaching the crest, these squares again received the fire of C. Halkett's and Maitland's brigade. At the same time the first brigade

[344] A minor point. But Houssaye says positively and precisely ten minutes. The source which he was using, however, indicates that the Guard remained for "about ten minutes" (letter of Lieutenant Sharpin, Dec. 6, 1834, in *W. L.*, p. 229). Other English officers usually indicate an even shorter period of time (letters of Major General Maitland, Nov. 24, 1834, of Ensign J. P. Dirom, Feb. 27, 1835, and Journal of Captain Powell, *W. L.*, pp. 244-245, 255, 258).

[345] Wellington or Lieutenant Colonel Saltoun or perhaps both, but the sources are somewhat contradictory (letters of Captain Powell, April 21, 1835, of Ensign Dirom, Feb. 27, 1835, in *W. L.*, pp. 255, 258).

[346] Letter of Major General Maitland, Nov. 24, 1834 (*W. L.*, p. 245).

of the English line curving down to Hougoumont, Adam's brigade, advanced and poured in a flank fire, while in the rear the Hanoverian brigade of W. Halkett "debouched from the hedges of Hougoumont and fired on the French from the rear." These little bands of Frenchmen, totaling now less than fifteen hundred and situated in the corner of the English line, were receiving from the front, from the flank, and from the rear the fire of perhaps four to six thousand men. It could not last. After five minutes of fire, upon the orders of its leaders, Adam's brigade charged. "Already much shaken by the formidable musketry and cannonade which they had passed through, chasseurs and grenadiers" broke in confusion and fled without order or discipline.[347] Adam's brigade continued its march diagonally across the slope toward the rear of La Haye Sainte.[348]

With the failure of the Guard everything crumbled. The advance and repulse of the Guard had occupied perhaps half-an-hour and it was now eight o'clock,[349] a few minutes before sunset.[350] While the attack of the Guard was in progress, the Prussian corps of Von Ziethen had engaged Durutte's division around Papelotte and Ter la Haye. At first the Frenchmen took the Prussians for Grouchy's troops, especially since in the confusion they had fired on English-Allied soldiers.[351] But the French were soon bitterly disillusioned, and the news that not Grouchy but the Prussians had appeared on the French right soon spread along the

[347] Letter of Captain Budgen, Dec., 1834 (*W. L.,* p. 300).

[348] Letter of Lieutenant Gawler, Dec. 22, 1834 (*W. L.,* p. 294); Kennedy, *op. cit.,* pp. 144-145.

[349] Letter of Lieutenant Gawler, Dec. 22, 1834 (*W. L.,* pp. 294-295).

[350] *Ibid.*

[351] Report of Colonel Van Zuylen von Neyevelt, Oct. 25, 1815 (Wommerson and De Bas, *op. cit.,* III, 343); "Bericht der hannoverschen 1. Neunpfunder-Batterie," "Bericht des 3. Bataillons des nassauischen 2. Regiments, December 28, 1835," "Erwiderung der Offiziere des nassauischen 2. regiments auf den Brief des Prinzen Bernhard von Sachsen-Weimar, July, 1815" (*P.-H.,* pp. 184, 212, 226).

entire French line.[352] In this situation, when the battalions of the Guard retreated and cries along the French line were heard: "All is lost! The Guard is repulsed," the other divisions—Donzelot's, Alix's, and Marcognet's—that were on or near the summit of the English plateau—hesitated and also withdrew down the slope.[353] Wellington, having perceived the confusion in the French lines and having ascertained that his left wing was in communication with Von Ziethen's corps, now ordered a general advance of the entire English line, and released his cavalry reserve.[354] At this order, the remnants of the English-Allied troops, Brunswickers, Hanoverians, Belgians, Dutch, English, and Scotch, left the plateau they had occupied so long, and descended the forward slope.[355] General Vivian's cavalry moved to the right, swung around Maitland's guards and galloped at full speed down the slope, followed to the right by Vandeleur's cavalry.[356] At the same time the Prussians who had recaptured Ter la Haye and Smohain, now in co-operation

[352] Ney to Fouché, June 26, 1815 (Cotton, *op. cit.*, p. 251).

[353] Kennedy, *op. cit.*, p. 148. Donzelot's and Marcognet's brigades were on the summit; Alix's division had probably been unable to dislodge Kempt's, Pack's, and Lambert's brigades (report of Major General Kempt to Wellington, June 19, 1815, in Wellington, *Supplementary Dispatches*, X, 537; "Bericht des 2. Leichten Bataillons der Deutschen Legion," in *P.-H.*, p. 109). But then perhaps Alix's brigade did barely gain the crest; see memorandum of Captain J. Leach, Nov. 22, 1840 (*W. L.*, p. 366).

[354] Ellesmere, *op. cit.*, p. 209.

[355] Letters of Major General Somerset, April 4, 1835, of Captain Rudyard, Jan. 6, 1835, Major General Maitland, Nov. 24, 1834, of Major Calvert, April 19, 1835, of Captain Campbell, March 15, 1838 (*W. L.*, pp. 42, 233, 245, 353, 377); Editor's notes (*ibid.*, pp. 320, 346); "Bericht der hannoverschen 4. Infanterie-Brigade, December 10, 1824," "Bericht der hannoverschen 5. Infanterie-Brigade, January 7, 1825," "Bericht des 8. Linien bataillons der Deutschen Legion" (*P.-H.*, pp. 89, 98, 126); report of Lieutenant Colonel C. van Delen, Nov. 11, 1815, of Colonel Detmers, of Major General Trip (Wommerson and De Bas, *op. cit.*, III, 369, 377-379, 407).

[356] Kennedy, *op. cit.*, p. 149; letters of Major General Vandeleur, of Lieutenant Colonel Sleigh, Nov. 11, 1841, of Major Barton, Nov. 3, 1834, of Major Luard, of Sir Hussey Vivian, June 23, 1815, and Jan. 18, 1830 (*W. L.*, pp. 106, 108, 116, 122, 149-150, 159); Editor's note (*ibid.*, p. 145); "Bericht des 1. Husaren-Regiments der Deutschen Legion" (*P.-H.*, p. 160).

with the English left wing, marched diagonally across the field toward Belle-Alliance.[357] Under the double, united pressure of the English and the Prussians, the French withdrew from La Haye Sainte and evacuated the wood of Hougoumont; some individuals turned and fled.[358]

The movement of withdrawal caught Napoleon by surprise, for during the attack of the Guard he had been informed of the initial success of the right-hand battalion and assured that victory was near. But he did everything possible to stem and organize the retreat. While the Guard was engaged with the English on the plateau, Napoleon had been in the valley arranging three additional battalions of the Guard to go to the support of their comrades.[359] When the Guard and then the French line retreated, Napoleon placed the three battalions in squares in the rear of La Haye Sainte and at right angles to the highway, the right-hand square resting on the road.[360] They were to serve as a center of rally. But squares, while impregnable to cavalry, presented a narrow front to an infantry line and to infantry fire. Napoleon, perceiving this as the English line advanced and also perhaps realizing that it would be easier to rally his troops farther back, ordered the three squares to fall back, and they began to retire up the long French slope.[361]

Wellington halted his advance infantry in the valley

[357] "Bericht über den Anteil der hannoverschen Truppen und der Deutschen Legion an der Schlacht bei Belle-Alliance," "Bericht der hannoverschen 4. Infanterie-Brigade by General-Major Best, December 10, 1824," "Tagebuch des nassauischen 1. Regiments," "Bericht des nassauischen 1. Regiments, June 21, 1815" (P.-H., pp. 56-57, 88, 199, 202); Kennedy, op. cit., p. 148; Mauduit, op. cit., II, 432-433; Müffling, op. cit., pp. 215-216; report of General Gneisenau in Wellington, Supplementary Dispatches, X, 505; report of General Von Ziethen (Wommerson and De Bas, op. cit., III, 501-502).

[358] Kennedy, op. cit., pp. 149-150; letters of Colonel Hepburn, Nov. 22, 1834, of Captain Leach, Nov. 22, 1840 (W. L., pp. 267, 367).

[359] Houssaye, op. cit., p. 402.

[360] Ibid., p. 402; Kennedy, op. cit., p. 145.

[361] Houssaye, op. cit., p. 404.

to reform his line.[362] While this was occurring,[363] Vivian's brigade of cavalry, consisting of about twelve hundred horsemen, reached the valley, passed the infantry, and at a very fast pace galloped up the French slope.[364] It passed to the right (west) of the three squares of the Imperial Guard, to the left of Reille's Second Corps,[365] and began to carry confusion to those French troops that were beside and in the rear of the three squares.[366] Napoleon launched at Vivian's brigade the only cavalry reserve which remained: the four hundred horsemen of his personal headquarters staff.[367] But, heavily outnumbered, they were submerged by the English charge.[368] After the charge Vivian's cavalry, now more loosely formed, sped on to saber the gunners and silence the French guns that were in the center along the French slope.[369]

Wellington, having reformed his infantry line, now began to ascend the long French slope;[370] the Prussians con-

[362] "Memorandum by Wellington upon the plan of the Battle of Waterloo, written in October, 1836" (Wellington, *Supplementary Dispatches*, X, 513); letters of Captain Powell, April 21, 1835, of Major General F. Adam, of Colonel Colborne (*W. L.*, pp. 255-256, 277, 285); "Bericht der hannoverschen 4. Infanterie-Brigade, December 10, 1824" (*P.-H.*, p. 89); Kennedy, *op. cit.*, p. 145.

[363] Or shortly before or shortly after. The evidence is very confusing. See letters of Sir Hussey Vivian, June 23, 1815, of Colonel Colborne, of Lieutenant Gawler, Dec. 22, 1834 (*W. L.*, pp. 149, 286, 294).

[364] Letters of Sir Hussey Vivian, June 23, 1815, of Major Taylor, Nov., 1829 (*W. L.*, pp. 149, 173-174); Editor's note (*ibid.*, p. 145).

[365] Letter of Sir Hussey Vivian, June 23, 1815 (*ibid.*, pp. 149-150); Napoleon, "Bataille de Mont-Saint-Jean," *Correspondance*, XXXI, 198.

[366] *Ibid.*

[367] Houssaye, *op. cit.*, p. 403.

[368] Vivian's cavalry probably also charged one or two other formations of cavalry (letters of Sir Hussey Vivian, June 23, 1815, of Major Taylor, Nov., 1829, of Lieutenant Colonel Murray, Jan., 1835, in *W. L.*, pp. 149-150, 174, 181-182).

[369] Letters of Sir Hussey Vivian, June 23, 1815, of Lieutenant Colonel Murray, Jan., 1835 (*W. L.*, pp. 149-150, 181-182).

[370] "Memorandum of Wellington upon the plan of the Battle of Waterloo written in October, 1836" (Wellington, *Supplementary Dispatches*, X, 513); Kennedy, *op. cit.*, p. 145; letter of Colonel Colborne (*W. L.*, p. 286).

tinued to move forward from Papelotte toward Belle-Alliance.[371] Under the pressure of that united advance, the troops on the French left, the Second Corps of Reille and the heavy cavalry of the Guard, which were protected on the flank by the Woods of Hougoumont and had been in the process of re-formation while the Guard was on the English plateau, retreated in good order.[372] But the infantry of the French center and right had ascended the English plateau with the Guard, had withdrawn with the Guard, and now in the valley had not had time to reform. Under the pressure of the double, frontal and lateral, Anglo-Prussian advance, French regiments of the center and right fell into disorder, officers lost contact with their men, and the tendency toward individual flight toward Belle-Alliance and down the Charleroi road gained momentum.[373] Suddenly, with Vivian's cavalry in their rear and in their midst, with Prussian cavalry squadrons breaking through on the right, with the Allied infantry advancing, the French center and right, except for Lobau's line by Planchenoit and a few squares of the Guard, in a spontaneous movement dissolved and fled.[374] Cannoneers abandoned their guns. Cavalrymen

[371] "Bericht der hannoverschen 4. Infanterie-Brigade, December 10, 1824" (*P.-H.,* p. 88).

[372] Charras, *op. cit.,* II, 79-80; Mauduit, *op. cit.,* II, 440; letter of Captain Barton, Nov. 3, 1834 (*W. L.,* p. 116).

[373] Houssaye, *op. cit.,* p. 399.

[374] In regard to this movement of dissolution, it is usually agreed that it was sudden, that it happened in a few minutes, and that it was a mass occurrence in which individuals, probably perceiving that the general situation was hopeless, thought they might as well save themselves. But sources and secondary accounts disagree on (1) the area involved in the dissolution and (2) the time of the dissolution. Concerning the first point the impression is usually given that the entire French Army dissolved and fled. But it is known that Reille's Second Corps and the heavy cavalry of the Guard at first retreated in good order; that east of the road the line of Lobau and the Sixth Corps, Duhesme and the Young Guard, and the two battalions of the Old Guard in Planchenoit continued to hold sometime longer; that the four squares of the Guard west of the highway, the two squares on the knoll of Rossomme, and the square in the Wood of Cantelet continued to fight until the end. When these troops who remained in order are deducted, what is left—the French center

threw away their iron cuirasses to lighten their flight. Many
infantrymen threw away their packs and ran. Others simply

and right, that is the divisions of d'Erlon's corps, the cannoneers of the one
hundred and fifty or more guns that were on the French slope, and the cavalry,
the cuirassiers of Kellermann and Milhaud, the lancers of Lefebvre-Desnoëttes,
who were probably in the left center. These, numbering perhaps thirty thousand
on entrance into battle but by now considerably reduced, had fought hard during
the day and were the first to flee.

As to the time of the dissolution, Napoleon in his bulletin of the battle placed
it after the repulse of the squares of the Guard on the English plateau, Ney
after the annihilation of the four squares of the Guard west of the highway.
The one is too early, the other too late. The dissolution occurred after the
English advance from the plateau. Mercer in his account wrote that the
English infantry had descended the forward slope, the English batteries had
ceased firing for fear of hitting their own soldiers, and the plain below was
covered with masses of troops both English and French. Mercer and a Captain
Walcot were both "looking out anxiously at the movement below and on the
opposite ridge when Walcot suddenly shouted out, 'Victory!—victory! they fly!—
they fly!' and sure enough we saw some of the masses dissolving, as it were, and
those composing them streaming away in confused crowds over the field,
whilst the already desultory fire of their artillery ceased altogether. . . . On
looking around I found we were left almost alone. Cavalry and infantry had
all moved forward" (Mercer, *Journal*, p. 180). The dissolution occurred after
the halt of the English line in the valley and just as it began to ascend the
long French slope. Wellington said in the memorandum written in 1836: "The
infantry was advanced in line. I halted them for a moment in the bottom,
that they might be in order to attack some battalions of the enemy still on the
heights. . . . The whole moved forward again in very few moments. The
enemy did not stand the attack. Some had fled before we halted. The whole
abandoned their position" (Wellington, *Supplementary Dispatches*, X, 513; the
memorandum also contains remarks concerning the activity of the cavalry, but
in that regard the reminiscences of Vivian and his men seem more accurate).
Wellington's memorandum is perhaps confirmed by Wellington's contemporary
dispatch in which he remarked: "I immediately advanced the whole line of
infantry, supported by the cavalry and artillery. The attack succeeded at every
point: the enemy was forced from his positions on the heights, and fled in the
utmost confusion" (Wellington to Earl Bathurst, June 19, 1815, in *ibid.*,
XII, 482). Wellington's remarks are confirmed by the letter of Sir John
Colborne: the 52d and 71st regiments of Adam's Brigade halted in the
valley, reformed, and the whole line charged up the hill; then they observed
"the enemy in great confusion, some firing, others throwing away their packs
and running to the rear" (letter of Colonel Colborne, in *W. L.*, p. 286). The
dissolution was simultaneous with or occurred shortly after Vivian's overthrow
of the four hundred horsemen of the French headquarters staff. This is apparent from the contemporary letter of Vivian to his wife (Sir Hussey Vivian to
Lady Vivian, June 23, 1815, in *W. L.*, p. 150). It is also indicated by the fact
that Vandeleur's cavalry brigade, which followed to the right of Vivian's
brigade some time, perhaps ten minutes, later, met no organized resistance to

quit and walked off the field. As the only avenue of escape, they all made for the Brussels-Charleroi highway. Infantry, cavalry, all arms mingled in utter confusion, without organization, a confused mass of thousands fled down the road and the adjoining fields.[375] In this manner, by the dissolution of the French center and right an immense gap—over a mile wide—was opened in the French position. The English continued to advance. The three squares of the Guard west of the highway with a fourth which Napoleon had placed halfway to Hougoumont over an hour before, surrounded and jostled by the enemy, retreated slowly, turned every fifty paces to reform and to use every favorable bit of ground, but were reduced, and by the time they reached the summit of Belle-Alliance were engulfed and disappeared.[376]

In the meanwhile, Lobau and the Sixth Corps, Duhesme and the Young Guard, and the two battalions of the Old Guard continued to maintain a dike to the east parallel to the road against the Prussian troops of Bülow and Pirch. Taking advantage of this circumstance, Napoleon now far-

---

speak of but only fleeing Frenchmen. That is, when Vandeleur's brigade reached the French slope, the dissolution and flight were already under way (letters of Captain Barton, Lieutenant Luard, Sir Hussey Vivian, Jan. 18, 1830, in *ibid.*, pp. 116, 122, 159; Hay, *op. cit.*, p. 189). Napoleon attributed the disorder to Vivian's brigade (Gourgaud, *Sainte-Hélène: Journal inédit,* French ed., I, 196-197).

[375] For a description of the dissolution: Mercer, *Journal*, p. 180; Ellesmere, *op. cit.*, p. 101; Stanhope, *op. cit.*, p. 246; letters of Lieutenant Colonel Murray, Jan., 1835, of Lieutenant Luard, of Captain Mercer, Nov. 26, 1834 (*W. L.*, pp. 182, 189, 221); Hay, *op. cit.*, p. 189; "Memorandum upon the plan of the Battle of Waterloo written in October, 1836" (Wellington, *Supplementary Dispatches,* X, 513); Wellington to Earl Bathurst, June 19, 1815 (*ibid.*, XII, 482); Ney to Fouché, June 26, 1815 (Cotton, *op. cit.*, p. 252); report of Colonel Van Zuylen von Neyvelt, Oct. 25, 1815 (Wommerson and De Bas, *op. cit.*, III, 349); "Bericht der hannoverschen 4. Infanterie-Brigade, December 10, 1824" (*P.-H.*, p. 89); "Témoin oculaire" bound with the *Near Observer*, pp. 120-121; Napoleon, "Bataille de Mont-Saint-Jean," *Correspondance*, XXXI, 198-199.

[376] Ney to Fouché, June 26, 1815 (Cotton, *op. cit.*, p. 252); Mauduit, *op. cit.*, II, 444.

ther back on the road on the knoll of Rossomme again tried
to stem the torrent of retreat. The two remaining battalions
of the Guard which he had left on the knoll, he stationed
in squares, one on each side of the road to halt the fugitives
and delay the English advance. He placed himself on horseback within one of the squares. But in the obscurity of
twilight and then in darkness nothing could be accomplished.[377] The fugitives went on by,[378] and as the English began to arrive, the fugitives and Vivian's cavalry
swirled and eddied around the two squares.[379] Under the
combined pressure of Prussians from the front and Prussians
from the side, furthermore, the left-hand end and center
of Lobau's line crumbled to swell the torrent.[380] To the
east only Planchenoit remained as an island of defense.
But Bülow's corps about nine o'clock splintered the French
defense of that village, rushed through to the road near the
position of the squares, and tumultuously blended in with
the fugitives, and the English-Allied and other Prussian
pursuers.[381] To the west of the highway, at about the same
time, the English overtook Reille's Second Corps and under
pressure it, too, disbanded.[382] It was now utterly dark. In
the confusion and tumult, the two squares of the Guard on
the road maintained the integrity of their formation and
the safety of Napoleon against fugitives who wished to
enter the squares for protection, against enemy pursuers
who tried to break them open.[383] On Napoleon's order the
squares retired slowly and disputed every foot of ground;[384]
but the second attempt at rally had failed. Napoleon, in
fact, had no compact reserve of any size to act as a rear

[377] Napoleon, "Bataille de Mont-Saint-Jean," *Correspondance*, XXXI, 199;
letter of Lieutenant Gawler, Dec. 22, 1834 (*W. L.*, p. 295).

[378] Charras, *op. cit.*, II, 81-82.

[379] Letter of Major Taylor, Nov., 1829 (*W. L.*, p. 175).

[380] Charras, *op. cit.*, p. 81.

[381] "Rapport des General Leutnant von Bülow, July 10, 1815" (Wommerson and De Bas, *op. cit.*, III, 536).   [382] Charras, *op. cit.*, p. 83.

[383] Houssaye, *op. cit.*, p. 410.   [384] *Ibid.*

guard. He and Ney had thrown nearly everything into the battle, and at the hour of disintegration, the possible reserves, the unused battalions of the Guard, were dispersed over the field. Partly as a consequence, what had been one of the bravest armies in the world was now just a crowd of perhaps fifty thousand trudging, sometimes running, in the dark down a highway and the adjacent fields. Napoleon marched with the two squares to the farm of Caillou.[385] Then, perceiving that the situation on the battlefield was beyond immediate remedy, he galloped off with his staff to attempt to organize a third stand farther back at Genappe, and then a fourth at Quatre Bras.[386] But these attempts also failed, and he thereupon set out for Charleroi,[387] to be carried by a flood of events to his second abdication and to St. Helena.

In the meantime, Blücher, who broke through with Bülow's corps, met Wellington behind Belle-Alliance; they were both on horseback: Blücher embraced and kissed the English leader, "exclaiming *Mein lieber Kamerad* and then *quelle affaire!*" which, as Wellington noted later, was pretty much all Blücher knew of French.[388] Wellington, discerning that the French Army was in full rout, now committed further pursuit to the fresher Prussians and halted his own weary English-Allied division.[389] With "trumpet blasts, drum rolls, hurrahs, and victory songs,"[390] the Prussians, especially the Prussian cavalry, joyously and remorselessly pressed the pursuit throughout the night.[391] Back on the English plateau, the few infantrymen and artillerymen who had not participated in the advance could hear the shouts,

[385] *Ibid.*, p. 411; Gourgaud, *Sainte-Hélène: Journal inédit* (French ed.), I, 503.

[386] Houssaye, *op. cit.*, p. 432.　　[387] *Ibid.*, p. 428.

[388] Stanhope, *op. cit.*, p. 245.　　[389] Kennedy, *op. cit.*, p. 150.

[390] "Bericht von General Major von Pirch" (Wommerson and De Bas, *op. cit.*, III, 508-510).

[391] Kennedy, *op. cit.*, p. 150; Blücher, *op. cit.*, p. 150; report of General Gneisenau (Wellington, *Supplementary Dispatches*, X, 505-506).

the clamor, the occasional fire of the Prussians pursuing, could hear the clamor diminish as it receded, and finally die away,[392] leaving the countryside silent, save for the groans of the wounded on the battlefield.

After the battle, there was the usual horror. In Mercer's battery, one third of his men were disabled, and 140 of his 200 fine horses lay dead, dying, or severely wounded. He was unable therefore, to share in the general advance, and that night he slept on the ridge close to his guns.[393] The next morning he arose at dawn.[394] The forward slope of the English position was strewn, almost carpeted with dead or dying who lay in and on the downtrodden grain.[395] Along and in front of the English right wing, where the struggle had been thickest, the observer was struck by the "actual masses of dead men and horses heaped together" for several hundred yards.[396] Among these dead bodies were "many wounded, so disabled as not to have the power to extricate themselves."[397] Mercer "had not been up many minutes when one of his sergeants came to ask if they might bury Driver Crammond. 'And why particularly Driver Crammond.' 'Because he looks frightful, sir; many of us have not had a wink of sleep for him.'" Mercer "walked to the spot where he lay and certainly a more hideous sight" could not "be imagined. A cannon shot had carried away the whole head except barely the visage, which

[392] Letter of Captain Taylor, Nov., 1829 (*W. L.*, p. 175); "Bericht des 3. Husaren-Regiments der Deutschen Legion" (*P.-H.*, p. 172). Inference from material contained in these two letters.

[393] Mercer, *Journal*, pp. 181, 185; letter of Captain Mercer, Nov. 26, 1834 (*W. L.*, p. 221).

[394] Mercer, *Journal*, p. 185.

[395] Letter of Captain Mercer, Nov. 26, 1834 (*W. L.*, p. 221); also Simpson, *op. cit.*, pp. 48, 104; letter of Major Barton (*W. L.* p. 116); Eaton, *op. cit.*, pp. 134, 137.

[396] The observer in this case was Hay, *op. cit.*, p. 200; also p. 189; likewise Mercer, *Journal*, p. 175; letter of Captain Mercer, Nov. 26, 1834 (*W. L.*, p. 219).

[397] Hay, *op. cit.*, p. 200.

still remained attached to the torn and bloody neck. The men said they had been prevented from sleeping by seeing his eyes fixed on them all night; and thus this one object had superseded all the other horrors by which they were surrounded. He was of course immediately buried."[398] Over by Hougoumont, which Mercer later visited, the trees were cut and splintered by cannon ball and shot, and the woods were choked with French dead. The farm buildings themselves were a shattered or a smoking ruin, the ashes or in some cases the blackened, swollen remains of those soldiers who had perished in the fire lay scattered about.[399] The farmhouses of La Haye Sainte, Ter la Haye, and Papelotte had likewise, though less extensively, suffered, and the villages of Smohain and Planchenoit were half-consumed, empty of their peasant inhabitants.[400] The English field hospital was in a large barn at Mont-Saint-Jean, and there the customary scenes of mutilation and suffering occurred.[401] Despite the unremitting toil of the surgeons, many wounded remained on the field until Wednesday, the third day after the battle, and suffered agonies of thirst and pain,[402] and Prussian patrols went around "shooting their own and French wounded soldiers who were beyond recovery" to put them out of misery.[403]

Among the participants and later among the historians of the Allied forces there was little dispute concerning the general nature of the campaign and the battle, although there was a more or less acrimonious discussion in regard to the

[398] Mercer, *op. cit.*, p. 185.

[399] *Ibid.*, p. 190; Stevenson, *op. cit.*, pp. 284-285; Simpson, *op. cit.*, pp. 102-105; Eaton, *op. cit.*, pp. 137-139.

[400] "Bericht des 3. Bataillons des nassauischen 2. Regiments, December 28, 1835," "Brief des Kompagnie-Chirurgen Wilhelm Schütte an seine Eltern über die Tätigkeit der braunschweigischen Truppen bei Quartre-Bras und Belle-Alliance, July 2, 1815" (*P.-H.*, pp. 212, 236); Simpson, *op. cit.*, pp. 85-87; Stevenson, *op. cit.*, p. 279; letter of Major Luard (*W. L.*, p. 122).

[401] Stevenson, *op. cit.*, p. 275.

[402] *Ibid.*, pp. 89-90; Hay, *op. cit.*, pp. 211-212.

[403] Hay, *op. cit.*, p. 211.

respective credit due the English and Prussian armies. Among the French participants, however, there was controversy and recrimination, partly because they had lost, partly because in the confusion of rout and change of government no one insisted on reports from the marshals and subordinate generals. To many actors on the French side who were unaware of the complex of maneuvers and errors of the campaign, the result seemed incomprehensible or to be explained by some superficial cause—treason and the like. Napoleon himself, who had lived that day in a world of sanguine unreality, did not at first understand what had occasioned the defeat. In the ache and disappointment of the first few days after the battle apparently the occurrence which stood out in Napoleon's mind was the major blunder of the afternoon—Ney's premature and unskilled employment of cavalry. When on arriving in Paris and in descending from his carriage he was greeted by a faithful councillor, the Duke of Vicence, Napoleon's first words were: "Ney behaved like a madman, he made me massacre all my cavalry!"[404] and this mistake was also underlined in the bulletin which Napoleon dictated concerning the campaign.[405] During the weeks following his abdication, however, when he was still in France under the surveillance of the French government, Napoleon gradually recovered that objectivity with which he was able to regard himself and his past actions. Remembering perhaps his dilatory, self-confident drifting into action on the morning of June 18, his physical inactivity in the early afternoon when he probably should have supervised personally the attack on the English,[406] he remarked to his warden, General Beker: "This battle was lost because to begin with me, no one did his duty."[407]

[404] Pontécoulant, *op. cit.*, p. 471.
[405] "Bulletin de l'armée, June 20, 1815," No. 22061, in *Correspondance*, XXVIII, 296-297.
[406] Mauduit, *op. cit.*, II, 360-361.   [407] Beker, *op. cit.*, p. 203.

At St. Helena, as he reflected on the campaign, the more detailed errors and might-have-beens became apparent. To his secretary, General Gourgaud, he commented on different occasions: "The men of 1815 were not the same as those of 1792. The Generals had become timid. . . .[408] I needed some one to command the guard. If I had had Bessières, or Lannes, in command of the guard, I would never have been defeated. . . .[409] It was a great mistake to have employed Ney. He had a distracted head. His past conduct deprived him of all energy. Carnot did not even wish me to make him peer. I would have acted wisely. . . .[410] On leaving Quatre-Bras, I should have left only Pajol, with the division of the 6th corps, in pursuit of Blücher, and taken all with me. . . .[411] I should have intrusted to Suchet the command I gave to Grouchy. . . . Suchet has more fire and knows better my manner of making war. . . .[412] I could not see the battle well, I wished to make, as at Montmirail, a perpendicular attack and conduct it myself, but the arrival of Bülow forced me to remain in a central position; Ney could not understand this attack. . . .[413] On seeing the great superiority of the Prussians, I should perhaps have retreated sooner. I would have lost then fifty or sixty cannon. My plan had succeeded: I had surprised the Prussians and the English, but what can you expect? a great battle is always a grave affair."[414] Other errors might have been listed: his imagination that he had totally routed the Prussians at Ligny, his careless handling of his relations with Grouchy, his easy assumption as to the weakness of the English line.

It is well to recall, however, that at Waterloo Napoleon did not simply make mistakes; he also exhibited some of

[408] Gourgaud, *The St. Helena Journal* (English ed.), p. 63.
[409] *Ibid.*
[410] Gourgaud, *Sainte-Hélène: Journal inédit* (French ed.), I, 520.
[411] *Ibid.*, I, 197.   [412] *Ibid.*, I, 502.
[413] *Ibid.*, I, 544.   [414] *Ibid.*, I, 504.

those qualities which had once made him one of the great commanders—easy mastery of the technical knowledge of his profession, cool and impassible courage, tenacity, an ability to inspire the utmost from the common soldier. In the opening of the campaign and in the plan of battle itself, he displayed a high level of intelligence and brilliance of conception. Save for the errors in the selection of his subordinates, all his mistakes were due to overconfidence, to the old-time tendency to take a too sanguine view of the situation, a tendency which had become exaggerated, and to the infirmities of the later years, inflexibility and fatigue. To the impartial observer, it is obvious of course that the battle was one of those affairs: if somebody had done something, if someone else hadn't done something, various people and various things, the outcome would have been different. But once the battle was over, the result was irretrievable, and a man, even a Napoleon, is sometimes caught in the stream of his activity and the nature of his character.

AFTERWORD ON METHOD

IN WRITING the Friedland chapter I wanted simply to see. I wished to see how close one could get to past reality; that is, how someone walked or talked, or thought and wrote, or rode. Then I desired to present the reality as I saw it in simple and nontechnical language that would enable the reader to see what I saw and would not screen him from what had gone on.

This undertaking at first did not seem difficult. Writing the true story of a Napoleonic battle seemed initially the simplest of historical problems. After all, as sources we usually have from both sides the communiqués of both commanders, the reports of the subordinate generals, the memoirs of subordinate officers, the diaries of common soldiers, and the notes of an observer. Since they testify about the same series of events, we often have at least two independent eyewitnesses testifying to the factuality of the same occurrences.

However, it turned out that there were obstacles to full unflawed vision. No one saw the battle as a totality. Each participant perceived only the events of his small circle. In the days before smokeless gunpowder that circle was small indeed. Then, too, eyewitnesses differed in the quality of their perceptions and understanding. The Belgian tavernkeeper who at Waterloo was at the side of Napoleon all day was admirably suited to observe the coming and going of aides-de-camp, the flow of command decisions. But he understood and hence really perceived and reported only simple concrete incidents: when Napoleon took snuff, when he turned pale. Even sophisticated eyewitnesses omitted much that a historian would like to know: what to the observer seemed inconsequential—what the soldiers ate for breakfast, for example—or routine—what tactical formation the French used in a given battlefield maneuver. In addition there were national styles perhaps of perception and certainly of presentation that inhibited full communication. To be sure, British soldiers in their personal accounts usually told their stories in rich, vivid, pictorial detail; it is a historian's great good fortune that a British observer, Robert Wilson, was present at the battle of Friedland. But educated French officers, whatever their perceptions, tended to write an abstract, generalized narrative that like an asphalt highway killed vivid, sensational life. Again, it is the historian's good luck that the French officer who had an eye for pictorial detail, General Lejeune (interestingly enough, a painter), was at Aspern-Essling; but he was an exception.

Then, another hindrance to vision, rare is the eyewitness who in his account placed himself in an unfavorable light. Deliberate falsification of the communiqué by the overall commander was standard operating procedure. Conscious or unconscious slanting of field reports of generals was not unknown. Memoirs were frequently acts of self-exculpation, and in any case reminiscence of distant events was often vague and inaccurate. Nor in the 1930s did my personal experience enable me always to appreciate what eyewitnesses were saying: I had not yet served in an army, and I have never been in a battle. Moreover, in my search for past reality the professional military historians were not then of much help, although doubtless I could have learned more from them than I did. They wrote a bland, impersonal, generalized narrative—the VI Corps did that, the V Corps did this, the enemy responded thus—that concealed more than it revealed and screened the reader from whatever was going on back there. And, apparently by a gentleman's agreement, they totally excluded the horror of the battlefield and the hospital.

So in rebellion against conventional, dehumanized military history, I ventured on my own. To establish factual accuracy, I applied the methods of historical criticism in which

I had been schooled. For each battle I broke up the sentences of each primary source into their component declarations. The hypothetical sentence *Grouchy hurried across the plain from Sortlack to Posthenen* contains at least four declarations: Grouchy hurried; across the plain; from Sortlack; to Posthenen. The declarations were then matched and dovetailed. History is a flowing jigsaw puzzle in which most of the pieces, the traces of the events, have been lost. To find one trace is a triumph, but often of doubtful certainty. To find two traces that concur heightens the certainty without extending our knowledge. To find two pieces that dovetail creates a third piece, often a relationship, that is more reliable than the first two pieces and enhances their reliability. Dovetailing proved especially useful in seeking to reconstruct the French side of Waterloo, since in the confusion of rout and the change of government the French officers did not submit reports that could be matched with the British and Prussian accounts. Matching and dovetailing led to estimates of the general reliability of each source. Thus the memoirs of Marbot, usually decried, proved to have high reliability for Friedland, where in items that can be checked, he made only one mistake, and for Waterloo, where his account dovetailed with what is known from other sources. The memoirs of Savary, often cited, proved singularly inaccurate. I also sought material not hitherto brought to light, and found it, for example, in the memoir-casebook of the Grand Army's great surgeon, Baron Larrey.

I needed then an artistic form that mirrored the reality I thought I saw. Since a battle is a flowing totality, an ongoing narrative with a minimum of analysis best symbolizes that flow. Suspense in the narrative was built on human expectation, since both expectation and suspense were in the battle itself. Where the sources permitted, the story moved by scenes. The narrative scenes ideally were communicated by words that appealed to the five senses of sight, hearing, touch, taste, and smell. Like the narrative scenes in the Gospels, "A woman at the well," for example, which for centuries in changing cultures evoked an image in the reader, the sentences in the battle scenes were whenever possible concrete but not too specific and intended to open vistas to the reader's imagination. An essay on the philosophy of style for a certain type of military history could be elaborated from this paragraph.

The volume, an exploratory personal experiment written from 1936 to 1942, can be viewed as a pioneer work in a broad movement of revolt against conventional military history. The rebellion started first in literature, with the novels of Stendahl (*The Charterhouse of Parma*), Victor Hugo (*Les Misérables*), Leo Tolstoy (*War and Peace*), Stephen Crane (*The Red Badge of Courage*), James Boyd (*Marching On*), and the fiction of World War I. The rebellion entered large-scale military history in the multivolume official history of the American Army during World War II. A philosophical reflection upon aspects of that history appeared in S. L. A. Marshall's *Men against Fire* (1947). In Napoleonic historiography the concurrent revolt and search for battlefield reality has been manifested in such works as Jac Weller, *Wellington at Waterloo* (New York: Crowell, 1967), David Howarth, *Waterloo: Day of Battle* (New York: Atheneum, 1968), John Keegan, *The Face of Battle* (New York: Viking, 1976), Gunther E. Rothenberg, *The Art of Warfare in the Age of Napoleon* (Bloomington, Ind.: Indiana University Press, 1978), and the relevant chapters of Steven Ross, *From Flintlock to Rifle: Infantry Tactics, 1740–1866* (Cranbury, N.J.: Associated University Presses, 1979).

The history of Napoleonic warfare has had its own history. It can be rapidly traced by indicating some of those major narrative accounts that in their day commanded the attention of successive generations of English and American readers. The first of these was the twenty-volume *History of the Consulate and Empire* written by the French politician Adolphe Thiers and published from 1845 to 1862. The great virtue of Thiers's story is that it retains the excitement of the original historical situation. Born in 1797 in Marseilles, Thiers grew up in the excitement of the Napoleonic epic. After he moved to Paris in 1821 he knew and interviewed many eye-witnesses of Napoleonic battles, and read their memoirs. The result was a partisan narrative of tremendous gusto. The French army is "our army," and Napoleon is the hero of events of epic proportions. Although Thiers recognized the decline of Napoleon's powers after 1807, he retained for him an unshakable admiration. However, the inexactitudes of memoirs, especially those emanating from St. Helena, and his own hero worship frequently led Thiers astray. His accounts of Friedland and Aspern-Essling are not too far off, but that of Waterloo, while fun to read, is to be distrusted at every page.

From Thiers the movement of Napoleonic military history writing was toward the expansion of documentation and greater objectivity. From 1858 to 1903 Napoleon's major orders and military decisions were published in editions of his general correspondence.[1] These were supplemented by Ar-

---

[1] Napoléon I, *Correspondance de Napoléon*, 28 vols. (Paris: Imprimerie impériale, 1858–1869); L. Lecestre, *Lettres inédites de Napoléon Ier (an VIII–1815)*, 2 vols. (Paris: Plon, Nourrit, 1897); L. Brotonne, *Lettres inédites de Napoléon Ier*

thur Chuquet's *Ordres et apostilles de Napoléon, 1799–1815,* 4 vols. (Paris: H. Champion, 1911–1912) and Ernest Picard and Louis Tuetey, *Correspondance inédite de Napoléon conservée aux Archives de la Guerre,* 5 vols. (Paris: Charles-Lavauzelle, 1912–1925). In 1882 the historical section of the French general staff began the massive publication of the more detailed orders of Napoleon's chief of staff Berthier and the corps commanders for the Egyptian, Marengo, Hohenlinden, Austerlitz, Jena, and Polish campaigns and for the Austrian war of 1809.[2] The pattern and high standard of these volumes were set by Paul-Jean Foucart in his publications on the first stages of the campaigns of 1806 and 1807 up to Friedland and continued by Charles Gaspard Saski in his three volumes on the campaign in 1809 through Aspern-Essling. Although the detailed dispatches are connected with only a minimum of narrative explanation, they enable the historian to follow the day-by-day concerns and anxieties of Napoleon's generals. Soon the historical sections of the German and Austro-Hungarian general staffs and their associates followed suit and began to sponsor substantial reports of Napoleon's campaigns, written in part from the manuscript dispatches in their war ministry archives. Thus we have Oscar von Lettow-Vorbeck's four-volume *Der Krieg von 1806 und 1807* (Berlin: Mittler, 1891–1896) and M. von Hoen, Hugo Kerchnawe, and Alois Veltze's four-volume *Krieg 1809* (Vienna: Seidel, 1907–1910). The 1880s and 1890s and the first fourteen years of the twentieth century also saw a surge of publication of the mem-

---

(Paris: Champion, 1898); idem, *Dernières lettres inédites de Napoléon Ier,* 2 vols. (Paris: H. Champion, 1903).

[2] Paul-Jean Foucart, *Campagne de Pologne,* 2 vols. (Paris: Berger-Levrault, 1882), *Iéna* (Paris: Berger-Levrault, 1887), and *Prenzlow-Lübeck* (Paris: Berger-Levrault, 1890); Clément Étienne de La Jonquière, *L'expédition d'Égypte,* 5 vols. (Paris: Charles-Lavauzelle, 1889–1907); Jean de Cugnac, *La campagne de l'armée de réserve en 1800,* 2 vols. (Paris: R. Chapelot, 1900–1901); Paul Azan and Ernest Picard, *La campagne de 1800 en Allemagne,* 3 vols. (Paris: E. Chapelot, 1907); Paul-Claude Alombert and Jean Colin, *La campagne de 1805 en Allemagne,* 6 vols. in 7 (Paris: C. Chapelot, 1902–1908); Charles Gaspard Saski, *Campagne de 1809 en Allemagne et en Autriche,* 3 vols. (Paris: Berger-Levrault, 1899–1902).

oirs of Napoleon's warriors, including those of the common soldier and officers of the lower ranks.[3] With this extended documentation it was possible to write more accurate accounts of the movements of army corps and divisions at Friedland (Lettow-Vorbeck), Aspern-Essling (Saski, Von Hoen, Kerchnawe, and Veltzke), and Waterloo (Henry Houssaye).[4] It was also possible for Theodore Dodge, a specialist in the history of the art of warfare, to prepare his *Napoleon* (New York: Houghton Mifflin, 1904–1907), a four-volume overall narrative of the campaigns of the French Revolution and Napoleon. Although Dodge's comments on Napoleon's generalship were commonplace, his story of Napoleon's actions and of the movements of army corps and divisions was well researched, intelligent, and basically correct. It is still interesting to read, if only to discover what Dodge has to say about a subject.

From about 1900 until today military historians of the Napoleonic period, while continuing to set the military record straight in innumerable specialized studies and biographies, have undertaken three major tasks: to understand Napoleon's personal style of making war, to integrate his military organization and procedures with the military developments of the eighteenth century and the French Revolution, and to discover and incorporate the experience of the common soldier. The controversy over his personal style of warfare turns on whether he was a schematic thinker who applied a few simple principles of operation to every campaign and battle or

[3] If we tabulate by decades 255 military memoirs listed in Jean Tulard's *Bibliographie critique des mémoires sur le Consulat et l'Empire* (Geneva: Droz, 1971) under the headings of "Allemagne (Campagnes de 1805, 1806, 1809, 1813)," "Espagne (Guerre)," "France (Campagne de)," "Friedland," "Russie (Campagne de)," and "Waterloo," they break down by date of first publication as follows: 1810–1819 (13), 1820–1829 (17), 1830–1839 (14), 1840–1849 (11), 1850–1859 (14), 1860–1869 (5), 1870–1879 (6), 1880–1889 (15), 1890–1899 (45), 1900–1909 (52), 1910–1919 (25, all from 1910 to 1913), 1920–1929 (9), 1930–1939 (9), 1940–1949 (0), 1950–1959 (10), 1960–1969 (9), 1970–1971 (1).

[4] Henry Houssaye, *Waterloo* (Paris: Perrin, 1893). It is best to use the later editions of this work, published after Houssaye had revised his account in response to the criticisms of A. Grouard of 1904 and 1907.

whether he was an imaginative improviser to whom each campaign and battle was a unique experience, problem, and opportunity. To the debate, which is as old as Baron Antoine Henri Jomini, a member of Marshal Ney's staff, General Hubert Camon, Basil H. Liddell Hart, and David Chandler have more recently contributed.[5] On the integration of Napoleon's procedures with the evolution of French military doctrine and practice, a succession of able monographs continue to enlighten us. To mention only a very few, they include Jean A. Colin, *L'éducation militaire de Napoléon* (Paris: R. Chapelot, 1901), Spenser Wilkinson, *The French Army before Napoleon* (Oxford: Clarendon Press, 1915) and *The Rise of General Bonaparte* (Oxford: Clarendon Press, 1930), Robert S. Quimby, *The Background of Napoleonic Warfare* (New York: Columbia University Press, 1957), and Steven Ross, *From Flintlock to Rifle: Infantry Tactics, 1740–1866.* Meanwhile, Harold Parker, Jac Weller, David Howarth, Jack Keegan, and Gunther Rothenberg, already mentioned in the afterword, were pioneering in portraying the experience of the common soldier. Profiting from these decades of source publication and research effort David Chandler prepared his magisterial *The Campaigns of Napoleon: The Mind and Method of History's Greatest Soldier* (New York: Macmillan, 1966). Although he neglects the experience of the common soldier as not germane to his subject, his book still stands as the best overall synthesis of our knowledge of the Napoleonic military epic. It is the book to own and to read.

To catch this movement of historical thought the student might well start by reading successive versions of the most

[5] Hubert Camon, *La bataille napoléonienne* (Paris: R. Chapelot, 1899); *La Guerre napoléonienne,* 5 vols. (Paris: R. Chapelot, 1907–1911); *Génie et métier chez Napoléon* (Paris: Berger-Levrault, 1930); *Quand et comment Napoléon a conçu son système de manoeuvre* (Paris: Berger-Levrault, 1931); *Quand et comment Napoléon a conçu son système de bataille* (Paris: Berger-Levrault, 1935). Basil H. Liddell Hart, *The Ghost of Napoleon* (New Haven, Conn.: Yale University Press, 1935); *The Strategy of Indirect Approach* (London: Faber and Faber, 1941). David Chandler, "Napoleon's Battle System," *History Today* 15 (1965), 75–86.

controversial battle, Waterloo. He might begin with the story in the last volume of Adolphe Thiers, *History of the Consulate and the Empire of France under Napoleon* (many editions), and vitriolic anti-Thiers, the fourth or later editions of Jean Baptiste Adolphe Charras, *Waterloo*, 4th ed. (Brussels: Lacroix, Verboeckhoeven, 1863). The reader will then be prepared to assess the narratives of Theodore A. Dodge, *Napoleon*, vol. 4, and the post-1907 editions of Henry Houssaye, *Waterloo*, as well as the more recent versions of Jac Weller, *Wellington at Waterloo*, David Howarth, *Waterloo: Day of Battle*, John Keegan, *The Face of Battle*, Henry Lachouque and Juan Carmigniani, *Waterloo* (New York: Hippocrene, 1978), and David Chandler: *The Hundred Days* (London: Osprey Publishing, 1980). The bibliography in Chandler's book will lead the reader still further into the intricacies of the subject.

Or, more systematically, the student might well start with three general works: Theodore Ropp, *War in the Modern World* (Durham, N.C.: Duke University Press, 1959), David Chandler, *The Campaigns of Napoleon*, and Gunther E. Rothenberg, *The Art of Warfare in the Age of Napoleon*. He might then turn to those authors who have dealt with the style of Napoleon's generalship, Hubert Camon, Basil H. Liddell Hart, and Chandler, whose works are cited in note 5 of this brief bibliographic essay. The reader will then be ready for the never-ending adventure of placing Napoleon within the context of his time. Here the books of Jean Colin, Spenser Wilkinson, Robert Quimby, and Steven Ross, already mentioned, are invaluable. These might be supplemented by outstanding biographies of Napoleon's marshals and opponents, such as John G. Gallaher's *Iron Marshal: A Biography of Louis N. Davout* (Carbondale: Southern Illinois University Press, 1976), S. J. Watson's *By Command of the Emperor: A Life of Marshal Berthier* (London: The Bodley Head, 1957), and Gunther E. Rothenberg's *Napoleon's Great Adversaries:*

The Archduke Charles and the Austrian Army, 1792–1814
(Bloomington, Ind.: Indiana University Press, 1982). As the
student plunges into the sources, Jean Tulard's *Bibliographie
critique des mémoires sur le Consulat de l'Empire* will guide
him as he listens to the siren voices of the authors of memoirs.

The best campaign and battle maps as well as an excellent
accompanying text are in V. J. Esposito and J. R. Elting, *A
Military History and Atlas of the Napoleonic Wars* (New
York: Praeger, 1964). It should be beside the student in all
his reading.

INDEX

Adam, Sir Frederick, 189, 196, 201 n.

Aderklaa, **53**

Albuera, battle of (1811), 107

Alexander the Great, 14

Alexander I, Emperor of Russia, mentioned, 5 n., 24, 31; allies with Napoleon in Peace of Tilsit, 23; at war against Napoleon, 99; is lukewarm ally, 31

Alix, Jacques Alexandre François Comte de Freudenthal, 156 f., 159 n., 192, 197, 197 n.

Alle River, mentioned, 3, 5 n., 10, 13; Russians forced to retreat across in battle of Friedland, 21 f.

Andréossy, Antoine François, Comte, 27

Angeli, Moriz edler von, 48 n., 54 n.

Angers, French military school at, 105

Anglesea, Henry William Paget, 1st Marquis of, 158, 158 n., 160, 168

Anglo-Allied Army (in battle of Waterloo), 114 n., 152 n., 189, 197

Arbuthnot, Sir Robert, 165 n.

Army of Italy (French), 7, 75

Army of the North (French), 7, 113

Aspern (town), mentioned, 55, 57-62, 64, 66 f., 71, 78; occupied by French forces, 57

Aspern-Essling, battle of (1809), mentioned, 24, 32 n., 48 n., 88, 98, 150; break in pontoon prevents French reinforcement, 62; condition of wounded after, 83 f.; estimate of, 83; field hospitals during, 72; fighting ceases, 78; losses on both sides, 82 f., 82 n.;

Austrian Army in: attacks French, 57 f.; attacks French center, 68 f.; bombards French line, 60, 64 f., 67 f., 71, 76, 96; disposition of, prior to battle, 52 f.; does not attack the Lobau, 82; gains ground in Aspern, 66; position of at end

of first day, 59; prepares for battle, 52-55; reaches Danube before French cross it, 48; reports French crossing of Danube, 40 n., 41 n.; scouts watch movement of French, 49; sharpshooters harass retreating French, 82; size of, 48 n.; skirmishes with French, 42, 52; storms Essling, 66; surrounds small French force, 35; suspends attack, 71;

French Army in: almost breaks Austrian line, 61; cavalry skirmishes with Austrians, 55; crosses Danube River, 40-54; delays in crossing Danube, 40-46; disposition of army, prior to battle, 31; forced to evacuate Essling, 70; Napoleon gives final orders for retreat of, 79; Napoleon prepares to take initiative, 59 f.; Napoleon supervises crossing of Danube, 42; Napoleon unaware of presence of Austrian Army, 56; position of, at end of first day, 58; problem of supplies, 33; retakes Aspern, 60; scarcity of food for wounded, 84; scarcity of munitions and supplies, 64-66, 68; size of French forces, 32, 32 n.; supplies distributed prior to battle, 39 n., 45; withdraws to Aspern-Essling line, 62; withdraws to the Lobau, 73, 81 f., 81 n.

See also Napoleon in battle of Aspern-Essling; Charles, Archduke of Austria, in battle of Aspern-Essling

Aspern-Essling line, 58, 60

Auerstädt, battle of (1806), 8

Auger, Pierre, 97

Augsburg, 26

Austerlitz, battle of (1805), 8, 112, 117

Austria, mentioned, 24, 28, 30 f., 39; declares war on Napoleon, 26; is de-

Brunswick, troops of in Waterloo campaign, 114, 188 f., 191, 193, 197

Brunswick-Oels, Friedrich Wilhelm, Duke of, leads uprising against Napoleon's regime, 29

Brussels, 101-103, 103 n., 105, 105 n., 108-111, 118, 121, 123, 125, 127, 130 f., 136, 145, 150, 154

Brussels highway, 134, 137, 141-143, 148, 151 f., 156, 158, 166, 175, 178, 193. *See also* Brussels-Charleroi road

Brussels-Charleroi road, mentioned, 124, 151, 182; French retreat down, 202. *See also* Charleroi-Brussels road

Brussels-Wavre highways, 142, 157

Bülow, Friedrich Wilhelm, Count of Dennewitz, 147, 148, 151 n., 162, 162 n., 174 f., 181, 181 n., 182, 202 f., 208

Butterworth (British gunner), 173

Byng, Sir John, Earl of Strafford, 189

Caesar, Caius Julius, 14

Caillou (farmhouse near Waterloo), 121 n., 127, 133, 135, 137, 190, 204

Cambacérès, Jean Jacques Régis de, 46

Cannes, Napoleon lands at, 100, 101

Cantelet, Wood of, 182, 200 n.

Capitaine de Chesnoy, Michel, cartographer, 135

Carnot, Lazare Nicolas Marguerite, 208

Carra (French officer), 43

Castellane, Esprit Victor Elisabeth Boniface, Comte, 40 n.

Caulaincourt, Armand Augustin Louis, Marquis de, Duc de Vicence, 31, 207

Cayenne, 43

Charlemont, 123

Charleroi, mentioned, 105, 105 n., 118, 204; Napoleon seizes, 118

Charleroi-Brussels road, mentioned, 109, 127, 139, 200; British retreat down, 110 f.

Charles, Archduke of Austria, mentioned, 26-28, 31, 38, 44, 48, 51, 74 f.; in battle of Aspern-Essling: attacks French center, 69 f.; decides to attack French Army, 57; determines not to stop French crossing of Danube, 54; disposition of his troops prior to battle, 52 f.; estimate of, in battle of Aspern-Essling, 83; his scouts report on movements of French, 49 f.; military skill of, 49; position at end of first day, 59; prepares for battle, 54, 54 n.; reaches Danube before French Army crosses river, 48; receives news of French crossing of Danube, 53; saves Austrian line, 61; size of his army, 48 n.; suspends attack, 71

Chassé (commander of Dutch-Belgian troops at Waterloo), 193

Chasseurs (French), 186 n., 190 n., 193-196

Château de Hougoumont. *See* Hougoumont, Château de

Chaumont, 132

Civita-Vecchia, 28

Claparède division (French), 32 n., 59, 61

Clarke, Henri Jacques Guillaume, Duc de Feltre, 39, 46 f.

Cleeves (British officer), 168, 193

Coalition (against Napoleon), invades France, 100; mobilizes army (1815), 101

Coignet, Sergeant (French officer), 64, 67

Colbert, Pierre David, 45 n.

Colonne infernale, la (French division commanded by Oudinot), 6

Condé, Louis II, de Bourbon, prince, the Great, Duc d'Enghien, 14

Confederation of the Rhine, 24

Constant, Benjamin, 116

Consul of France, Napoleon as, 8

Corbais, 132, 145

Cossacks, in battle of Friedland, 18

Couture, 155 n.

Crammond (British wagon driver), 205

Danube River, mentioned, 26 f., 31 f., 38, 40, 43, 45 n., 47, 49, 52, 54, 56, 59, 68, 74 f., 78 f., 83 f., 99; break in pontoon bridge delays French, 55, 62, 63 n.; construction

of pontoon bridge across, 37, 39;
crossed by French forces prior to
battle of Aspern-Essling, 40-46, 48,
50-52; French troops sent across prematurely are surrounded, 35; inadequacy of Napoleon's maps of, 33,
33 n.; Napoleon crosses, 47 f.; Napoleon recrosses to French side, 79 f.;
pontoon bridge across cannot be repaired, 68; problem of getting
French Army across, 33; reconnaissance for building bridge across, 33;
rises to flood stage, 68 f., 72; width
of at Kaiserebersdorf, 37 n.
Danzig, 25
Daru, Pierre Antoine Noël Bruno,
Comte, 45, 68
Davout, Louis Nicolas, Duc d'Auerstaedt, Prince d'Eckmühl, mentioned,
16, 28 n., 31, 45, 45 n., 59 f., 63 n.,
67 f., 74, 114, 121, 121 n., 122 n.,
157 n.; broken pontoon delays his
crossing of Danube, 62
Demaré, François, 90
Demont division (French), 32 n., 39 n.,
59 f.
Deutsch-Wagram, 53
Ditmer (Belgian officer), 194
Dörnberg, Wilhelm Caspar Ferdinand,
Freiherr von, 29
Domon, Jean Siméon, Baron, 141 f.,
147, 174
Donauwörth, 26
Donzelot, François Xavier, Comte, 156-
159, 159 n., 192 f., 197, 197 n.
Dorsenne, Jean Marie François Lepaige,
Comte, 65
Drouot, Antoine, Comte, 115, 135, 182,
183 n.
Duchand, Augustin Jean Baptiste, 191,
194
Duchy of Warsaw, 25
Duhesme, Philippe Guillaume, Comte,
180, 200 n., 202
Dumas, Mathieu, Comte, 81 n.
Durutte division (French), 137, 156 f.,
161, 179, 192, 196
Dutch troops in battle of Waterloo,
112, 114, 134, 156, 189, 193, 197

Dutch-Belgian troops in battle of
Waterloo, 193
Du Plat (German officer), 189
Dyle River, 132 f., 139, 145, 146 n.,
149-151

East Prussia, mentioned, 3; agriculture in, 4
Ebersberg, 32 n.
Ebersdorf, 35, 37, 40 n., 45 n., 79 n.,
80, 83 f., 98
Egypt, 8
Eibersbrunn, 52 n.
Elba, mentioned, 100, 193; Napoleon
escapes from, 100
Elbe River, 29
Elector of Hanover, 114
Eloy, Captain (French officer), 145,
146 n.
Empire (French), mentioned, 7; administrative problems of, 30, 43 f., 82
England. See Great Britain
English Channel, 28
Enzersdorf, 77
Enzersfeld, 52 n.
Erlon, Comte d' (Drouet, Jean Baptiste), 109, 115, 120, 125, 127, 137,
141, 142-144, 153 n., 162 n., 164,
164 n., 165, 177-179, 185 f., 192,
201 n.
Espagne, Bertrand, 17
Essling (town), mentioned, 57, 59-62,
64, 66-68, 70, 71 n., 76, 87; French
forced to evacuate it, 70 f.; French
occupy it, 57
Eton, 105
Eugène de Beauharnais, 24, 27, 39
Europe, mentioned, 3, 24, 86, 100,
112; ports of, closed to British goods,
99
Exelmans, Remy Joseph Isidore, Comte,
mentioned, 119, 121, 123, 130-132;
loses line of Prussian retreat, 130
Eylau, battle of (1807), 8; Napoleon's
headquarters at, 4, 11

Ferrari (cartographer), 129 n., 135,
155 n.
Fifth Corps (Austrian), 52, 55
First Consul, Napoleon as, 8
First Corps (Austrian), 52, 55

First Corps (French), 120, 127, 137, 141, 143, 179
First Corps (Prussian), 183
Fischamend, 33 f.
Flahault de La Billarderie, Auguste Charles Joseph, Comte, 57, 155 n., 169
Fleurus, 119, 120 n., 121
Fontainebleau, 99
Fortresses, of Northern France, 108, 118
Fouché, Joseph, Duc d'Otrante, 30, 46
Fourth Chasseurs (French), 186 n., 190 n., 193
Fourth Corps (Austrian), 52, 55
Fourth Corps (French), in battle of Aspern-Essling, 32 n., 59; in battle of Waterloo, 122, 123
Fourth Corps (Prussian), 147
Fourth Grenadiers (French), 186 n., 193 f., 195
Foy, Maximilien Sébastien, 15, 144, 192
France, mentioned, 7 f., 24 f., 43, 102, 106, 108, 111 f., 115; Coalition prepares to invade (1815), 101; fortresses in north of, 108, 118; invaded by armies of the Coalition, 100; Napoleon recovers control of (1815), 101
Franck, Jean Pierre, 86
Frazer, Sir Augustus Simon, 172
Frederick II, the Great, King of Prussia, 14
French Army, mentioned, 4, 5 n., 11, 15, 17, 31 f., 39, 106 f., 129, 134 f., 207; Army of Italy, 7, 75; artillery, 19, 25, 155 f.; cavalry, 7, 9-11, 17, 25, 28, 32, 45, 48, 111, 127, 129, 137; cuirassiers, 137, 141, 156, 160 f., 166, 170, 191; hussars, 4; infantry, 9, 17, 25, 45, 48, 129, 137, 156; position at Donauwörth 26. *See also* Aspern-Essling, battle of, French Army in; Friedland, battle of, French Army in; Waterloo, battle of, French Army in
French people, do not support Louis XVIII, 101; remain loyal to Napoleon, 101; weary of war, 100
French Republic (first, 1792-1799), 8

French Revolution, 7, 14
Fresnaye, Major ————La (French officer), 148, 150, 153 n., 154
Friedland (town), mentioned, 3, 9, 11, 13, 18, 22-24; burned during battle of, 21; fighting in the town, during battle of, 21; preliminary military operations in vicinity of, 4, 5 n., 6
Friedland, battle of (1807), mentioned, 10 f., 23, 112, 117, 165
  French Army in: artillery fire during, 20; disposition of reserves in, 16 f., 20 n.; disposition of troops in, 17; objectives of attack, 18; precarious position of, in early hours of battle, 10-12; reinforcements arrive, 12-14; tactical problems of, 9;
  French victory in, 21 f.; Napoleon comments on victory, 23; hour at which fighting ended, 22 n.; political consequences of, 23;
  Russian Army in: mentioned, 5 n., 6, 9-11, 11 n., 13, 16, 18, 19-22; dangers of position of, 13; losses in, 23; Napoleon comments on route of, 23; strength of, 16; withdrawal of, 20 f.
Friedland bridge, mentioned, 6, 13, 16, 18; Russians retreat across, 21
Friedland forest, 4, 9, 12 f.
Friedland plain, 3, 5, 9, 13
Friant, Louis, Comte, 193
Fririon, François Nicolas, Baron, 70
Frischermont, 105, 155 n., 175
Frischermont, Wood of, 105

Gachot, Edouard, 46 n.
Galicia, 39
Gascon, characteristics of a, 7, 76
Gate of Namur, 102
Gembloux, 119, 121, 123, 127, 129-132, 134, 138, 144, 146, 150, 155 n.
Genappe, 105, 109, 127, 135 f., 204
Gentinnes, 138
Gérard, Etienne Maurice, Comte, 115, 129, 131 f., 151, 151 n., 155 n.
German Army, officers of lead uprisings against Napoleon's regime, 29
German Legion, 189

German troops in battle of Waterloo, 112, 134, 156, 178, 188 f.

Germans, 4

Germany, mentioned, 25 f., 100, 115; rises against Napoleon, 99; unrest in, 28

Gery, 138

Gneisenau, August Wilhelm Anton, Graf Neidhardt von, mentioned, 108; asks Wellington to join in attack on Napoleon, 110; good strategist, 108

Gould, Colonel (British officer), 171 f.

Gourgaud, Gaspard, Baron, 115 n., 151 n., 163 n., 184 n., 208

Grand Armée (French invasion of Russia), 106

Great Britain, mentioned, 24, 106; at war with Napoleon, 99, 101; Continental ports closed to goods of, 99; King of, 114; Napoleon's hatred of, 126, 127 n.; prepares expeditionary force, 28; treatment of prisoners of war, 112

Grenadiers (French), 10, 12, 17, 186 n., 193-196

Gross-Ebersdorf, headquarters of Archduke Charles, 49, 52, 52 n.

Gross-Enzersdorf, mentioned, 51, 57, 60; occupied by French forces, 57

Grouchy, Alphonse Frédéric Emmanuel Marquis de (son of Emmanuel Grouchy), 8

Grouchy, Emmanuel, Marquis de, mentioned, 5 n., 7-9, 115, 127 f., 132 n., 136, 145-149, 149 n., 151 n., 153-155, 155 n., 162, 162 n., 174, 196, 208; his ability not rewarded, 8; his mistakes, 132 f., 133 n., 150 f.; in battle of Friedland, 10 f., 17; in battle of Waterloo, 119, 119 n., 121 n., 122 f., 123 n., 129, 129 n.; loses contact with Prussian Army, 130; mistakes direction of Prussian retreat, 119 f.; sends reports to Napoleon, 130-132, 144 f., 144 n., 150, 153 n., 154; military operation in Italy, 8

Grünhof, 17

Guard. See Imperial Guard (French)

Guides (French), 47

Gurwood, John, 155 n.

Guyot, Claude Etienne, Comte, 141, 170

Hagenbrunn, 52

Hal, 111 f.

Halkett, Sir Colin, 189, 191, 193-195

Halkett, W. (commander of Hanoverian troops at Waterloo), 189, 196

Hamburg, 25

Hannibal, 14

Hannut, 131

Hanover, Elector of, 114

Hanoverian Legion, 114, 188 n., 189, 196 f.

Harlet, Louis, Baron, 193

Haxo, François Nicolas Benoît, 137

Haye Sainte, La (farmhouse near Waterloo), mentioned, 104, 111, 129 n., 137, 140, 156, 160, 163, 163 n., 164 n., 165 f., 169, 180, 183 n., 185-187, 191, 198, 206; British garrison at, lacks ammunition, 176; British regain, 161; French fail to take advantage of, 191; French repelled from, 165; French storm British position at, 156 f.; French take, 176

Henrichsdorff, mentioned, 4, 5 n., 9 f., 10 n., 17; operations in, during battle of Friedland, 10 f.

Henrion, Christophe, Baron, 193

Hessian troops, 29

Heurteloup, Nicolas, Baron, 84

Heymés, Colonel (French officer), 179

Hill, Rowland, 1st Viscount Hill, 111 n.

Hiller, Johann, Freiherr, mentioned, 50 f., 53; urges attack before French complete Danube crossing, 53

Hoen, Maximilian, Ritter von, 37 n., 41 n.

Hohenlinden, battle of (1800), 8

Holland, 25

Homburg, 29

Horn, 48 n.

Hougoumont, Château de (near Waterloo), mentioned, 104, 111 f., 140, 143, 151, 153 n., 166, 180, 185-187, 189, 192 f., 196, 198, 200, 202, 206;

his comments on his errors at Waterloo, 120 n., 164 n., 207 f.; his comments on the battle, 151 n., 162 n., 163 n., 179 n., 182 n., 183 n., 184, 184 n., 185 n., 201 n.; his hatred of the British, 126, 127 n.; his immediate views on the battle, 207; his optimism prior to the battle, 128, 128 n., 135; his plan of battle, 141 f., 152; his plan of campaign, 118-121; his plans to break British line, 163 f., 164 n., 165 n., 190; holds reserves to meet Prussians, 179; ignores reported union of British and Prussian armies, 136; ignores Soult's advice, 136; leads Imperial Guard against British position, 185, 191 f.; learns Grouchy's real position, 148 n., 155; learns true direction of Prussian retreat, 127 f., 130-132; fails to interpret it, 128; leaves battlefield of Ligny, 119; moves troops to meet Coalition armies, 108; Ney reports on British position, 121; orders Grouchy to pursue Prussians, 122 f., 127; orders his troops into final position, 137; orders Ney to attack British, 124; personally reconnoitres British position, 133, 137; prepares for final attack on British, 182; proceeds to battle on fragmentary reports, 121, 121 n.; proclamation to his soldiers before, 112 f.; Prussian retreat erroneously reported to, 120; questions Prussian prisoner, 147; realizes entire Prussian force is at hand, 183 f., 183 n., 184, 184 n.; receives Grouchy's reports, 133 f., 144 f., 144 n.; replies to Grouchy's report, 138 f.; reviews troops before battle, 121; revises orders to Grouchy, 123; sees danger of Prussian-British union, 145; sends Imperial Guard against Prussians, 180 f.; sends in cavalry reserve, 170; supervises defense against Prussians, 175; tells troops

Grouchy has arrived, 185; troops loyal to him, 113;

increased territories of, after Peace of Tilsit, 24;

knowledge of problems of supply, 15, 33;

makes peace with Austria, 99;

military skill of, 14, 16, 26, 33;

mistakes of, 15, 120 n., 164 n., 207 f.;

scorns idea of danger from Prussia, 30, 44, 47;

uses conscription to raise troops, 25; war with Great Britain, 99

Nassau, troops of in Waterloo campaign, 114, 189, 189 n.

Netherlands, The, 106

Neu-Polla, 48 n.

Neustadt, 32, 32 n.

Ney, Michel, Duc d'Elchingen, Prince de la Moskowa,

decline in tactical skill of, 165;

in battle of Friendland, 16-18, 20 f., 20 n.;

in battle of Waterloo: 109, 114, 118, 120 f., 121 n., 122, 122 n., 124-126, 135, 142 f., 151 n., 152, 162 n., 163 n., 164 n., 165, 169, 204, 208; asks Napoleon for reinforcements, 179; comments on battle, 201 n.; is unable to take advantage of weak British line, 179; leads final assault on British line, 186, 191; marches on foot in final assault, 193; sends French cavalry in too soon, 166, 170, 207; sends Imperial Guard against strongest part of British line, 191 f.;

in Spanish campaign, 28

Nivelles, 111 n.

Nivelles road, 141, 143, 153 n.

Nosocomial fever, 88

Nussdorf, 32 n., 34, 34 n., 35 f., 48, 51 f., 55

Ompteda, Christian Friedrich Wilhelm, Freiherr von, 189, 192

Ostend, 105 n.

Reille, Honoré Charles Michel Joseph, 115, 125 f., 137, 141, 143 f., 164, 164 n., 179, 185, 199 f., 200 n., 203

Reneveck barracks hospital (Vienna), 86, 92 f., 95, 98

Reserve Corps (Austrian Army), 52

Restoration (of Bourbon dynasty in France), 113

Rhine River, 24, 27, 75, 100

Rochefort, 117 n.

Roi-d'Espagne (inn at Genappe), 136

Rome, 28

Ropes, John Codman, 152 n., 155 n.

Rosas, 44

Rossomme (farm near Waterloo), 137, 183 n.

Rossomme, Knoll of, 142, 146, 182, 200 n., 203

Rovigo, Duc de, 63 n. *See also* Savary, Anne Jean Marie René, Duc de Rovigo

Russia, mentioned, 24, 31, 106; allied with Napoleon, under Peace of Tilsit, 24; closes ports to British shipping, 24; defeated by Napoleon (1813), 100; is lukewarm ally of Napoleon, 31; Napoleon's invasion of, 99; opens ports to British goods, 99

Russian Army, mentioned, 4, 5 n., 12 f., 15, 17, 21, 23, 69; artillery, 19; cavalry, 4, 10 f., 11 n., 18; does not cross Austrian frontier, 31; infantry, 11 n.; invades France (1813), 100; marches against Austria, 39, 44

Russian Imperial Guard, in battle of Friedland, 20 n., 23

Rustam, a Mameluke, 80

St. Bernard pass, 8

Saint Cyr, Laurent Gouvion, Marquis de, 43

St. Helena, 122 n., 151 n., 164 n., 184 n., 204, 208

Saint-Hilaire, Louis Vincent Joseph, le Blond, Comte, 63

Saint-Hilaire division (French), 32 n., 39 n., 59, 61

Saint-Lambert, 139, 145-148, 149 n., 150, 150 n., 163, 174

Saint-Lambert, Forest of, 146

St. Petersburg, 39

Saint-Poelten, 31, 32 n., 45

Saltoun (Fraser, Alexander George, 16th Baron Saltoun), 195 n.

Sart-à-Walhain, 130-132, 138, 145, 150 f., 153 n., 155, 155 n.

Sauvenières, 129-131, 134, 138

Savary, Anne Jean Marie René, Duc de Rovigo, 16, 40 n., 41 n., 42 n. 63 n.

Savoy, King of, 8

Schill, Johann Heinrich von, 29

Schneidergrund (sandbank in Danube River), 43, 46

Schönau. 50

Schönbrunn, 34, 40, 40 n., 41 n., 86

Schwechat, 37 n.

Scotch troops, in Waterloo campaign, 156, 160, 197

Second Chasseurs (French), 193

Second Corps (Austrian), 52, 55

Second Corps (French), in battle of Aspern-Essling, 32 n., 59 f.; in battle of Waterloo, 125 f., 129, 137, 141-143, 179, 200, 203

Ségur, Philippe Paul, Comte, 63 n., 75 n.

Seymour (British officer), 183 n.

Seyring-Reuhoff, 53

Sharpshooters, Austrian, 81, 81 n., 82; French, 137, 177, 186, 191; use of, in battle of Friedland, 9

Silesia, 29

Sixth Corps (Austrian), 50, 54

Sixth Corps (French), 120, 122, 126, 137, 141-143, 148, 163, 174, 200 n., 202, 208

Smissen, Van der (Belgian officer), 194

Smohain, mentioned, 104, 111 f., 156, 175, 180, 197, 206; French take, 179

Soignes, Forest of, 102, 104, 122, 128, 136, 138, 140, 142

Somerset, Lord Robert Edward Henry, 158, 160, 178

Songis, Nicolas Marie de, mentioned, 33, 39 n.; reports on site for bridge across Danube, 34

Sorauren, battle of, 107

French cavalry, 166 f., 186; French deserter informs Wellington that Napoleon will attack, 190; general advance begins, 197 f.; holds lines at Quatre Bras, 109, 118; merits of position of, 141, 141 n.; numbers in Waterloo campaign, 113; pursues French Army, 202-204; rain favors withdrawal of, 111; takes final position, 112; weakest army in Waterloo campaign, 114; Wellington prepares to meet all contingencies, 112; Wellington reorganizes British lines, 186-188, 188 n.

comment on battle, 208 f.;

comparison of armies engaged in, 113 f.;

controversial details concerning, 152 n., 153 n., 186, 206 f.;

devastation caused by, 206;

effects of rainstorm on, 129, 129 n., 134 f., 142;

French Army in: cavalry fails to break British squares, 168, 170, 175; common soldiers fight well, 156; composed of veterans, 113; dissolves in confusion, 199 f., 200 n., 201 n.; distrusts officers, 113; faith in Napoleon, 113; final assault partially succeeds, 192-194; final position of, 141 f.; Imperial Guard in confusion, 194 f.; Imperial Guard repulsed, 196; makes frontal attack, 156; mistakes direction of Prussian retreat, 119 f.; moves out to meet enemy, 108; Napoleon at Ligny and Quatre Bras, 108; Napoleon optimistic concerning battle, 128, 128 n., 135; Napoleon orders Grouchy to pursue Prussians, 123; Napoleon's plan of campaign, 118; Napoleon's proclamation to his army prior to, 112 f.; Ney sends cavalry in too soon, 166, 169; no rear guard to cover retreat, 204; other units disintegrate after repulse of Guard, 197; outnumbered by

Allies, 113; rainstorm breaks as attack begins, 125; reaction to approaching Prussian Army, 184, 198; sharpshooters and artillery decimate British line, 177 f.; 189, 192; strikes before Allies are in position, 108; takes La Haye Sainte, 176; takes up position against British, 124;

Hougoumont château attacked, 144, 152, 154;

numbers of troops engaged in, 113, 114 n.;

Prussian Army in: advances on French flank, 163, 175; attacks French divisions, 196, 198; breaks through French lines, 200, 203; composed of veterans, 113; enters battle, 174; Grouchy pursues, 123, 130; hampered by mud, 150; is perceived by Napoleon and French Army, 183 n., 184 n.; loses Planchenoit, 181; main body of moves up, 183 f., 190; Napoleon plans to attack it first, 118; numbers in Waterloo campaign, 113; position at Waterloo, 108, 112; pursues fleeing French, 204 f.; takes Planchenoit from French, 180; withdraws after French attack at Ligny, 108 f., 118-120, 128;

weather improves, 136 f.;

wounded, condition and care of, 205

Wavre, 109-112, 121, 128, 130-133, 133 n., 134, 136, 138 f., 145-150, 154, 157

Wavre road, 142, 157, 159

Wellington, Arthur Wellesley, 1st Duke of,

mentioned, 25, 28, 101, 105, 108, 113, 123, 126, 129 n., 130 f., 133, 133 n., 134-136, 143, 145, 147, 151 f., 155 n., 164 n., 174 f., 187 n., 191, 194 n., 195 n., 198 f.;

appearance of, 107;

career in India, 106;

in battle of Waterloo: agrees to attack Napoleon with aid of one

Prussian corps, 110; comments on the battle, 201 n.; conceals infantry, 158; has never fought Napoleon before, 107; his calmness throughout battle, 186 f.; his plan of battle, 187; is present at all points of danger, 186; maintains close contact with Blücher, 174; meets Blücher after battle, 204; meets French cavalry charge, 166 f.; merits of position chosen by, 141, 141 n.; moves British troops into position, 111 f., 140; orders advance of entire British line, 197; receives information that Napoleon will attack, 190; reinforces decimated lines, 178 n.; reinforces right wing and center, 187 f., 188 n.; reorganizes lines when Prussians enter battle, 187; withdraws advanced artillery, 166; in Peninsular campaigns, 106; life and character of, 105 f.; military skill of, 106 f.; military training of, 106